100 HEADLINES
THAT CHANGED
THE WORLD

100 HEADLINES THAT CHANGED THE WORLD

James Maloney

ROBINSON

Constable & Robinson Ltd
55-56 Russell Square
London WC1B 4HP

www.constablerobinson.com

First published in the UK in 2012 by Robinson,
an imprint of Constable & Robinson Ltd

A copy of the British Library Cataloguing in Publication Data
is available from the British Library

ISBN 978-1-78033-481-3

Printed and bound in the UK

10 9 8 7 6 5 4 3 2 1

CONTENTS

Introduction	1
Penny Postage Pictures	7
Gold Mine Found	10
Massacre Of English At Delhi	13
Discovery Of A Subterranean Fountain Of Oil	17
The War Begun	20
Important Assassination Of President Lincoln	23
Audible Speech By Telegraph	26
The Indian War	29
Edison's Electric Light	32
Jesse James, The Bandit, Killed	35
The Whitechapel Horrors	38
The Woman's Suffrage Bill Assented To	41
Lumière's Cinematographe	44
Oscar Wilde In Jail	47
War Declared Boers Commence Hostilities	51
Wireless Signals Across The Ocean	54
Dayton Boys Emulate Great Santos-Dumont	57
The Conquest Of The South Pole	60
Titanic Sunk	63
Sensational Derby Suffragist's Mad Act	66
Heir To Austria's Throne Is Slain	69
Last Barrier In Canal Is Removed	72
Five Days Inside The Cordon	75
Abdication Of Czar	78
How London Hailed The End Of War	81
Whole Country Goes Dry	84
Mr. Macdonald's Crowded Day	87
The "Televisor"	90
Seek Congressional Medal Of Honor For Lindbergh	93
Greatest Crash In Wall Street's History	96

Ghandi Seized By British	99
Hitler Made Chancellor Of Germany	102
Edward VIII Abdicates	105
Owens Completes Triple As 5 Olympic Marks Fall	108
Hindenburg Burns In Lakehurst Crash	111
Britain's First Day Of War	114
175 Nazi Planes Down	117
Japan, U.S. At War	120
VE-Day – It's All Over	123
First Atomic Bomb Dropped On Japan	126
State Of Israel Is Born	129
Mao Heads Peiping Regime	132
Truman Orders U.S. Air, Navy Units To Fight In Aid Of Korea	135
The Crowning Glory: Everest Is Climbed	138
Why You Are You	141
Ruth Ellis To Hang	144
First Blows By Navy And R.A.F	147
Soviet Fires Earth Satellite Into Space	150
21 Dead 7 Manchester Utd Players Perish In Air Crash	153
Birth Control Pill Approved By Commission	157
The Innocence Of Lady Chatterley	160
Man Enters Space	164
East German Troops Seal Border With West Berlin	167
We Blockade Cuba Arms	170
Profumo Quits	173
Kennedy Slain On Dallas Street	176
3,000 Fans Greet British Beatles	179
U.S. Forces Out of Vietnam	182
4 Children Die, 160 Missing in S. Wales Horror	185
Man With A New Heart	188
Martin King Shot To Death	191
How Bobby Was Shot!	194
Man On The Moon	197
Up, Up And Away!	200
Three Spacemen Are Home Safe	203

The Death Steps	206
13 Killed As Paratroops Break Riot	208
Nixon Resigns	211
King Elvis Dead	214
Test Tube Mother Has Girl	217
Mrs Thatcher Takes Over	219
Bomb On Boat Kills Lord Mountbatten	223
Poland Yields On Independent Trade Unions	226
John Lennon Shot Dead	229
Pope Shot	232
Rare Cancer Seen In 41 Homosexuals	235
GOTCHA	237
Murder	240
Worldbeater!	243
Explosion Stuns Nation	246
Nuclear Nightmare Is Here	249
Hundreds Die As Jumbo Jet Plunges Into village	252
Our Day Of Tears	255
Crackdown In Beijing	258
Mandela Goes Free Today	261
Capital Sarajevo Racked By Serb-Muslim Civil Strife	264
Scientists Clone Adult Sheep	267
Diana Dead	270
Clinton Admits To Lewinsky Relationship	273
U.S. Attacked	276
Bloodbath On Holiday Island	279
The Tyrant Is Now A Prisoner	282
We Saw The Sea Coming, We All Ran. But God Saves Little'	286
Katrina Storms Ashore	289
Microsoft Says Goodbye To Bill Gates	292
Obama Makes History	295
World Transfixed By The Great Escape	298
The Day That Shook Japan	301
Got Him!	304
Steve Jobs Dead	307

INTRODUCTION

As a journalist as well as an author with a keen interest in history and a fascination with newspapers, I found compiling this book was an absolute joy for me. I soon realised that there was no shortage of headlines from which to choose. The problem was what to leave out. This wealth of riches meant that some momentous events did not find their way into the pages of this book.

I had been very aware from the outset that my final choice of *100 Headlines* would cause disagreement, incredulity and possibly some anger amongst readers. How could such-and-such be left out? Why has *that* been included? Did that really *change* the world? It would be impossible to please all, perhaps even the majority, so in the end I have just had to please myself.

I could quite easily have filled the book with war and conflict or natural disasters, murder or scientific discoveries. All have been plentiful over the years. But I have striven to bring variety, and so we have tragedies co-existing with medical breakthroughs, heroic feats, political disasters and wonderful inventions.

Sadly, there have been all too many tragedies in history. I have had to be highly selective in choosing which to include. My criterion has not been solely based on the number of deaths or injuries in an incident. Nor have I adhered doggedly to global impact. I have endeavoured to bring together a selection of headlines that caused shock, disbelief and a considerable amount of emotional outpouring at the time of their happening. And so we have the likes of the 1958 Munich air disaster, which tore apart the young Manchester United football team – the most exciting team of the era – or the devastating Boxing Day tsunami of 2004, which saw the loss of over 200,000 lives. General Custer's last stand finds a place, as do the First and Second World Wars. And so on.

The main theme of the book is that headlines – or events – should have changed the world. Some of the chosen headlines clearly did change the world, while others may have had a less obvious impact. Ultimately the choice is subjective. It could also be argued that everything and anything changes the world to some degree.

This is a book of headlines, the stories behind them and the impact they would have on the future of the world. I have delved into the world's newspaper archives and found some remarkable articles on famous events such as the sinking of the *Titanic*, the assassination of Abraham Lincoln and the serial murders of Jack the Ripper. But some things I imagined I might include I had to abandon because I was unable to find a headline. These are mostly inventions, scientific discoveries and medical advances that were not fully appreciated at the time and so, outside of scientific, medical and other specialist publications, they received little or no attention in mainstream newspapers. For some I have managed to find a later headline with which to write a retrospective piece. This I did with the advent of Microsoft, for example, by including it under a headline announcing Bill Gates's departure from the company he set up.

The Internet, social networking sites and 24-hour TV and radio news have changed the way we hear the news. But in this book, many of the headlines you see were the main source of information at the time. News travelled at a slower pace in decades past and so major events were often not reported in newspapers until days – sometimes weeks – later.

Old newspapers' front pages were very different from today's. Many of them had classified adverts on the front and the news stories, however major, were 'buried' inside in small columns easily overlooked in the 'wall of print'.

While it is true that newspaper readership has declined as the electronic media have flourished, the printed word still carries great impact. Newspapers are both fascinating social documents of the time and records of history. There is nothing like seeing and holding an old newspaper in your hands, knowing that the very paper itself was there when the event actually happened – be it the first man to set foot on the moon or the Russian revolution of 1917. It feels like living history.

Newspapers have been around in one form or another for hundreds of years. The ancient Romans can probably lay claim to distributing the first form of public news in the form of bulletins carved in metal or stone and prominently displayed for all to read. In 59 BC Julius Caesar informed the public about social, political and military events with information written on large white boards and placed in prominent places. In 8th-century China, hand-written newsheets were distributed. And in 1556 the Venetian government published *Notizie scritte*, for which readers paid a small coin, or 'gazzetta', hence the popular newspaper name of *Gazette*.

But the newspaper as we might recognise it did not begin to appear until the 17th century as printing presses became more widespread and newspapers appeared more regularly.

The arrival of the telegraph in 1844 meant that information could be relayed much more quickly. This enabled newspapers to be more timely and relevant in reporting distant events. They became the most important means of communication and, as more and more national and local newspapers appeared, the headlines became increasingly bigger and more attention-grabbing in an attempt to entice people to buy them. *100 Headlines That Changed The World* features some of the most memorable banner headlines with the stories behind the headlines retold in as concise a form as possible to put the headline in context and explain how these stories from the past helped to shape the world that we live in today.

PENNY POSTAGE PICTURES

(Liverpool Standard, 12 May 1840)

THE PENNY BLACK was the world's first adhesive
postage stamp used in a public postal system. It was
issued in Britain on 1 May 1840, for official use from
6 May, and it marked a turning point in social history.

Prior to 1840, the post service was too expensive for most people to use. The cost of sending a single letter could equate to a working man's daily wage, or more. Postage was charged by the number of sheets of paper used and the distance travelled. And it was paid by the recipient. But all Members of Parliament and Lords had the right to frank and receive a number of letters free.

The expense meant it was difficult for family or friends living long distances apart to communicate with each other. Sending letters was, therefore, a privilege of the wealthy, but to save money it became common practice to cram as many words as possible onto both sides of a sheet of paper. There was no such thing as an envelope. Letters were simply folded and sealed with wax. There were no pillar boxes, so it would have to be taken to a post office. If the addressee lived in a remote area they might never receive the letter. And the recipient of a costly letter could simply refuse delivery.

GUMMED LABELS

All of this began to cause some concern to the government in the 1830s. Some maintain that James Chalmers, a bookseller and printer from Dundee, first came up with the idea of pre-paid gummed labels. But it was Rowland Hill, a teacher turned civil servant from Kidderminster, Worcestershire, who is widely credited with the invention of the adhesive stamp and the basis of the modern postal system.

BROKEN HEARTED

Hill, so the story goes, was inspired to begin planning a whole new postal system when he came across a sobbing young woman, broken hearted because she had no money and could not afford to pay for a letter that had been sent to her by her fiancé.

In 1835, Hill embarked on a study of the existing postal system and, two years later, he produced a pamphlet called 'Post Office Reform: Its Importance and Practicability.' The mainstay of Hill's reform proposals was a penny post, which meant that any letter weighing less than half an ounce (14 grams) could be sent anywhere in Britain for one penny.

The Postmaster General, Lord Lichfield, was startled by such a radical concept and commented, 'Of all the wild and visionary schemes which I ever heard of, it is the most extravagant.' But merchants and reformers backed Hill, seeing the benefit of allowing the common man to be able to afford to send letters.

Hill's pre-paid system advocated the use of stamped 'covers' consisting of 'a bit of paper just large enough to bear the stamp, and covered at the back with a glutinous wash'. This was to eventually become the Penny Black. He also suggested the use of envelopes.

CONTROLLER OF STAMPS

Hill appointed his older brother, Edwin, as the first Controller of Stamps, a position he would retain for the next 32 years. Edwin also invented a machine for making envelopes. The covers (stamps) were designed by artist William Mulready, based on an engraved head of the reigning monarch, Queen Victoria, as a young woman. The black background included the word 'POSTAGE' at the top of the stamp and 'ONE PENNY' at the bottom, along with flourishes around the borders and ornamental stars. Stamps would be printed in sheets of 240 that could be cut by the postmaster or postmistress using scissors or a knife.

But the rather sombre design was disliked by some and the

Liverpool Standard newspaper in a lengthy article headlined, 'Penny Postage Pictures' criticised the stamp, describing, 'little bits of stuff like sticking plaster, with a dirty looking bust of Her Majesty, for dabbing on the back of a letter.' It added, 'Perhaps Rowland Hill, Esq. or the artist W. Mulready, Esq. R.A. can explain, but for our part, we give up the attempt in despair.'

The Penny Postage Bill was passed by Parliament on 17 August 1839, whereby prepayment would become the standard for sending letters and the basic cost would be a one-penny stamp.

The Penny Black first went on sale on 1 May 1840, although they were only valid for postage from 6 May 1840. It was followed a day later by the Two Penny Blue. This new postal system became an instant success with a huge increase in people sending letters, which provided lucrative revenue.

RED INK PROBLEMS

But the Penny Black was in use for a little over a year. The red cancellation mark that was used on the stamp was found to be hard to see on a black background and the red ink was easy to remove, making it possible to re-use stamps after they had been cancelled.

In 1841, it was determined that black ink was more robust and so the Treasury switched to the Penny Red and issued post offices with cancellation devices with black ink.

By the end of 1840, more than 160 million letters had been sent in Britain and by the turn of the century, the figure had rocketed to 2.3 billion.

STAMPS SPREAD WORLDWIDE

The use of an envelope brought added privacy to letter writing, which encouraged people to write more confidential messages, including 'love letters'.

Adhesive postage stamps were gradually introduced throughout the world. The head of the reigning monarch has featured on British stamps ever since. Because the Penny Black and Two Penny Blue were the world's first postage stamps, they did not name their country of origin and British stamps are still the only ones in the world that carry on this tradition. ●

GOLD MINE FOUND

(*Californian*, 15 March 1848)

RUMOURS OF GOLD in California had existed for years but it wasn't until gold was discovered at Sutter's Mill that the Gold Rush began. People from all over the United States and from around the world made their way to this sleepy backwater and changed the face of California for all time.

On 4 January 1848, James Marshall, who was building a sawmill for Swiss emigrant John Sutter in Sacramento, found what he thought might be gold along by the river. He took it back to show Sutter and tests showed that it was, indeed, gold.

Worried that the find would bring an onrush of prospectors to his land and that his own workforce would desert him, Sutter asked his workers to stay quiet about the find. But word soon got out.

When this local newspaper report relayed the story of the find at Sutter's Mill, hordes of gold-hunting Californians began to make their way to the area. And after major newspapers began to report the find, President James Polk, speaking to Congress on 5 December 1848, confirmed that gold had been discovered in California. It was then that 'gold fever' broke out in earnest.

MINER FORTY-NINERS

By 1849 the rush was on. Many miners or 'forty-niners', as they were nicknamed after the year of their arrival, expected to find rivers overflowing with gold and were unprepared for the gruelling necessity for panning and digging.

Gold was found throughout much of California and made some rich, but many went away with little or nothing at all. As more and more people arrived, those with an entrepreneurial flare gave up the hunt for gold and, instead, used their skills as carpenters, traders, builders and teachers, to service the mining industry

ANGER AT FOREIGNERS

As gold became increasingly more difficult to find, anger and fighting broke out. Americans became incensed that foreigners were raping their lands and drove them out of mining camps so that they had to set up camps of their own.

California had become a possession of the U.S. following the war with Mexico but was not a formal territory. It was a pretty lawless place and anyone who found gold was quickly surrounded by others. Thieves, thugs and conmen found their own 'shortcut' ways of getting their hands on the treasure.

Claim laws had to be set on which pieces of land individuals were allowed to mine. And camps set up claims officers to patrol mines and settle disputes.

Gradually, California was being transformed. Towns and cities were chartered and roads and houses and stores built. A state constitution was drawn up, elections were held and representatives sent to Washington, D.C., to negotiate the adoption of California as a state.

POPULATION EXPLOSION

Before the gold rush, California was largely inhabited by missionaries and Native Americans – a total of about 2,000 people. By late 1849 its population had grown to 15,000, and by 1853 there were over 300,000 people living there.

When silver was discovered in Nevada in 1859, the miners headed there and the California Gold Rush came to an end

Many of the communities that had been built – full of shacks, shops and saloons – became 'ghost towns.' But, by this time, California had a growing economy of farming and commerce with many staying on to take advantage of the rich agricultural land and business opportunities.

CALIFORNIAN DREAM

Roads, schools, churches, railways and civic organisations were created throughout the land. On 9 September 1850 California became part of the United States of America. The phrase 'Californian Dream' was used to describe the varied opportunities to flourish and prosper in this new golden state.

The population quickly expanded, especially with the coming of the trans-continental railroad link in 1869, and today more people live in California than in any other state.

They still hunt for, gold, too with tourists and hobbyists panning gravel in streams across the state and there are almost 25,000 official active gold mining claims. Despite the high price of gold, however, the meagre amounts that are extracted today are not likely to bring on another bout of gold rush fever. ●

MASSACRE OF ENGLISH AT DELHI

(*Daily Telegraph*, 29 June 1857)

A REBELLION WITHIN the Indian Army caught the British government by surprise when it escalated across the country and gained the support of thousands of citizens.

Britain, as the colonial power, was used to acquiescence amongst Indian troops and had failed fully to appreciate the warning signs over the years that all was not well. And when the troops finally took a stand, there was shock and outrage at what was seen as a betrayal.

The *Daily Telegraph* reported how from Calcutta to Lahore the troops of the Bengal Presidency were in 'open or undisguised mutiny'.

Variously described as 'The Indian Mutiny', 'The Great Rebellion', 'The Sepoy Uprising' or 'India's First War of Independence', it was a result of mounting tension among Indian troops over unfair treatment from European officers.

It began on 10 May 1857 when sepoys (native Indian soldiers) of the British East India Company's army, in the town of Meerut, shot their British officers and marched on Delhi. Word of the uprising quickly spread and other sepoys rebelled in different parts of India.

THE SEPOY SOLDIERS

The background to the rebellion was a series of incidents which led to mounting grievances, resentment and anger. The sepoys were a combination of Hindu and Muslim soldiers who made up the bulk of the army in the East India Company (which effectively governed India).

The forces were divided into three Presidency armies – the Bombay, the Madras and the Bengal.

There had been some early resentment amongst the soldiers when the army's campaign to annex more land forced them to serve in distant areas such as Burma in the Anglo-Burmese Wars of 1856. There were more grievances when, under the General Service Act, new recruits would no longer receive a pension on retirement. Another cause of friction was the increasing number of European officers in the battalions, which made promotion for the rank and file increasingly slow and difficult. The Bengal Presidency had extra cause to feel bitter because they were paid less than Bombay and Madras.

NEW CARTRIDGES

The final spark which ignited this seething pressure can of resentment was the issue of new paper cartridges to use with the new Enfield rifles. The cartridges came pre-greased and to load the rifle, sepoys had to bite the cartridge open to release the powder. But the tallow used to grease the paper was believed to be made with cow and pig fat, upsetting the religious sensibilities of both Hindus and Muslims.

On 26 February 1857 the 19th Bengal Native Infantry (BNI) refused to use the cartridges and their angry colonel confronted them on the parade ground, backed with artillery. But after some negotiation, the artillery was taken away and the next morning's parade was cancelled.

LONE REBEL COURT-MARTIALLED

A month later, a 29-year-old sepoy of the BNI named Mangal Pandey told his colleagues he was going to rebel against his commanders. On hearing of his intent, Sergeant-Major James Hewson went to investigate, only to have Pandey shoot at him.

Pandey had failed to incite others to join him in the rebellion but they showed their support in refusing orders to arrest him – save for one man, Shaikh Paltu, who managed to restrain him.

Pandey was court-martialled on 6 April and hanged two days later. The regiment was disbanded and stripped of its uniforms for its failure to act.

On 24 April, all apart from five of the 90 men of the 3rd Bengal Light Cavalry at Meerut refused to accept the cartridges. Retribution was severe. On 9 May, 85 men were court martialled and most were sentenced to ten years' imprisonment with hard labour.

The entire garrison was put on parade to witness the men being stripped of their uniforms and placed in shackles. As they were marched off to jail, some of them chided their comrades for their lack of support.

There was some protest in the city amongst civilians, with fires started in several of the buildings.

OFFICERS KILLED

The following day, the 3rd Cavalry, broke into revolt. Officers were killed when they tried to curtail them. Then European civilians' quarters were attacked with 50 Europeans killed, including soldiers, four male civilians, eight women and eight children.

The sepoys freed their 85 imprisoned comrades from jail, along with 800 other prisoners, and marched towards Delhi in the evening.

With other rebellions breaking out across India, garrisons were beleaguered for several months before the British could send reinforcement troops.

Early on 11 May the 3rd Cavalry reached Delhi and called for Emperor Bahadur Shah in his palace, to acknowledge and lead them, which he later did. Meanwhile, the house of the Chief Magistrate was destroyed and European officials and their families were killed by sepoys or other crowds of rioters.

Panicking British officers felt they could trust no one and opened fire on their own sepoys, managing to turn some potentially faithful men into enemies.

SIEGE OF DELHI

It wasn't until the beginning of July that British troops arrived on the outskirts of Delhi and established a base on the ridge to the north of the city. Heavy artillery rained down on the rebels in what became known as 'The Siege of Delhi' and by mid-September the city had been retaken. Bahadur Shah was arrested and many Indian citizens and sepoys were killed in retaliation.

A shocking incident had taken place in June when rebel sepoys in Cawnpore took 120 women and children hostage and killed them when they realised that all was lost.

In Lucknow, the besieged British Residency was rescued when a small column of relief soldiers managed to overcome the rebels.

REBELS DEFEATED

The last of the rebels were defeated in Gwalior in June 1858.

The bloodshed had sent shockwaves throughout colonial Britain, which had hitherto taken India for granted. The rebellion led to the dissolution of the East India Company with direct control of the region being assumed by the British Government in the form of the new British Raj. •

DISCOVERY OF A SUBTERRANEAN FOUNTAIN OF OIL

(*New York Tribune*, 8 September 1859)

THE PRESENCE OF OIL around Titusville in Pennsylvania had been known for years. Native Americans had been using it in medicinal remedies and by the mid-19th century it was being refined into kerosene for lamp oil.

Early methods of extracting it included digging trenches along Oil Creek or collecting it from seeps in the ground, but it was slow and laborious and not very efficient.

Knowing that there were big bucks to be made from oil, a group of investors formed the Pennsylvania Rock Oil Company and hired former railroad conductor Edwin Laurentine Drake to help them extract it. He had no engineering background and was principally hired because he was entitled to free rail travel, which would save the company money.

In his mid-30s, he retired due to ill health but, when the company became Seneca Oil with some new backers, he was tempted to return by its president, New Haven banker James M Townsend. His mission was to extract oil on a large scale basis at Titusville.

SINKING A SHAFT

Drake, who was hired at $1,000 dollars a year, had been frustrated by his earlier attempts and this time he decided on a new method based on that used by salt-well drillers. He would bore into the ground and sink a shaft straight to the source.

He was given the title of 'Colonel' to impress Titusville residents but they were less than respectful when he and his team arrived in March 1858.

At that time Titusville was a sleepy town, mostly involved in lumber, and the locals laughed at him for digging for oil – it was something that nobody had ever done. His effort was quickly dubbed 'Drake's folly', as they were convinced it wouldn't work.

After setting up the rig, drilling started in early August 1859, using a steam engine to drive a heavy iron bit into the ground to break the rock. The work was slow, averaging just a couple of feet a day, and the Seneca Oil directors were losing faith and interest, but Drake persevered.

PENNSYLVANIA OIL RUSH

On 27 August the drill bit had reached a depth of 69.5ft (21m) when the workers stopped for the day. But they hadn't realised that they had finally made it. The next morning when Drake's driller, Billy Smith, looked into the hole he saw crude oil rising up.

He excitedly rushed to tell Drake that they had struck oil and 'Drake's folly' became the prototype for future oil well construction. It was the first commercially viable oil well in the United States, producing 25 barrels a day and was the beginning of the Pennsylvania oil rush.

The town's population of 250 swelled to 10,000 as eight refineries were built between 1862 and 1868, spawning an ever-growing oil support industry.

BOOM TOWNS

New towns grew out of what were previously small settlements, oil wells springing up around the unimaginatively named Petroleum Center, while nearby, Pithole grew from nothing to have more than fifty hotels, three churches and a population of at least 20,000.

Prior to the oil boom, Titusville, which was originally called Edinburgh when Jonathan Titus founded the settlement in 1796, had around 250 residents, most of whom were involved in the lumber business. The town very quickly expanded to have a population of more than 10,000 and, unlike Petroleum Center and Pithole which became almost ghost towns when their oil ran dry, Titusville is still thriving today, albeit with a greatly reduced population.

OIL MILLIONAIRES

The first oil millionaire was Jonathan Watson, who owned the land where Drake's well was drilled. He was soon joined by many other millionaires but Drake was not one of them. He was to die an invalid, confined to a wheelchair and virtually penniless.

The Seneca Oil Company, which was now earning a fortune, paid him off with $2,167 in June 1860. Drake's subsequent business ventures were not a success. He lost what money he had made in bad investments and by May 1866 he was so down on his heels that he wrote to a friend asking for money. His wife supported their family by sewing dresses and taking in boarders.

In 1873, the state of Pennsylvania, by way of thanks for founding the oil industry, granted him an annuity of $1,500. He died on 9 November 1880. ●

THE WAR BEGUN

(New York Herald, 13 April 1861)

THIS SUCCINCT HEADLINE marked the start of the bloodiest war in American history, which was to last four years and result in the deaths of around 600,000 people.

The article was a despatch from Charleston, on the previous day which read, 'Civil war has at last begun. A terrible fight is at this moment going on between Fort Sumter and the fortification by which it is surrounded.'

Hostility between those in the North and South had been going on for years. The agricultural South favoured strong state government and relied on slaves to work on their land, while the more industrial North wanted a unifying federal government and sought to curtail the use of slaves.

The election of Abraham Lincoln as President in November 1860 was the final trigger for war between the two sides. Lincoln wanted to limit the expansion of slavery, but not abolish it. He was sworn in on 4 March 1861, and in his inaugural address he stated he had no intention to invade Southern states, nor did he intend to end slavery where it existed, but that he would use force to maintain possession of Federal property in the South.

SOUTHERN STATES SECEDE

The South did not want a Republican to be its President and abhorred Lincoln's views. As a result many Southern states left the Union. South Carolina had been the first to secede on 20 December 1860, now several others followed. Civil war was brewing as the two sides began to build up their armies.

THE BLUE AND THE GREY

The Union's soldiers in the North were called either 'Federals', 'Northerners' or 'Yankees' and wore blue uniforms. And the Confederacy in the South dressed in grey uniforms and were often referred to as 'Rebels' or 'Johnny Rebs'.

One of the Federal government's key forts in the South was Fort Sumter, because controlling it was integral to controlling Charleston harbour, one of the busiest ports in the South.

In charge of the fort was Major Robert Anderson, who sent a message to Lincoln that their supplies were running low in the fort and would only last six more weeks. Lincoln ordered new supplies to be delivered but the Confederates were determined to drive the Union out of their states and increased the pressure on the weakened Fort Sumter.

DEAL REJECTED

On 11 April 1861, Confederate General Pierre Beauregard demanded that Major Anderson evacuate the fort. Anderson played for time, saying he would leave the fort at noon on 15 April. But as Beauregard was aware that supplies would be delivered by then, he rejected the deal and at 4.30am the following day, he gave the order to open fire on the fort.

Short of ammunition, as well as food, the Federals did not return fire until about 7am. The firing stopped at night before re-starting the following day. When a cannonball set the barracks alight, Anderson agreed to a truce at about 2pm.

STRAY SPARK TRAGEDY

Incredibly, no one on either side had been killed. But when Anderson was allowed to stage a 100-gun salute to the U.S. flag, a pile of cartridges blew up from a spark, killing two of his men.

In the aftermath, Lincoln called for 75,000 men to enlist in the army to protect Federal property in the South and the Confederates were also swelled by eager young men willing to fight for their rights.

BLOODIEST BATTLE

A number of inconclusive engagements were fought during 1861-62 as the Confederates repulsed Union attempts to capture their capital at Richmond, Virginia, although the Confederates were defeated in Maryland at the Battle of Antietam in September 1862.

In 1863, General Robert E. Lee struck north and was eventually halted by Union forces at Gettysburg in Pennsylvania, where more lives were lost than in any other battle of the war. Union forces fared far better in the west and, when western commander Lieutenant General Ulysses S. Grant took charge of Union forces in the east, it spelled the end for the Confederacy.

After four years of warfare, including ferocious battles for Atlanta and Richmond, Robert E. Lee ultimately surrendered to Grant on 9 April 1865 at Appomattox Court House in Virginia.

As a result, slavery was outlawed throughout the nation and the role and influence of the Federal Government was enormously enhanced. •

IMPORTANT ASSASSINATION OF PRESIDENT LINCOLN

THE PRESIDENT SHOT AT THE THEATRE LAST EVENING

(*New York Herald*, April 15 1865)

IT WAS THE NEWS that shocked the nation. Many could scarcely believe it and crowds took to the streets in alarm and bewilderment.

The long-running American Civil War was just coming to a close as the victorious President Abraham Lincoln took time out with his wife, Mary, to enjoy a night at the theatre. But it would prove to be his final act as the curtain came down abruptly on his extraordinary life.

The Lincolns and their guests, Major Henry Rathbone and his fiancée Clara Harris, arrived at Ford's Theatre in Washington, D.C., at 8.40pm on Good Friday, 14 April 1865, to watch the British play *Our American Cousin*.

THE PRESIDENT BOWS

As they walked across the balcony to the Presidential Box, the wealthy theatregoers broke out into a round of applause, because of the satisfactory end of the Civil War. A delighted Lincoln paused to bow to the audience before continuing on his way.

The curtain went up and the play got under way and the audience enjoyed much of the humour. Then, during the third and final act a man made his way through a corridor to Lincoln's box, armed with a derringer and a hunting knife, and shot him in the back of the head at the moment when a particular line was said in the play which routinely elicited the biggest laugh.

The sound of the laughter partially muffled the gunshot and for a while the audience didn't quite know what had happened until they saw the President slump forward in his seat. Mary screamed and Major Rathbone grappled with the gunman but was stabbed in the arm. The attacker then leapt from the box to the stage, eleven feet below. He landed awkwardly, snapping the fibula bone in his left leg just above the ankle. Stumbling across the stage, he brandished his knife at the startled audience, and shouted, '*Sic Semper Tyrannis!*' (Latin for 'Thus always to tyrants', and the state motto of Virginia).

THE GUNMAN
ESCAPES

He made his escape backstage and out onto the street where he had left his horse with a theatre employee, and rode off.

A couple of doctors in the audience rushed to the President's aide but on seeing the bullet hole in the back of his head, they knew the wound was fatal. However, he was still breathing and so needed to be moved. They thought better of a bumpy carriage ride back across town to the White House and instead he was carried across the street to William Petersen's boarding house, where he was laid on a bed in a first-floor room.

Here a vigil took place for the dying President. The New York Herald reported how he was surrounded by his Cabinet, many in tears. As the news spread, people thronged the streets outside, anxious for more information.

Meanwhile, some members of the theatre's orchestra had identified the gunman as the actor John Wilkes Booth. He had performed throughout the country and was the lead in several of Shakespeare's plays. He had also played at Ford's Theatre on 12 occasions and so knew the layout well.

Booth was a Southern sympathiser who was incensed by Lincoln and his Emancipation Proclamation, which freed all slaves within the Confederacy.

By January 1865, he had organised a group of co-conspirators to capture Lincoln when he attended a play at a hospital just outside Washington and hold him in return for the release of Confederate prisoners of war. But the plot was foiled when the President changed his mind about attending.

CONFEDERATE SURRENDER

With numbers of the Army of Northern Virginia – the main army of the Confederacy – having dwindled to 35,000, General Robert E. Lee accepted the inevitable against General Ulysses S. Grant's Union soldiers of 120,000. He surrendered on 9 April , thereby ending the war.

But Booth refused to give up the fight and decided on drastic action. When he heard that Lincoln would be going to Ford's Theatre with General Grant, he saw it as a perfect opportunity to kill them both. At around the same time his gang of co-conspirators would kill Vice President Andrew Johnson and Secretary of State William Seward.

In the end, Grant didn't attend and Rathbone took his place. Lincoln died on the morning of 15 April, aged 56. No attempt to kill Johnson was made and Seward was stabbed at his home but it failed to kill him.

Booth was discovered 11 days later with a co-conspirator in a barn at a farm in rural Virginia by Union soldiers. After Booth had shouted that he would not be taken alive, one of the soldiers crept up behind the barn and shot him dead.

Abraham Lincoln was the first American president to be assassinated. He left a lasting impression on the United States, preserving the Union, cementing democracy and laying the foundation for the abolition of slavery. He is widely regarded as being the greatest President in American history. •

AUDIBLE SPEECH BY TELEGRAPH

PROF. A. GRAHAM BELL'S DISCOVERY

SUCCESSFUL AND INTERESTING EXPERIMENTS BETWEEN BOSTON AND CAMBRIDGEPORT

(*New York Times*, 21 October 1876)

A REPORTER FROM the *New York Times* was impressed by a demonstration given by Alexander Graham Bell and his assistant, Thomas Watson, on the evening of 9 October, 1876.

Telephones were placed at either end of a telegraph line from an office in Boston to a factory in Cambridgeport – two miles away. It was the first, long-distance, two-way telephone call.

'Articulate conversation then took place through the wires,' said the report. 'The sounds, at first faint and indistinct, became suddenly quite loud and intelligible. Mr Bell in Boston and Mr. Watson in Cambridge then took notes of what was said and heard, and the comparison of the two records is most interesting, as showing the accuracy of the electrical transmission.'

As with most inventions, there were several others working on similar ideas at the same time but Bell is credited with inventing the first practical telephone, having submitted an application for his model on 14 February 1876, just two hours before his rival, Elisha Gray.

WRITTEN SYMBOLS

Born in Edinburgh, he developed an interest with forms of communication from his father and grandfather, who both taught elocution. His mother was deaf and his father pioneered a method of communication called 'Visible Speech' – a set of written symbols designed to aid the deaf in speaking.

By the time the family emigrated to Canada in 1870, Bell junior was also teaching the deaf to communicate and later travelled to Boston in the U.S. to give lectures on Visible Speech.

He became professor of vocal physiology at Boston University in 1873. A year later he met an experienced electrical designer and mechanic named Thomas Watson and he hired him as his assistant in experimenting with the idea of transmitting speech over telegraph wires.

Their work eventually led to their succeeding in making their first telephone message on 10 March 1876, when Bell, in his Boston laboratory, summoned his colleague via the device from the next room with the now famous words, 'Watson, come here. I want to see you.'

In his journal, Bell later wrote, 'To my delight he came and declared that he had heard and understood what I said.'

The following year, Bell and Watson went on a tour of the Northeast, demonstrating their invention with great success to enraptured audiences.

The Bell Telephone Company was founded in 1877 and by 1886 over 150,000 people in the U.S. owned telephones.

CLARITY IMPROVED

In the succeeding years, there were numerous developments to improve clarity of telephone conversations and the distance over which they could be made. But the Bell Company, which used a liquid microphone transmitter, was nearly eclipsed by Thomas Edison's rival telephone company, which had patented a superior carbon version that enabled the telephone to be used over longer distances without needing to shout into the mouthpiece. Bell were saved when it developed a carbon device of its own.

Bell's invention had made him very wealthy and, inspired by Edison's huge scientific laboratory at Menlo Park in New Jersey, he set up Volta Laboratories, which later became Bell Labs. In 1885 a team working under him here developed an improved version of Edison's phonograph, called the graphophone, playing recorded sounds with the use of wax cylinders. He also experimented with kites and hydrofoils. But it would be the telephone that would mark his name in history. •

THE INDIAN WAR

GENERAL TERRY'S OFFICIAL REPORT OF THE CUSTER MASSACRE

(*Helena Daily Herald*, 14 July 1876)

T **HE MASSACRE OF General George Armstrong Custer's battalion in the Battle of the Little Bighorn was the worst U.S. Army defeat of the day.**

Yet it was to portray the man responsible for the disaster as a hero and the popular description of the battle, Custer's Last Stand, captured the imagination of generations for ever more.

This newspaper article, three weeks after the defeat, reported General Terry's official account of the massacre and the general tone is one of gallantry against overwhelming numbers.

CUSTER THE SHOWMAN

Custer had built a reputation fighting for the Union Army in the Civil War and became one of the youngest generals at the age of 23. He had also found a flair for publicity and showmanship. Keen to show his bravery he put himself forward for battles, petitioned for promotion and sought to capture attention with swagger and bravado. He also caught the eye with his 'dandy' style of dressing which included the likes of shiny cavalry boots, tight olive-coloured trousers, a wide-brimmed hat and a red neckerchief. At the end of the war he fought the Indians and took to wearing buckskin outfits. But despite his vanity, Custer had the respect of his men by fearlessly leading from the front, unlike some other officers.

GOLD IS DISCOVERED

The white settlers' expansion had continually pushed out the Plains Indians from their lands. The U.S Government 'allowed' the Plains Indians to live in certain areas, or 'reserves' but not in others, regularly reneging on treaties and agreements. And when gold was discovered in the Black Hills in Dakota, the U.S. decided to drive away all remaining free Plains Indians. The government set a deadline of 31 January 1876 for them to report to their designated reserves or be considered 'hostile'.

Tension was high and Sitting Bull called a gathering of Sioux and Cheyenne Indians at Ash Creek in Montana in late 1875 with the intention of fighting for their rights. Two victories in clashes with the U.S. Army the following spring spurred their confidence.

LITTLE BIGHORN RIVER

The 7th Cavalry, a unit of around 500–600 men, led by Custer, departed from Fort Lincoln on 17 May 1876 as part of a larger army force determined to round up remaining free Indians.

On 25 June, Custer's scouts sighted the large Indian encampment along the Little Bighorn River – where Sitting Bull and various Indian tribes had gathered.

Custer divided his men into three battalions. One, led by Major Marcus Reno, was to cross the river at the south end, attacking the encampment from the east, while Custer and his men would head west to attack from the other end. Captain Benteen's men would advance south and west to cut off any retreat through the upper valley.

But Custer had underestimated the size of the Indian contingent – an estimated 1,800 warriors – as well as the difficulty of the terrain, which was full of hills and ravines.

When Reno's men made their charge on the encampment, they were met by a massive counter-attack and after a brief ten-minute skirmish, they made a hasty retreat, taking cover in the trees along the river.

To the north and west, Custer and his 208 men – many of whom had crossed the river – were met head on by Cheyenne and Sioux Indians, who forced them back. Meanwhile, another force, largely Oglala Sioux under Crazy Horse's command, swiftly moved downstream in a sweeping arc, enveloping the Army in a pincer movement.

Custer ordered his men to shoot their horses and stack the carcasses to form a wall. But they were far outnumbered and in less than an hour they had all been killed.

Meanwhile, Reno and Benteen's now combined force continued fighting for another day until the Indians learned that a further two columns of soldiers were on their way, and fled.

CORPSES MUTILATED

When the main column under General Terry arrived two days later, the army found most of the soldiers' corpses stripped, scalped and mutilated. Custer's body had two bullet holes, one in the left temple and one just above the heart. Inexplicably, he had not been scalped. Some believe that because he was dressed in buckskin instead of blue uniform, the Indians may have not thought he was a soldier. Another explanation is that his hair had been cut short for battle, which may have made scalping difficult. A more romantic view was that his bravery had been respected.

The Indians had achieved their greatest victory at Little Bighorn, but retribution was swift. Within a year, the Sioux nation was defeated and broken. ●

EDISON'S ELECTRIC LIGHT

(*New York Times* 28 December 1879)

ON 21 OCTOBER 1879, prolific inventor Thomas Edison – who had invented the phonograph in 1877 – developed a practical electric light at his laboratory in Menlo Park, New Jersey.

Shortly after, he invited a *New York Times* reporter into his laboratory to witness the spectacle which was to make gas lamps redundant.

The reporter described how he was shown a glass globe containing a thread of carbonised paper held by two platinum clamps from which two wires ran outwardly through a small glass tube contained within a larger one leading out of the glass globe. Inside the tube the platinum wires were met by two copper ones connecting with the conductors of the electricity. Edison explained to him how the carbonised paper became incandescent by a current of electricity. He then proceeded to give a demonstration.

Edison was standing under a chandelier in which two of the bulbs were already burning. He removed one of them and the light went out. When he replaced it, the light shone brightly once more.

BRILLIANT INCANDESCENCE

The reporter was enraptured by what he saw. 'Mr. Edison then, by turning a screw in the lamp, brought the light down to a spark, turned it off completely, as gas can be turned off, and turned it on again to a brilliant incandescence by a twist of his fingers. He certainly demonstrated that in his own laboratory at Menlo Park, the electric light is as obedient to his will as the gas light is to the general public. The light from each lamp is of about the power of an ordinary gas-jet, but Mr. Edison claims that by increasing the electricity, he can raise the power to 15 gas-jets.'

Edison had a total of eighty-four lights burning in his laboratory, all supplied with electricity by an 80 horsepower engine in the basement.

He told the reporter, 'The electric light is perfected and all the problems which have been puzzling me for the last 18 months have been solved. I expect to have every house here lighted and a number of street-lamps going within 10 days.'

LIGHT BULB NOT EDISON'S

Never one to hide his light under a bushel, Edison had not, in fact, invented the light bulb but, by improving on the work of others before him, had come up with a practical version.

It was English inventor Joseph Swan who received the first patent for the incandescent light bulb in 1879 and his home in Gateshead

was the first in the world to be lit by one. Swan had reported success to the Newcastle Chemical Society and at a lecture at Sunderland Technical College in February 1879 he demonstrated a working lamp.

But Edison and his team at Menlo Park focused on producing a light bulb that was more robust and that would burn for longer.

The former salesman had his mind on commercial success: mass producing the bulbs and designing a system for the generation and distribution of electricity to illuminate streets, businesses and homes.

Edison continued to improve his design and by 4 November 1879, filed for a U.S. patent for an electric lamp using 'a carbon filament or strip coiled and connected to platina contact wires'. It was granted on 27 January 1880.

COURT BATTLE AVOIDED

Edison made the first public demonstration of his 'own' incandescent light bulb on 31 December 1879.

To avoid a possible court battle with Joseph Swan, he teamed up with him to form a company called Ediswan, which allowed Edison to sell the lights in America while Swan retained the rights in Britain.

WIZARD OF MENLO PARK

On New Year's Eve 1879, Christie Street, just outside Edison's Menlo Park laboratory, became the first street in the world to be lit by incandescent lamps, using a power system devised by Edison.

By the summer of 1880, the man sometimes known as 'The Wizard of Menlo Park' was mass producing light bulbs and had wired up two houses. The first was the nearby home of mathematician Francis Upton, who worked for Edison, and the second was the boarding house run by Sarah Jordan who was the widow of one of Edison's former business partners. Some of Edison's single employees lodged at the house and it was where Edison's entire team came together for social occasions.

Edison's business went from strength to strength as he demonstrated how electricity could be delivered to homes, to deliver power for domestic lighting, from a central generating station. He applied for around 400 patents for inventions devised at Menlo park over the years. Within ten years the wizard had outgrown Menlo Park and moved into a purpose-built facility in West Orange, New Jersey, which would be the inventor's headquarters until his death in 1931 at the age of 84. •

JESSE JAMES, THE BANDIT, KILLED

(*New York Tribune*, 4 April 1882)

A PAGE FIVE ARTICLE datelined 'St Joseph's Mo [Missouri] April 3', begins... 'A great sensation was created in this city this morning by the announcement that Jesse James, the notorious bandit and train robber, had been shot and killed here.'

It goes on to say how crowds rushed to the quarter of the city where the shooting occurred, anxious to see the body.

That his killing made national news showed how this most notorious of outlaws had become famous in his own lifetime. And he was to become a legendary figure after his death.

He was born in Clay County, Missouri, on 5 September 1847, and his father, Robert, was a prosperous commercial hemp farmer and Baptist minister who owned more than 100 acres of farmland and six slaves.

He travelled to California during the gold rush to minister the mining community and died there when Jesse was three years old. Jesse, his older brother, Frank, and younger sister, Susan, were then brought up by their mother, Zeralda.

GUERILLA FIGHTERS

After the outbreak of the Civil War he and Frank joined a band of Confederate guerrilla fighters whose other members included brothers Cole and James Younger. As well as attacking

Union troops the band also robbed mail coaches and shot supporters of Abraham Lincoln.

After the war Jesse and Frank became outlaws, forming the James-Younger gang, which included their former guerrilla Confederates, Cole and James, along with Bob Younger. Other members were Bill Chadwell, Clell Miller and Charlie Pitts.

On 13 February 1866, the gang robbed a bank at Liberty, Missouri, and over the next few years they took part in twelve bank robberies, seven train robberies, four stagecoach robberies and various raids on stores.

As well as their home state of Missouri, they were also active in West Virginia, Alabama, Arkansas, Iowa, Kansas and Minnesota. During these robberies at least eleven citizens were killed by the gang.

ROBBERY GOES WRONG

But the gang was virtually wiped out on 7 September 1876 during a robbery attempt on the First National Bank at Northfield, Minnesota. Residents who realised what was happening opened fire. Chadwell, Miller and Pitts were killed and the three Younger

brothers wounded and captured. Only Jesse and Frank escaped.

They went into hiding in Nashville and Frank appeared to settle down but a restless Jesse began to recruit a new gang in 1879 which included brothers Robert and Charlie Ford and Dick Liddel.

But Jesse was nervous and didn't trust his new gang like he did his former Confederate guerrilla colleagues.

During a robbery of train passengers as it slowed down to pass through an area of Missouri known as Blue in September 1881, the gang killed the conductor and a pensioner. The enraged governor of Missouri, Thomas Crittenden, offered a reward of $10,000 for the capture of Jessie James dead or alive. Robert Ford contacted Crittenden and offered his services.

LIVING IN DISGUISE

Jesse was living with his wife and children in a house at St Joseph, Missouri, under the pseudonym of J. D. Howards, and had asked the Ford brothers – whom he trusted more than others in his gang – to live at his house for extra protection.

Dick Liddel feared that Jessie wanted to kill him after he and

Robert Ford shot dead his cousin, Wood Hite. He turned himself in at Kansas City and told them what he knew about the James gang.

Ford knew he had surrendered but kept it secret from Jesse. When, three weeks later, he found Jesse reading a newspaper report about it while at home on the morning of 3 April 1882, Jesse accused him of knowing about it because he was in the neighbourhood at the time.

SHOT DEAD

Jesse glared at him but then seemingly changed his mood, saying it didn't matter. Ford, however, was certain that he was a marked man. Jesse was pretending not to mind because he didn't want to shoot him while his wife and family were at home. Jesse took off his gun belt and threw it on the bed. Then he stood on a chair to dust a picture on the wall and Ford took his chance to shoot him behind the ear while his back was turned.

Ford was arrested for murder but two hours later he was reprieved after Crittenden stepped in to give him his reward.

The legend of Jesse James grew and grew after his death with 'dime novels' of the 'James Gang' adventures in which he took on the mantle of a latter-day Robin Hood who stole from the rich to give to the poor. He was eulogised in songs and there have been numerous films about him over the years, all of which have kept him alive as an enduring icon of popular culture. •

THE WHITECHAPEL HORRORS

(*London Evening News*, 1 October 1888)

A DOUBLE MURDER in the early hours of 30 September 1888 sent terror through Whitechapel in the East End of London as the legend of Jack the Ripper gained pace and spread around the world.

The body of Elizabeth Stride was found by the steward of a working men's club in Dutfield's Yard near Berner's Street. Her throat had been cut. Just three-quarters of an hour later, a second body, Catherine Eddowes, was discovered with her throat cut in Mitre Square, Aldgate, along with an abdominal mutilation.

'LEATHER APRON'

Fear throughout the area had already been heightened by two similar murders – those of Mary Ann Nichols and Annie Chapman on 31 August and 8 September. Lurid newspaper accounts had nicknamed the attacker 'Leather Apron' – the description given to police by local prostitutes of a violent man who would demand a share of their earnings. But that was to change when a letter, dated 25 September 1888, was posted to the Central News Agency. The frenzied writing included the line, 'I am down on whores and I shant quit ripping them till I do get buckled.'

It was signed, 'Jack the Ripper'.

After the letter was forwarded to the police, the name was made public and excited people's imagination – not least that of headline writers. The double murder that occurred just days later intensified the general frenzy. The name Jack the Ripper stuck as news spread through the country and abroad.

And there was more to come, as on 1 October a postcard was sent to the agency, written in spidery red ink, which spoke of the 'double event' and again signed off as Jack the Ripper.

FIEND IN HUMAN SHAPE

The sales of newspapers soared as people were eager to hear the latest about 'this fiend in human shape'. His nerve and outrageous audacity in making such brutal attacks in the centre of London shocked the public.

The *London Evening News* reported, 'The public cannot fail to be impressed with one fact – the apparent bravado of the assassin. He seems to revel in brutality and the more energetic the police become in tracking him, the more contemptuously does he defy their efforts.'

From the similarity of the murders – cut throats and disembowelment – Jack seemed to be accountable for the murders of Nichols, Chapman, Stride and Eddowes. Police believed that he had been interrupted in his attack on Elizabeth Stride by the arrival of the local club steward in his trap and had to flee before completing the usual mutilation.

Some believed that The Ripper may also have murdered two other Whitechapel women, Emma Elizabeth Smith and Martha Tabram, who were both savagely attacked with a knife earlier in the year.

SCOTLAND YARD CALLED IN

The killing spree was considered too much for the Whitechapel police, headed by Detective Inspector Edmund Reid, and so Scotland Yard was called in, along with City police. But although many suspects were questioned and trails followed, they all ultimately led to nothing.

On 9 November, Mary Jane Kelly was found lying on her bed in the single room where she lived in Miller's Court, Spitalfields. Her throat had been cut, her abdomen virtually emptied of its organs and her heart was missing.

Throughout the period from 1888 to 1892, there were 11 women murdered in Whitechapel. No one can say for sure how many were the work of Jack the Ripper, but it is generally considered that five can be reasonably attributable to him – Mary Nichols, Annie Chapman, Elizabeth Stride, Catherine Eddowes and Mary Jane Kelly. All were killed between 31 August and 9 November 1888.

RIPPER REMAINS A MYSTERY

No one was ever convicted of the murders and the identity of Jack the Ripper has remained a mystery, although there has been a deluge of books and documentaries from those claiming to have identified the killer.

The murders drew attention to the poor living conditions of humble women in unsanitary and unsafe areas of the East End of London who had few options when it came to earning money, resulting in many turning to prostitution.

In the aftermath, some of the worst slums were demolished, there was improved lighting and charities were set up to help people through their hardship. •

THE WOMAN'S SUFFRAGE BILL ASSENTED TO

(*Auckland Star*, 19 September 1893)

NEW ZEALAND became the first self-governing country in the world to grant all women the right to vote in parliamentary elections.

The Governor, Lord Glasgow, signed the new Electoral Act into law in September 1893, following increasing pressure from suffragettes and their supporters.

The movement was spearheaded by Kate Sheppard. Born in Liverpool in 1847, she emigrated to settle in Christchurch in her early twenties. In 1885 she helped form New Zealand's Women's Christian Temperance Union, which advocated women's suffrage as a means to fight for liquor prohibition. But it was suffrage that was to become an end in itself for Sheppard.

She led an intensive seven-year campaign for the right for women to vote, speaking eloquently at public meetings, lobbying politicians with telegrams and letters and writing many pamphlets to keep the debate alive. Opposition was fierce but the suffragists gained increasing support when women outside the temperance movement joined them.

Sheppard argued, 'We are tired of having a "sphere" doled out to us, and of being told that anything outside that sphere is "unwomanly".'

BILLS FAIL IN PARLIAMENT

Such was the growing support that it could not be ignored and in 1878, 1879 and 1887 bills or amendments extending the vote to women only narrowly failed to pass in Parliament.

The WCTU compiled a series of petitions from the public in support of their aims which they presented to Parliament. In 1891 over 9,000 signatures were gathered, in 1892 almost 20,000 and in 1893 nearly 32,000.

A number of New Zealand's leading politicians, including John Hall, Robert Stout, Julius Vogel, William Fox and John Ballance, supported women's suffrage. But there was considerable opposition both in and out of Parliament.

Scaremongers warned that meddling with the 'natural' gender roles of men and women could have terrible consequences. And the powerful liquor industry, fearing the WCTU's aim to prohibit alcohol, lobbied sympathetic Members of Parliament and organised counter-petitions.

WHEELBARROW PETITION

The massive third petition was transported theatrically to Parliament in a wheelbarrow and the 766-foot-long scroll was unrolled across the chamber of the House of Representatives with dramatic effect. It was the largest petition ever presented to Parliament. The bill was passed on 8 September 1893 by 20 votes to 18.

But the long battle was still not over as new anti-suffrage petitions were circulated and some members of the Legislative Council petitioned the Governor to withhold his consent. It was not until 11 days later that Lord Glasgow signed the bill into law. Suffragists celebrated throughout the country, and congratulations poured in from campaigners in Britain, Australia, the United States and elsewhere.

Suffrage opponents had warned that delicate 'lady voters' would be jostled and harassed in polling booths by 'boorish and half-drunken men'. But the election on 28 November of that year, when 65 per cent of women took the chance to vote for the very first time, was described as the 'best-conducted and most orderly' ever held.

Even so, New Zealand women still had a long way to go to achieve political equality. They would not gain the right to stand for Parliament until 1919, and the first female Member of Parliament, Elizabeth McCombs, was not elected until 1933.

THE WHITE CAMELLIA

During the campaign for women's suffrage, those who supported the

1893 Electoral Bill were presented with a white camellia to wear in their buttonhole. The white camellia has since become a symbol of women's suffrage in New Zealand.

Sheppard continued to work at home and abroad for women's rights – from contraception to freedom from the corset. She became president of the National Council of Women of New Zealand and editor of the *White Ribbon*, the first newspaper in New Zealand to be owned, managed and published solely by women. In 1909 she was elected honorary vice president of the International Council of Women.

She died on 13 July 1934, a year after she saw Elizabeth McCombs, enter Parliament. •

LUMIERE'S CINEMATOGRAPHE

(*Sydney Morning Herald*, 22 September 1896)

THE LUMIERE BROTHERS, who can justifiably claim to have 'invented' the cinema, were wowing audiences the world over with their moving pictures in the late 19th century.

Their exuberant father, Antoine, worked as a sign painter before becoming interested in an article about a new technique for manufacturing photographic dry plates, pioneered by the Belgian chemist Van Monkhoven.

He set about making his own plates in his small studio in Lyon, but with little success. Frustrated, he turned to his bright teenage son, Louis, who excelled at science at the technical school he attended with his brother, Auguste.

At the age of 17, Louis was able to improve on Van Monkhoven's design, creating a new form of dry plate which was far more sensitive.

The brothers started to work for their father – Louis as a physicist and Auguste as a manager – and

as photographic portraits became a fashionable trend, the Lumières became very wealthy. To meet the demand for their product, they opened a big new factory in the Lyon suburb of Monplaisir.

CREATIVE VISIONARY

The brothers took control of the company around 1882 but Antoine continued to be a creative visionary source and in the autumn of 1894 he was inspired when a friend showed him one of Thomas Edison's new Kinetoscopes. These were popular novelty arcade devices. By dropping a coin through the slot of the heavy wooden cabinet, the spectator activated a small motor inside that moved spools of celluloid. An electric light flashed onto the film and, by peering down through a lens, the spectator was able to watch crude moving pictures – usually performing animals, boxing matches and circus performers.

An excited Antoine hurried to Louis and told him they should be making film like this. Determined to eclipse Edison by taking a share of this new market, he decided that they would need to develop a camera and projector of their own. The problem lay in moving the strip of film smoothly through a camera. But it was Louis who, once again, found the solution. He adapted the sprocket mechanism of the newly popular sewing machine to move a strip of film along. It was housed in a wooden box which acted as both camera and projector.

THE CINEMATOGRAPHE

Significantly, by projecting pictures onto an exterior screen, they were able to be watched by groups of people instead of just one. They named the device the cinematographe, derived from the Greek word for movement. It was the birth of cinema.

Although Auguste gave credit to Louis, the successful machine was patented in France on 13 February 1895 in both of their names.

In March they used it to shoot a short film of their employees called, *La Sortie des Usines Lumière* (*Workers Leaving the Lumière Factory*).

Later that month, the Lumières arranged intimate screenings of the film for French scientific institutions and then arranged for a larger public viewing in the basement of the Salon Indien du Grand Café in Paris on 28 December.

Just hours before this first show, Antoine was still desperately drumming up support for the event which was payable on admission. Only 33 people turned up. At first they saw a series of still pictures projected onto a screen and there were some disgruntled noises about this lack of innovation. But then one of the pictures, a horse and cart, started to move towards them. It was followed by other moving vehicles and people walking down a street. It was an incredible sight.

EVERYDAY SCENES

The series of ten short films screened were of such simple everyday scenes as Auguste Lumière and his wife feeding their baby, a gardener using a hose and the workers leaving the

Lumière factory. Each lasted around 50 seconds.

News of the films swept across France and overseas. Before long, 2,500 people a day were queuing to watch them.

The Lumières made over 200 cinematographes and employed agents to demonstrate them around the world, shooting scenes and screening them.

OVERWHELMING RESPONSE

One of the first overseas shows was organised in London by the illusionist Felicien Trewey, a friend of Antoine, at the Marlborough Hall on Regent Street on 20 February 1896. Such was the overwhelming response that the show soon transferred to the far bigger Empire Theatre in Leicester Square, where it would play for almost eighteen months.

The *Sydney Morning Herald* contained a small report about the cinematographe's arrival in Australia, having been 'drawing the crowds at the Empire Theatre, London'. Following its success at a private viewing at the Lyceum Theatre in Sydney, it would shortly have a public exhibition. •

OSCAR WILDE IN JAIL

(*Daily Inter Ocean*, 6 April 1895)

THE TRIAL OF OSCAR WILDE was eagerly followed around the world, the sensational revelations making the story compulsive reading as Wilde went from complainant to defendant in the blink of an eye.

The famous playwright and poet had delighted audiences with his comedy plays *The Importance of Being Earnest, Lady Windermere's Fan* and *A Woman of No Importance*.

And he had charmed high society with his flamboyant dress and sparkling wit. But at the height of his fame things took a downward turn when he decided to prosecute the Marquis of Queensberry for libel after he accused him of 'posing as a sodomite'.

The Chicago newspaper, *The Daily Inter Ocean*, reported the sensational moment at London's Old Bailey Court when, on 5 April 1895, Wilde withdrew his libel action, thereby practically admitting the truth of Queensberry's accusation.

WILDE ARRESTED

He was arrested at the Cadogan Hotel shortly after the court closed and spent the night in a cell at Bow Street Police Station. His name was promptly withdrawn from play bills and advertising from two theatres, the St James and the Haymarket, where his plays were running.

While at university at Oxford, Wilde, a brilliant scholar, took a keen interest in the philosophy of aestheticism, which he later portrayed in his stories and poems that were published in magazines.

On 29 May 1884 he married Constance Lloyd, and they settled in a house in Chelsea, West London, and had two sons, Cyril and Vyvyan. Wilde began an affair with a young man named Robert Ross in 1886 and afterwards with 22-year-old Oxford undergraduate Lord Alfred Douglas, the son of the Marquis of Queensberry. Wilde was then 38.

MALE PROSTITUTES

Acts of homosexuality were at that time illegal and it was the rather self-centred Douglas who introduced Wilde to London's 'underground' world of young male prostitutes.

The Marquis of Queensbury, a Scottish nobleman born John Sholto Douglas, was a founder of the Amateur Athletics Association and a very keen boxer, having given his name to boxing's 'Queensbury Rules'. He was absolutely furious about his son's 'friendship' with Wilde and demanded that it end, but Alfred stubbornly refused to stop seeing Wilde.

Queensbury was determined that Wilde should not be allowed to lead his son astray. His eldest son, Francis, was widely rumoured to be having a homosexual affair with the Prime Minister, Lord Roseberry, and, in October 1894, Francis was to die in a mysterious hunting accident. Queensbury had no qualms about confronting Oscar Wilde.

In June 1894, Queensberry visited Wilde at his home and told him, 'I do not say that you are it, but you look it, and pose at it, which is just as bad. And if I catch you and my son again in any public restaurant I will thrash you.'

At the premiere of *The Importance of Being Earnest*, at St James's on 14 February 1895, Queensberry arrived determined to publicly insult Wilde by throwing a bouquet of rotting vegetables onto the stage. But Wilde had been tipped off and had him barred from entering the theatre.

Four days later, Queensberry left his calling card at Wilde's club, the

Albemarle, inscribed, 'For Oscar Wilde, posing somdomite [sic]'.

Wilde, encouraged by Alfred and against the advice of his friends, initiated a private prosecution against Queensberry, who was arrested on a charge of criminal libel.

THE TRIAL BEGINS

The trial opened on 3 April 1895 amidst great publicity and excitement in the packed public and press galleries. Queen's Counsel for the defence, Edward Carson, questioned Wilde about his acquaintances with younger, lower-class men. Wilde insisted they were just friends but admitted lavishing gifts on them.

He responded to many of Carson's questions with his usual mix of wit and aesthetic intellect, which, although entertaining, did not help his plight.

The following day at court, Carson announced that he had located several male prostitutes who were to testify that they had had sex with Wilde. Sir Edward George Clarke, Wilde's counsel, left the courtroom to consult with Wilde who was in another room. On his return he dramatically announced

the withdrawal of the case on behalf of his client.

QUEENSBURY NOT GUILTY

The jury, as directed by Justice Collins, found Queensberry not guilty of libel and he left court triumphant, smiling and surrounded by friends. A warrant for the arrest of Wilde was quickly applied for. He was arrested at the Cadogan Hotel and spent the night at Bow Street police station.

Wilde wrote a letter to newspapers in which he said, 'It was not possible to prove my case without putting Lord Alfred Douglas in the witness-box against his father. Lord Alfred was extremely anxious to go into the box but I would not allow it. Rather than put him in such a painful position I determined to retire from the case, bear upon my own shoulders whatever shame and ignominy might result from not prosecuting the Marquis of Queensberry.' He was placed on remand at Holloway Prison until his trial opened at the Old Bailey on 26 April. Wilde pleaded not guilty and the trial ended with the jury unable to reach a verdict.

WILDE JAILED

The final trial on 25 May was presided over by Mr Justice Wills and here Wilde was convicted of gross indecency and sentenced to two years' imprisonment. He was first incarcerated in Pentonville, then Wandsworth and later Reading.

Wilde's health suffered badly in prison and after his release on 19 May 1897 he moved to France and was reunited with Alfred at Rouen three months later. They lived together in Naples for a few months towards the end of the year but Wilde was a broken man who had lost everything and after Queensberry threatened to cut off Alfred's funds, he returned home.

By 25 November Wilde had developed cerebral meningitis. He was now living in a dingy hotel in Paris, alone and with very little money. He died on 30 November 1990. •

WAR DECLARED BOERS COMMENCE HOSTILITIES

(*Grocott's Daily Mail*, 12 October 1899)

THIS SOUTH AFRICAN newspaper reported the start of a gruelling three-year war which would result in great suffering and many deaths and change the face of the country.

Hostilities between Britain and the descendants of Danish settlers, the Boers (farmers), had broken out in 1880 in the first Boer War. This was in the wake of around 15,000 Boers making the 'Great Trek' out of the British-owned Cape Colony across the Orange River into the interior of South Africa between 1835 and 1847.

They established two independent republics – the Transvaal and the Orange Free State – which were recognised by Britain in 1852 and 1854.

In 1867 diamonds were discovered near the confluence of the Orange and Vaal Rivers, prompting a diamond rush.

BOER ARMED RESISTANCE

British Colonial Secretary, Lord Carnarvon proposed a confederation of South African states in 1875. The Boers began armed resistance against annexation of the Transvaal in 1880 and the republic was reinstated.

In 1886 gold was discovered in the Transvaal but the republic did not have the manpower or industrial base to be able to properly mine it and so the Boers reluctantly agreed to the immigration of fresh waves of uitlanders (foreigners), mainly from Britain, who came to work there. This resulted in the number of uitlanders in the Transvaal eventually exceeding that of Boers, which caused resentment and conflict.

In September 1899 Britain sent an ultimatum to the Boers, demanding full equality for those uitlanders resident in the Transvaal.

BOERS THREATEN WAR

Paul Kruger, the President of the Transvaal, issued his own ultimatum, giving the British 48 hours to withdraw all their troops from the border. If they did not then the Transvaal, allied with the Orange Free State, would declare war against the British.

On 11 October 1899, the second Boer War broke out after Britain rejected the ultimatum.

The Boers attacked British-held territory in Natal and the Cape Colony, besieging their garrisons at Ladysmith, Mafeking and Kimberley.

In the New Year reinforcements of British troops arrived under the command of Lord Roberts in an attempt to relieve the sieges.

The siege of Mafeking was to last 217 days before it was finally relieved on 17 May 1990. Colonel Robert Baden-Powell, in command of the defence of the town, was hailed as a hero back home in Britain, where people were overjoyed with the news.

Once Natal and the Cape Colony were secure the British were able to invade the Transvaal and the republic's capital, Pretoria, was captured on 5 June 1900.

SCORCHED EARTH POLICY

In November Lord Herbert Kitchener, who succeeded Roberts as commander in South Africa, implemented a 'scorched earth' policy in which towns and farms in the republics were burnt or ravaged, destroying crops and livestock. Citizens – especially women and children who had been made homeless – were confined in appalling conditions in camps.

Kitchener's reasoning behind this policy which caused great suffering was that the commandos would no longer be able to obtain food from women on the farms, and would surrender in order to reunite their families.

The war struggled on for another two years before the Boer forces finally surrendered on 31 May 1902. The peace settlement, the Treaty of Vereeniging, brought to an end the Transvaal and the Orange Free State as Boer republics. But the British granted the Boers £3 million for restocking and repairing farm lands and promised eventual self-government. In 1910 the four provinces – Cape, Natal, Transvaal and Orange Free State – were incorporated into the Union of South Africa, a dominion of the British Empire. On 31 May 1961 the nation became a republic, under the name of the Republic of South Africa. •

WIRELESS SIGNALS ACROSS THE OCEAN

(*New York Times*, 15 December 1901)

A **FAINT SOUND OF three taps heard over a radio receiver in Newfoundland, Canada, marked a new era of global communications.**

Guglielmo Marconi had managed to transmit a radio signal across the Atlantic and defied fellow scientists who thought it could not be done.

Born in Bologna, the son of a wealthy Italian father and Irish mother, he became interested in science at school and carried out many experiments in the attic at home. It was here that his fascination with wireless telegraphy began. Having read about German scientist Heinrich Hertz's work with electromagnetic waves, Marconi hit on the idea of sending messages as signals through the air instead of along wires in the telegraph and telephone.

One night in 1895 he called his mother into the attic to show her how he was able to press a switch on a transmitter to send out radio waves to a receiver about nine metres away and ring a bell. He was later able to send messages in Morse code between a transmitter and receiver in the garden, two kilometres apart.

Marconi quickly realised the commercial possibilities that lay ahead but he could find little interest in his home country, which seemed content with the current system of transmission by telegraph lines and underwater cables.

SIGNALS OVER LONDON

His mother felt that his best opportunities lay in England and they came to London in 1896. That July he sent signals a mile over central London and by September, two miles across Salisbury Plain. Marconi's main aim was to use his system as a means for helping ships in distress. In May 1897 he transmitted across the Bristol Channel and in December from the Isle of Wight to a ship in the English Channel.

He formed the Wireless Telegraph and Signal Company Limited with his cousin Henry Jameson Davis.

In 1898 Marconi installed radio equipment on the Royal Yacht so that Queen Victoria, who was staying at Osborne House on the Isle of Wight, could communicate with the Prince of Wales (later Edward VII), lying off Cowes, who was convalescing on board.

Marconi's system was first used as a practical aid to the ship in distress on 11 March 1899 when a ship went aground on the Goodwin Sands, in the English Channel off the east coast of Kent, amidst a thick fog. The South Goodwin Lightship fired gun signals but this system often failed because when wind was blowing offshore the guns could not be heard on land. However, on this occasion they were heard by the East Goodwin Lightship, which communicated by wireless telegraphy to the South Foreland Lighthouse, and from there telegraphic messages were sent to the authorities.

INTERNATIONAL MESSAGES

Marconi pushed the boundaries further when, on 27 March 1899, he transmitted the first international wireless message across the Channel from Wimereux near Bologne, France, to the South Foreland Lighthouse.

Marconi had become something of a celebrity by now and, with a flair for showmanship, he set out to perform his biggest experiment yet – transmitting signals across the Atlantic.

It was an enormous financial gamble costing around £50,000 and there were many who said it could not be done because of the curvature of the earth.

At Poldhu in Cornwall, he set up a powerful radio transmitter and an aerial system at Cape Cod in Massachusetts. But after bad weather damaged the aerial Marconi and his assistant, George Kemp, at short notice, switched the location to the appropriately named Signal Hill in St John's, Newfoundland, Canada.

Here Marconi and his assistants set up a radio receiver connected to a makeshift aerial consisting of 500 feet of wire supported by flying kites. It was nowhere near as powerful or sophisticated as the set up at Poldhu but Marconi felt it sufficient for his needs.

Marconi and Kemp sat in a hut at Signal Hill on 12 December waiting for a pre-arranged signal from the station at Poldhu – three dots, the Morse code for the letter 's', chosen for its simplicity. At 12.30pm (GMT), Marconi heard three faint clicks in his telephone connected to the radio receiver. The clicks had come all the way from Cornwall.

MURDERER CAPTURED

In 1909 1,700 lives were saved through wireless distress calls when two liners collided and one of them sank off the coast of the USA. The following year saw more success when Marconi's wireless system made headline news after it was used to apprehend Dr Hawley Crippen, who was fleeing England with his lover, Ethel Le Neve, after murdering his wife and burying the body in his cellar. The captain of the SS *Montrose* asked his Marconi operator to send a brief message to England: 'Have strong suspicions that Crippen London cellar murderer and accomplice are among saloon passengers. Accomplice dressed as a boy. Voice manner and build undoubtedly a girl.'

A detective from Scotland Yard boarded a faster ship and arrested him before SS *Montrose* docked in Montreal. •

DAYTON BOYS EMULATE GREAT SANTOS-DUMONT

(*Dayton Daily News*, 18 December 1903)

THIS RATHER UNDERWHELMING headline 'celebrated'
one of the greatest human achievements in history –
the power of flight.

It was on page eight of the *Dayton Daily News*, newspaper of the home town of brothers Orville and Wilbur Wright.

Brazilian aviator Alberto Santos-Dumont had become a celebrity from pioneering and flying steerable air balloons and although the newspaper spoke of the Wrights emulating him, they had actually ushered in the modern age of aviation.

The brothers had become interested in flying at an early age. In 1878 their father had given them a toy helicopter powered by rubber bands. They played and experimented with it and built their own versions of the toy. They also learned the fundamentals of flight by playing with kites. After opening a bicycle sales and repair shop in Dayton in 1892, they began making their own bikes and this mechanical knowledge of movement and steering led them to building gliders.

GLIDER PILOT KILLED

But it was the widely publicised fatal crash of famed German glider pioneer Otto Lilienthal in 1896 that really focused their attention on flight. They built and experimented with gliders at Kitty Hawk, North Carolina. They chose this location because of the steady winds there which would lift their gliders whilst the sand dunes offered a soft landing ground.

FIRST FLYING MACHINE

The Wrights' third glider, built in 1902, was a dramatic success and they were able to make numerous controlled flights in it – the best lasting for twenty-six seconds. They were convinced that they were close to powered flight and the following year they began experimenting with a piloted 'flying machine' at Kitty Hawk.

The *Wright Flyer* was a biplane which had light timber wings spanning 40ft 4in (12.3m) covered with canvas. It was 21ft 1in (6.4m) long, 9ft 4in (2.8m) high and weighed 605lbs (274kg).

It was fitted with two propellers mounted behind the wings and connected to a small gasoline engine. Underneath this sat the navigator, who controlled a rudder of canvas which could be moved from side to side and up and down.

On 14 December 1903 they were ready to make the first attempt at powered flight at Kitty Hawk. A flip of the coin had decided that Wilbur would pilot the *Wright Flyer* but it stalled during take-off and they had to repair it before trying again three days later.

This time it was Orville's turn in the pilot seat. It was launched from a trolley on a track on an incline. As it gathered speed, Orville started up the engine, which worked the propellers, and it was lifted into the air, obtaining an altitude of 60ft and flying for 120ft in 12 seconds.

AIRCRAFT DESTROYED

The brothers took turns each in the pilot seat for the next three flights that day. The longest was the final flight with Wilbur at the controls managing 852ft in 59 seconds. But it landed badly, damaging the front rudder. After removing the rudder and carrying the machine back to camp, the brothers stood discussing the flights with their team when a gust of wind turned the machine tumbling over and over, smashing it beyond repair.

But it mattered little. The Wright brothers had discovered the secret of flight. During the design and construction of their experimental aircraft they also pioneered many aspects of future aeronautical engineering such as the use of a wind tunnel.

Not everyone, however, was convinced of the Wright brothers' claims to have achieved powered flight, despite the fact that they had witnesses. In France, where there was great enthusiasm for aeronautics, many simply refused to believe that the Americans had been the first to fly, and maintained that the French would win the race to conquer the sky.

Wilbur and Orville were reluctant to travel to Europe as they thought that others would simply steal their ideas. Alberto Santos-Dumont made the first European heavier-than-air flight in France in 1906, piloting an aeroplane he had designed, rather than the balloons that had made him famous. The Wright brothers shied away from competitions and the prizes that were being offered to pioneer aviators, instead concentrating on improving their aircraft and patenting it.

It was not until Wilbur visited France in 1908 and demonstrated how the Wright brothers' latest machine could stay aloft, by now for many minutes, under complete control, that all of Europe, including even the French, acknowledged the superior engineering of the Dayton boys' flying machine. •

THE CONQUEST OF THE SOUTH POLE

(*Manchester Guardian*, 9 March 1912)

AFTER A BRUTAL **and heroic trek across the frozen wastelands of Antarctica, British explorer Captain Robert Scott and his team, who were striving to be the first to reach the South Pole, finally reached their destination... only to find Norwegian rival Roald Amundsen had beaten them to it.**

News of the Norwegian expedition's achievement took several months to reach Europe. This report in the *Manchester Guardian* rather grudgingly congratulates Amundsen on his success but sows a hint of doubt into his story.

'Whether Amundsen was the first to reach the South Pole remains, of course, to be seen; no word has yet come of Captain Scott, and until we know whether he reached the Pole, and, if so, when, the question who is the victor in the race remains uncertain.'

The two expeditions had employed very different strategies. Amundsen relied on dogs and sledges to transport supplies over the ice while Scott preferred ponies and mechanical sledges. But the ponies suffered in the cold and the mechanical sledges failed and so the men ended up pulling them. The Norwegians eschewed the usual thick woollen clothing for wolfskin fur suits that had been adapted from Inuit garments, in addition to Burberry suits made of a lighter gabardine material.

SCIENTIFIC RESEARCH

Scott's agenda was to continue his scientific research, which he had undertaken on his *Discovery* expedition of 1901–4 which reached further south than anyone before them and had turned him into a national hero. But Amundsen focused on being the first to reach the South Pole. These are just some of the factors that led to success for the Norwegians and failure and tragedy for the British who were to die on their way home.

Amundsen and his team left Oslo on 3 June 1910 aboard the ship *Fram*, heading south. At that time Norway was a relatively new nation having only achieved its independence from Sweden in 1905. They needed diplomatic support from Britain and so the expedition was kept secret for fear of upsetting the British.

They arrived at the eastern edge of the Great Ice Barrier on 14 January 1911 and set up base camp named Framhein. After a first attempt at reaching the Pole failed,

Amundsen set off with four others, Olav Bjaaland, Helmer Hanssen, Sverre Hassel and Oscar Wisting, on 19 October. They arrived at the South Pole on 14 December 1911 and left behind their tent and a letter stating their accomplishment, in case they did not return home safely. The team reached Framhein on 25 January 1912 and news of their success became public after they sailed to Hobart, Australia, on 7 March.

TERRA NOVA SETS SAIL

The British expedition left West Indian Dock, London, aboard the ship *Terra Nova* on 1 June 1910, on the start of her voyage to Antarctica. On arrival in January 1911 they set up base camp in Ross Island. Scott made his selection of the men who were to accompany him on the final stage – Petty Officer Evans, Lieutenant Bowers, Dr Wilson and Captain Oates – and they set off on 1 November.

Ten miles from their destination, Bowers saw a black speck on the horizon. Later they came across sledge and ski tracks and the imprints of dog paws. When they arrived on 17 January 1912, they entered the tent and read

Amundsen's note, which confirmed that he had arrived a month earlier and had now departed.

A crushed Scott wrote in his journal that evening, 'Great God! This is an awful place and terrible enough for us to have laboured to it without the reward or priority.'

From the start of the return journey, Evans was weak and continued to deteriorate in the arduous conditions.

LOST SUPPLY DROPS

Amundsen had placed well-marked depots of food and supplies en route, while Scott had fewer and badly marked depots that often could not be found in the blizzards. Evans had cut his hand some weeks before on one of the sledge runners and it had swollen and turned gangrenous. He died on the Beardmore Glacier on 17 February.

By March Oates was suffering from severe frostbite. Scott described in his journal how Oates had said he couldn't go on but they refused his suggestion of leaving him behind in his sleeping bag and encouraged him to trek on with

them. But on the morning of 17 March he awoke and commented, 'I am just going outside and may be some time.' He then walked out into the howling blizzard and they never saw him again.

Scott, Wilson and Bowers all died from exposure and hunger while sheltering from a blizzard in their tent on 29 March 1912.

The last entry to Scott's journal on that day read, 'We had fuel to make two cups of tea apiece and bare food for two days on the 20th. Every day we have been ready to start for our depot 11 miles away, but outside the doors of the tent it remains a scene of whirling drift. I do not think we can hope for any better things now. We shall stick it out to the end, but we are getting weaker, of course, and the end cannot be far. It seems a pity, but I do not think I can write more. R Scott. For God's sake look after our people.'

Eight months later, on 12 November 1912, a search party found the tent, the bodies and Scott's diary. The bodies were buried under the tent, with a cairn of ice and snow to mark the spot. •

TITANIC SUNK

TERRIBLE LOSS OF LIFE FEARED
COLLISION WITH AN ICEBERG

(*The Times*, 16 April 1912)

CRACKS WERE appearing in the once mighty British Empire and the 'old world' of privilege, power and prosperity enjoyed by the upper-classes was about to be rocked by the outbreak of World War I.

But glamour and overt affluence was still to be had and none more so than a first-class transatlantic ticket aboard the White Star Line's new pride and joy, the RMS *Titanic*.

It was billed as the largest passenger steamship in the world and offered luxurious First Class accommodation, with large state-rooms, a Parisian café, a swimming pool and restaurant. What's more, special watertight compartments made her 'practically unsinkable'.

The *Titanic*'s maiden voyage from Southampton to New York City on Wednesday, 10 April 1912, attracted some of the most eminent people of the day as millionaires, businessmen, industrialists, aristocrats, politicians and bankers waved

family and friends a final farewell from the upper decks before departing on the trip of a lifetime.

But as well as the wealthy, the *Titanic* offered many working-class people the chance to try a new life in America with reasonably priced accommodation in Third Class, tucked away in the lower decks.

ICEBERG COLLISION

Four days into the journey, the unthinkable happened. The ship struck an iceberg at night, piercing the starboard side and popping out rivets. At first, everyone remained calm. This, after all, we the unsinkable *Titanic*. But one of the passengers aboard was Thomas

Andrews, a naval architect who worked for Harland & Wolff, the Belfast shipyard that had built *Titanic*. He was part of the company's 'Guarantee Group', a team of experienced engineers and tradesmen who sailed on every Harland & Wolff ship's maiden voyage to troubleshoot problems, iron out teething difficulties and suggest practical improvements to the design.

Andrews very quickly realised that the extent and position of the damage spelt disaster. He knew that if the watertight compartments in the ship's bow flooded, the water would rise up above the level of the compartments and flood the whole ship. That the ship would sink was, as he put it, 'a mathematical certainty.' It was just a matter of time.

Titanic struck the iceberg at 11.40pm on 14 April. By 2.20am the following morning, just two hours and forty minutes later, she would be gone. The ship's captain, Edward Smith, ordered 'mayday' signals to be broadcast.

The nearest ship to pick up the distress signal was the *Carpathia* but she was 58 miles (93 km) away and, despite travelling at full steam, she would not reach the area until three and a half hours later.

PASSENGERS PANIC

As the *Titanic* began to sink there was increasing panic aboard and lifeboats left the ship only partially full. The first to pull away, with a capacity of 65, contained 27 people. Another, with a capacity of 40, left with just 12. Third class passengers couldn't find their way to the upper decks where the lifeboats were stored and many were still below deck when the ship sank.

In less than three hours, *Titanic* had sunk and the lucky ones who had managed to get in lifeboats, spent three hours on the freezing cold water before *Carpathia* was spotted on the horizon with the coming of dawn and took them aboard.

The official British inquiry concluded that Titanic had sunk after colliding with an iceberg due to excessive speed of 22 knots.

The incident was to bring about many changes in maritime regulations. It was found that the provision of lifeboats was woefully inadequate. Just 20 boats could hold a maximum of 1,178 people. But on board the *Titanic* was a total of 2,201 passengers and crew. In the end, just 711 people were rescued.

THE AFTERMATH

No proper lifeboat drill had taken place and that would become a legal requirement, as would easier access throughout all future ships for passengers following the revelation that just 25 per cent of those in Third Class, below decks, were saved, compared with 62 per cent and 41 per cent in First and Second, respectively.

Other changes would be in hull and bulkhead design, improved life-vests and improved radio communications.

The sinking of the *Titanic* shook the world's confidence in the infallibility of modern technology and underlined the importance of safety and common sense. •

SENSATIONAL DERBY SUFFRAGIST'S MAD ACT

KING'S HORSE BROUGHT DOWN WOMAN AND JOCKEY INJURED

(*Morning Post*, 5 June 1913)

SUFFRAGETTE Emily Wilding Davison hit the headlines when she caused a sensation at the Derby by throwing herself in front of the King's horse.

The *Morning Post* described it as a 'mad act'. Jockey, Herbert Jones, survived the tumble but Davison died from her injuries four days later.

On the day of 4 June 1913, cheering crowds lined the packed course for the prestigious event. As the horses galloped towards the famous Tattenham Corner,

Davison ducked beneath a barrier and rushed across the course, where she attempted to grab the bridle of the King's horse, Anmer, as it rounded the corner.

The horse knocked her down and the impact fractured the base of her skull. The horse did a somersault on the ground and dragged Jones for a short way before he managed to free himself. He suffered concussion and minor injuries and refused hospital treatment.

Davison was taken by ambulance to Epsom Cottage Hospital, where she later died without regaining consciousness. She was wearing a suffragist flag of purple, white and green wrapped round her waist at the time of the incident and was a well-known activist in the movement for female emancipation.

FORMER SCHOOLTEACHER

Born in Blackheath, southeast London on 11 October 1872, she studied at Royal Holloway College and at Oxford University. In November 1906 she joined the Women's Social and Political Union (WSPU), founded by Emmeline Pankhurst. Three years later she gave up her job as a schoolteacher and went to work full-time for the suffragette movement.

She became increasingly militant and some members of the WSPU did not look favourably on her somewhat maverick behaviour.

She was arrested and imprisoned on numerous occasions. Her long list of convictions included those of causing a disturbance, burning post boxes, throwing stones and hiding in the House of Commons in the crypt and air shaft on three occasions.

In 1909, she was sentenced to a month's hard labour in Strangeways Prison in Manchester after throwing rocks at the carriage of Chancellor of the Exchequer David Lloyd George. Her customary way of protest for imprisonment was to go on hunger strike but this time the prison officers tried to force-feed her.

Davison pushed her cell furniture against the door to prevent them from entering. An irate warden climbed a ladder outside, pushed a hosepipe through the window and turned on the water. She remained defiant until the door was eventually forced open.

LEGAL ACTION

On her release, James Keir Hardie, the leader of the Labour Party, complained in the House of Commons about the hosepipe treatment. Davison was encouraged to take legal action and on 19 January 1910, Judge Parry pronounced in her favour, awarding damages of forty shillings.

There was mixed feeling about her intention at the Derby. Some witnesses felt that it was an accident and that she had just been making her way across the course to the centre in order to see a friend and had mistakenly thought that all the horses had passed. But others were convinced that it was a deliberate act. Even Emmeline Pankhurst and her daughter, Sylvia, were not united in their beliefs.

Sylvia argued, 'Emily Davison and a fellow-militant in whose flat she lived, had concerted a Derby protest without tragedy – a mere waving of the purple-white-and-green at Tattenham Corner – which, by its suddenness, it was hoped would stop the race. Whether from the first her purpose was more serious, or whether a final impulse altered her resolve, I know not. Her friend declares she would not thus have died without writing a farewell message to her mother.'

But Emmeline was in no doubt. In her autobiography, *My Own Story*, she wrote, 'Emily Davison clung to her conviction that one great tragedy, the deliberate throwing into the breach of a human life, would put an end to the intolerable torture of women. And so she threw herself at the King's horse, in full view of the King and Queen and a great multitude of their Majesties' subjects.'

WOMEN WIN THE VOTE

A combination of the events surrounding World War I, continuing protest by the suffragettes and the growth of the Labour Party eventually led to women being granted the vote. As the law stood at the end of the war, only men who had been resident in the country for twelve months prior to a general election were entitled to vote. This effectively disenfranchised a large number of troops who had been serving overseas in the war.

With a general election imminent, politicians were persuaded to extend the vote to women. The 1918 Representation of the People Act was passed, which allowed women to vote with the caveat that they were over the age of 30 and owned property. Although 8.5 million women met these criteria, it only represented 40 per cent of the total population of women in the U.K.

It was not until the Equal Franchise Act of 1928 that women over 21 were finally able to vote on the same terms as men. •

HEIR TO AUSTRIA'S THRONE IS SLAIN

WITH HIS WIFE BY A BOSNIAN YOUTH TO AVENGE SEIZURE OF HIS COUNTRY

(*New York Times*, 29 June 1914)

THE ASSASSINATION OF the Archduke Franz Ferdinand and his wife whilst visiting the Bosnian capital of Sarajevo set in motion a chain of events that led to the start of the Great War.

The Archduke and his wife, Duchess of Hohenberg, were shot dead in their car in an incident that would have far-reaching consequences around the world.

Bosnia and Herzegovina had been under Austro-Hungarian occupation since 1878 and was annexed by the mighty empire in 1908. The majority of the population were Serbs, furious with Austrian rulers who wanted unification with neighbouring Serbia.

Franz Ferdinand, nephew of the aged Emperor Franz Josef, who had been made head of the army, knew of the hostility and potential danger prior to his visit to Bosnia, where he had been invited to inspect the manoeuvres of the Austrian Army Corps stationed in the province.

On the morning of 28 June 1914 he and the Duchess were in

a car as it processed through the capital. There were many Serbian flags raised as a sign of protest.

FAILED BOMB ATTACK

He caught sight of a bomb being thrown at the car and managed to swipe it away with his hand. As his car moved on and the bomb fell to the ground, it exploded by the following car in the procession, injuring the occupants, Count von Boos-Waldeck and Colonel Morizzi, along with six spectators.

The Archduke's car increased speed and took him to a reception at the Town Hall where he was officially received by the Major.

Afterwards he asked to be driven to hospital to visit Col. Morizzi, who had been taken there after the bomb incident.

The driver took a wrong turning and as he slowed to turn around a second assassin took his chance and fired shots from a pistol. One struck the Duchess in the abdomen, while another hit the Archduke in the neck and pierced the jugular vein. Both died shortly after.

The men behind the assassination were part of the Black Hand, a Serbian nationalist secret society who had sent seven of their members to mingle with spectators during the Archduke's procession in Sarajevo to kill him.

The bomb had been thrown by a Serbian compositor named Gabrinovics. He was arrested within 20 minutes of the incident. The gunman was 19-year-old Gavrio Princip.

Austro-Hungary strongly suspected that the killing of the Archduke was part of a wider political plot involving the Serbian government and so it took the opportunity to try to crush the nationalist movement with military force.

It issued a list of demands designed to undermine Serbia's sovereignty, accusing the government of complicity in the assassination and insisting on delegates of the Austro-Hungarian government taking part in the investigation against those involved in the assassination plot.

WAR IS DECLARED

Although Serbia agreed to implement most but not all of the demands, Austro-Hungary declared war three days later on 28 July 1914.

But a set of historic alliances between countries throughout

Europe caused a domino effect. Serbia had ties with Russia and whilst not really expecting that Russia would be drawn into the dispute other than by words of protest, the Austro-Hungarian government sought assurances from her ally, Germany, that she would come to her aid should Russia join the war.

Germany, under Kaiser Wilhelm II, was becoming increasingly aggressive in its plans to extend its empire and had been building up its navy, which alarmed other powerful maritime nations such as Britain and France.

Germany readily agreed to help Austro-Hungary but when Russia unexpectedly committed military to aid Serbia, other countries were drawn into the conflict, one by one. France, which was bound by treaty to Russia, found itself at war with Germany and Austro-Hungary.

After Germany invaded Belgium on 4 August, Britain, which had an alliance with both Belgium and France, declared war against Germany on the same day. The move also brought in countries within her empire such as Australia, Canada, India and New Zealand.

Japan, honouring a military agreement with Britain, declared war on Germany on 23 August 1914.

The stage was thus set for a war that would cause great bloodshed and would last for four years. •

LAST BARRIER IN CANAL IS REMOVED

(*Oakland Tribune*, 10 October 1913)

THE HEADLINE IN THIS Californian newspaper referred to the longest and greatest technological achievements of the age.

In Washington, U.S. President Woodrow Wilson pressed a button in the Oval Office at 2pm on 10 October 1913, sending a signal to Panama to blow the Gamboa dyke, thus removing the last practical obstruction in the creation of the huge waterway known as the Panama Canal.

In a project that was first begun more than 40 years before and had cost the lives of over 27,000 workers, the Atlantic and Pacific Oceans were at last joined by a Trans-Isthmian waterway.

But the dream of such a thoroughfare had gone back much further into history. In the early 1500s explorer Christopher Columbus had searched in vain for a route in Panama that would take him from one ocean to another.

In 1534, Charles I of Spain ordered the first survey of a proposed canal route through the Isthmus of Panama to facilitate their ships in plundering the riches of Peru, Ecuador and Asia.

INHOSPITABLE TERRAIN

Others pondered the idea of a link over the centuries and in 1835 U.S. Army Colonel Charles Biddle was sent on an exploratory mission to evaluate its feasibility. But after four days in the sweltering, mosquito-infested jungle, he returned saying that the inhospitable terrain made it impractical.

It was to be another 40 years before construction finally began in 1879, led by the French entrepreneur Ferdinand de Lesseps, who had managed the successful Suez Canal project.

Following the Suez model, de Lesseps' plans were for a canal to be built at sea level across the Central American isthmus. But the mountainous Panamanian jungle was very different from the flat desert at Suez. Labourers had to cope with snakes, mosquitoes carrying yellow fever and malaria, collapsing hillsides, quagmires and insanitary conditions. More than 22,000 workers died.

The slow process and increasing cost resulted in his company being declared bankrupt in 1889.

NEW CANAL PLAN

Ten years later, the U.S. began, once more, to see the advantage of controlling a waterway linking the two oceans. After becoming President in 1901, Theodore Roosevelt put the plan into operation.

A payment of $40 million bought the rights to what was left of the French

canal but the constantly changing Colombian government, which was then the colonial power in Panama, refused to sell the land to the U.S.

Roosevelt abandoned attempts at negotiation and, instead, aided Panamanian revolutionaries in their fight for independence by providing a fleet of warships to both coasts of Panama, preventing Colombia from landing troop reinforcements.

He was then able to cut a deal with the new independent nation, paying $10 million in 1903 for the land needed for the canal.

Work began and, after initial deaths amongst the workforce, improved conditions were put in place in which swamps were drained, running water and sewage pipes laid and adequate accommodation built.

The French plan to build a canal at sea level was dumped for a lock-and-lake canal that would utilise the power of the rainy climate and the mighty Chagres River.

But the work was still tough and during American construction more than 5,000 died.

LANDSLIDE PERIL

One of the toughest challenges was the Culebra Cut that was to form a valley through the highest point on the route – the continental divide. More than 300,000 tonnes of rock had to be dug out and disposed of. It was prone to frequent landslides, setting the work back by months.

The Panama Canal officially opened to the world's shipping on 15 August 1915, each ship taking an average of nine hours to pass through the 50-mile (80km) long crossing from ocean to ocean.

Under American control the canal allowed their battleships easy transit between the two seas and confirmed the U.S. as a twentieth century superpower. ●

FIVE DAYS INSIDE THE CORDON

THE INSURRECTION AS SEEN FROM WITHIN THE CITY

(*Guardian*, 2 May 1916)

AN UPRISING AGAINST British rule in Ireland lasted seven days before it was crushed by troops. Yet it became the impetus for change and an enduring symbol of nationalism.

With the outbreak of World War I, Irish militants saw the opportunity to take advantage of Britain's preoccupation with fighting the Germans to mount their own battle – for independence.

In May 1915 a military committee (later the military council) was formed, consisting of Patrick Pearse, Joseph Plunkett and Éamonn Ceannt, who were all members of the Irish Republican Brotherhood and of the Irish Volunteers. Later, Seán MacDiarmada, Tom Clarke, James Connolly and Thomas MacDonagh also joined.

In January 1916 the seven men planned to mount a joint insurrection by members of the Irish Volunteers, the Irish Citizen Army and Cumann nam Ban, and to seize key locations in Dublin and proclaim an Irish Republic with themselves as its provisional government.

On Easter Monday the military committee led around 1,600 poorly armed men to take over the General Post Office in Sackville Street, which was to be used as their headquarters, and also to Liberty Hall, St Stephen's Green, the Four Courts, Boland's Mill and Jacob's biscuit factory.

IRISH REPUBLIC PROCLAIMED

Outside the GPO, Pearse proclaimed the establishment of the Irish Republic and hoisted two Republican flags, to the bewilderment of locals going about their normal day.

When two troops of British cavalry arrived to investigate the commotion, they were fired upon. There were a few other skirmishes that day but the following day extra British troops arrived and the shelling of the rebels' defences began in earnest. As the week progressed, more and more troops arrived and it became obvious what the outcome would be.

The British crushed the rebellion with superior numbers and firepower, forcing them to surrender in order to save further

lives. By the end of the fighting, 64 insurgents had died as well as 132 soldiers and police and around 230 civilians. Some 2,000 were wounded.

The high rate of civilian casualties was due to a combination of indirect fire from artillery and because they were directly attacked by both sides. The British troops tended to treat all of the Irish as enemies but, in truth, many resented the actions of the rebels in taking over the city where they lived and worked. And when they resisted orders, they were set upon.

SENTENCED TO DEATH

The seven signatories of the Proclamation and eight others were court-martialled and executed by firing squad. A sixteenth man, Roger Casement, was tried in open court in London and hanged in Pentonville Prison for his part in negotiating a shipment of arms from Germany. In the event, the ship carrying the weapons, disguised as a Norwegian fishing trawler, was intercepted by the Royal Navy.

Ninety-seven others were also sentenced to death, but had their sentences commuted to various terms of imprisonment. All of them were released within a relatively short period, the last in June 1917.

Although most Irish nationalists had considered the insurrection to be a foolhardy undertaking, doomed to failure, the Easter Uprising was to change people's views. The bravery and patriotism shown was seen as commendable and certain atrocities committed by the British troops, such as the execution of six civilians at Portobello Barracks, caused widespread and continuing anger which served to unite people against Britain. And the calls for independence became louder.

The Irish Volunteers became the Irish Republican Army and together with the political party, Sinn Féin, they pushed for independence, resulting in the Act of Partition, which came into effect in 1922. The mainly Protestant counties of Ulster would remain part of the United Kingdom, as Northern Ireland, while the predominantly Catholic counties in the south were given a measure of independence as the Irish Free State, before gaining full independence as the Republic of Ireland in 1948. •

ABDICATION OF CZAR

IS FOLLOWED BY THAT OF GRAND DUKE MICHAEL, WHICH ENDS ROMANOFF DYNASTY IN RUSSIA

(*Asheville Citizen*, 17 March 1917)

ON 3 APRIL 1917, exiled Russian political activist Vladimir Lenin returned to St Petersburg on a train from Finland and precipitated a second revolution in Russia, which ushered in the Communist era and brought about the shocking execution of the Royal Family.

In February of that year, resentment of Tsar Nicholas II's autocratic rule, the unfair balance of wealth between landowners and ordinary working people, along with Russia's involvement in an unpopular war, were causing much anger and ill-feeling.

Poor living conditions amongst the working class were exacerbated by the men being sent off to fight in the Great War. In the first few days of the war at the Battle of Tannenberg, the Russian army was comprehensively beaten, suffering 120,000 casualties to Germany's 20,000. Further losses continued and by 1916 morale amongst the soldiers, as well as on the home front, was at an all-time low. The Tsar was being blamed for the situation.

FOOD SHORTAGES

On 23 February there was a protest in St Petersburg against food shortages, which led to workers going on strike. The Tsar ordered the military to intervene but he could no longer count on their loyalty and many refused. With protests and looting breaking out, the Tsar felt his position untenable and abdicated his throne in March, handing power to his brother, Michael. But he deferred the throne until properly elected, leaving the country without a head of state and bringing an end to the Romanov dynasty.

A Provisional Government was quickly formed by leading members of the Russian parliament, the Duma, led by Alexander Kerensky, until elections could be held. But Kerensky, to the dismay of the public and soldiers, did not want to end the war.

LENIN RETURNS

Into this heated arena entered Lenin, who had been aided in his secret return by the Germans in the hope that he would unite the people to overthrow the Provisional Government and take Russia out of the war.

Throughout the spring and summer, Lenin made rousing public speeches, calling for Russia's withdrawal from the war, better working conditions, more food and the redistribution of wealth.

Some soldiers on the Eastern Front deserted and returned home, using their weapons to seize land from the nobility.

On 19 July, Kerensky gave orders for the arrest of leading members of the Bolshevik party campaigning against the war, which included Lenin and fellow activist Leon Trotsky.

The following month, the Royal Family were placed in the former Governor's mansion where they lived in considerable comfort.

Kerensky was forced to ask the Bolsheviks for military aid when he feared his Minister of War, Kornilov, was aiming for a military dictatorship. By the autumn, the Bolsheviks were growing in stature and Lenin knew the time was right to seize power from the Government.

BOLSHEVIK TAKEOVER

On 24 October 1917, a coup d'état took place as the Bolsheviks stormed the city, taking up strategic posts and meeting with little resistance. By the following day every key building in St Petersburg was under their control, except the Winter Palace where Kerensky and other ministers were holed up with a small guard. But after Kerensky fled, the Palace was taken on 26 October. Lenin's revolution had been achieved with the minimum of bloodshed. But the country was plunged into a civil war between the Red Guard (Communists) and the White Army (a loose alliance of Nationalists, Imperialists and other anti-Bolsheviks) which was to last four years at the cost of millions of lives before the Reds triumphed, establishing the Soviet Union in 1922.

ROYAL FAMILY IMPRISONED

In the meantime, the Russian Royal Family had been moved to the town of Yekaterinburg in the spring of 1918, where they were confined to the house of a successful local merchant which had been commandeered by the Bolsheviks. Here their guards treated them badly, with little or no respect.

The intention was to put the Tsar on trial but the civil war was raging and by mid-July a contingent of the White Army was approaching Yekaterinburg. Fearing that the Royal Family would be rescued, their guards were ordered to execute them.

In the early hours of 17 July 1918, the Tsar, his wife, five children and servants were herded into the cellar of their prison house and shot. Those who did not die straight away were viciously bayoneted. •

HOW LONDON HAILED THE END OF WAR

(*Daily Mirror*, 12 November 1918)

THERE WERE THOSE on both sides who thought that the Great War would last for a few months and it would all be over by Christmas. Few imagined that it would drag on through four long and bloody years.

When the Allied victory finally came over the Central Powers there was a huge sigh of relief and a great outpouring of celebration and euphoria.

The front page of the *Daily Mirror* was taken up with a montage of images from central London depicting the King and Queen on the balcony of Buckingham Palace, a soldier kissing his loved one, and a little girl waving a flag.

It had been a war fought mainly in the trenches, which had seen some epic battles at the Somme, Passchendaele and Gallipoli

amongst others, and an estimated 10 million military deaths.

The end unravelled quickly as the final Allied push towards the German border began on 17 October 1918 and resistance collapsed. Turkey signed an armistice at the end of October and Austro-Hungary followed on 3 November.

ARMISTICE SIGNED

On 9 November the Kaiser abdicated and, two days later, Germany signed an armistice in a railroad car outside Compiégne, France, agreeing to a cessation of fighting along the entire Western Front to begin at precisely 11am that morning. The Great War was at an end.

In London, huge crowds took to the streets in celebration. Outside Buckingham Palace they chanted, 'We want the King' until he appeared with the Queen on the balcony.

The Royal couple waved to the crowd to joyous cheers. Later in the day they re-appeared and King George V gave a short speech saying, 'With you I rejoice and thank God for the victories which the Allied arms have won, bringing hostilities to an end and peace within sight.' A band played 'God Save the King', 'Tipperary' and 'Auld Lang Syne'.

CHURCH BELLS RING

Church bells, silent throughout the war, sounded their joyous peal. Crowds formed at Trafalgar Square, Downing Street, Admiralty Arch and Mansion House. And The Strand was packed with people walking up and down. Revellers sang and waved flags and clambered aboard double-decker buses.

In the afternoon, the King and Queen drove through the City and again received a tremendous ovation. The following day they attended a service of thanksgiving at St Paul's Cathedral and celebrations continued throughout the week.

For the next few months the Allies, led by the 'Big Three' of David Lloyd George, Georges Clemençeau and Woodrow Wilson, the leaders of Britain, France and America, negotiated a peace treaty at the Palace of Versailles in Paris.

Negotiations were difficult with each of the Big Three wanting different things. Finally the Germans were shown the Treaty and they were appalled by the unfairness of it. But there was to be no negotiation.

AIR FORCE BANNED

The main points of the Treaty were an establishment of the League of Nations which excluded Germany; German troops banished from the Rhineland; The Saar, with its rich coalfields, given to France for 15 years; Alsace-Lorraine returned to France; fertile farm lands in eastern Germany given to Poland; all colonies placed under League of Nations mandates; Germany not allowed to unite with Austria; the army restricted to 100,000 men, navy to six battleships and no submarines and the banning of an air force; Germany to pay reparations which was eventually settled at 132 billion reichsmarks (around 22 billion pounds).

German hatred and resentment of the punitive terms agreed at Versailles was later to give rise to the Nazis and World War II twenty years later. •

WHOLE COUNTRY GOES DRY

(*Washington Times*, 16 January 1919)

THE NEWS ARTICLE which accompanied this headline announced that the nation would be 'bone dry within a year from today' following the ratification of the prohibition amendment making it illegal to consume, sell and transport alcohol in the U.S.

The ban came into effect on 17 January 1920 and was to last for 13 years, causing an upsurge in violence and criminal behaviour as those still wanting a drink turned to the black market and racketeers.

The ban evolved as a consequence of the activities of a combination of pressure groups, and as a result of America's involvement in World War I. The Anti-Saloon League in particular had campaigned hard that alcohol was damaging American society. And many vocal religious groups announced it was against God's will. Other active organisations included the Women's Church Federation, the Women's Temperance Crusade and the Department of Scientific Temperance Instruction

WARTIME PROHIBITION

After the U.S. joined the Great War in April 1917, a wartime prohibition act was passed which banned the sale of beverages with an alcohol content greater than 2.75 per cent. This was said to have been done to save grain for the war effort. It led to the Volstead Act of 1919, which established the enforcement of prohibition. Finally, the 18th Amendment to the Constitution of the United States made prohibition throughout the country the law after it was certified on 16 January 1919.

But there were many people who objected to prohibition and sought to carry on drinking alcohol. In this climate, illegal drinking dens flourished, becoming known as 'speakeasies'. These were usually bars that claimed to sell soft drinks but served alcohol behind the scenes.

THE BLACK MARKET

Chicago, in particular, became notorious for gangsters making millions of dollars from selling illicit liquor and doing battle with others who wanted a part of the lucrative black market trade. Al Capone and his rival Bugs Moran indulged in frequent gang warfare. The most infamous incident was the St Valentine's Day massacre in 1929 when Capone's men, disguised as police, 'raided' a trucking warehouse which served as Moran's headquarters. They lined seven men up against a wall and shot them dead with machine guns, firing more than 150 bullets into the victims. The photographs of the dead and bloodied bodies that appeared in newspapers shocked the public.

By the end of the decade, Capone controlled around 10,000 speakeasies in Chicago and ruled the bootlegging business. In addition he owned bookmakers, gambling houses, brothels, horse and race tracks and nightclubs.

Gangland violence, intimidation, theft, protection rackets and murder proliferated and the 1,500 prohibition agents commissioned to enforce the law were overwhelmed. Many also turned a 'blind eye' in exchange for a pay-off.

'BATHTUB GIN'

Making alcohol at home was very common with home-distilled spirit known as 'bathtub gin' in the northern cities and 'moonshine' in the south.

Stores sold grape concentrate with warning labels that listed the steps that should be avoided to *prevent* the juice from fermenting into wine.

With violence on the increase, the black market booming and the law being increasingly difficult to administer, public feeling against prohibition began to change.

In 1929 the Wickersham Commission reported that Prohibition was not working. On 23 March 1933 President Franklin D. Roosevelt signed the Cullen – Harrison Act, which allowed the manufacture and sale of alcohol of 4 per cent proof. And on 5 December of that year, prohibition was repealed with the 21st Amendment. •

MR MACDONALD'S CROWDED DAY

(*Guardian*, 23 January 1924)

A RATHER LOW-KEY headline in the *Guardian* detailed James Ramsay Macdonald's busy schedule on the previous day, which included two visits to Buckingham Palace where he was sworn in as Britain's first Labour Prime Minister.

Born on 12 October 1866 in Lossiemouth, Morayshire, Scotland, the illegitimate son of a crofter, MacDonald worked as a teacher locally and then moved to London where he became a clerk at the House of Commons.

He became increasingly interested in politics and joined the Fabian Society where he met many high-profile socialists of the day such as George Bernard Shaw, Emmeline Pankhurst and H. G. Wells. In 1893, a group of independent socialists, including James Keir Hardie, formed a new national working-class movement called the Independent Labour Party.

MacDonald joined in 1894 and the following year was selected as the ILP candidate for Southampton.

ANTI-WAR CAMPAIGNER

MacDonald was bold in speaking out against the Boer War, which he viewed as a consequence of imperialism. He wrote that, 'Further extensions of Empire are only the grabbings of millionaires on the hunt.' But his resolution to condemn the war at a meeting of the Fabian Society was defeated. Following this failure he, along with thirteen others, resigned from the Fabian Society.

Hardie, the leader of the Independent Labour Party, and George Bernard Shaw of the Fabian Society, realised that the way for socialists to win seats in parliamentary elections would be to form a new party made up of various left-wing groups.

On 27 February 1900, representatives of all the socialist groups in Britain met with trade-union leaders at the Congregational Memorial Hall in Farringdon Street, and the Labour Representation Committee (LRC) was formed with MacDonald as the secretary.

The LRC put up fifteen candidates in the 1900 general election and between them they won 62,698 votes. Two of the candidates, Keir Hardie and Richard Bell, won seats in the House of Commons.

1906 ELECTION VICTORIES

The LRC did much better in the 1906 general election with 29 successful candidates winning their seats, including MacDonald as MP for Leicester. On 12 February, the group of MPs decided to change the name from the LRC to the Labour Party. Hardie was elected chairman and MacDonald was the party's secretary.

After the 1910 election, when 40 Labour MPs were elected to the House of Commons, MacDonald became party chairman. His opposition to the Great War caused him much criticism, particularly in the right-wing press, which labelled him a traitor.

But by the early 1920s, MacDonald was the dominant figure in the Labour Party, impressing people with his mix of intelligence, moderate and practical policies, oratory skills and imposing presence. At the 1922 general election he was elected to represent Aberavon, and the Labour Party won 142 seats, eclipsing the Liberals as the main opposition to the governing Conservative Party.

No party won an overall majority in the general election of December 1923, with the Conservatives taking 258 seats, Labour 191 and the Liberals 159. The Conservatives kept power, but lost a vote of confidence in the House of Commons in January 1924.

PRIME MINISTER RESIGNS

The Prime Minister, Stanley Baldwin, went to Buckingham Palace to tender his resignation to King George V. Shortly after, MacDonald was summoned to the Palace and the King asked him to form a government.

MacDonald was cheered by a group of supports as he left. Later that evening he returned to the Palace as Prime Minister to present to the King his list of government appointments.

McDonald later recalled that the King had complained about the singing of the historic socialist songs, *Red Flag* and the *La Marseilles*, at the Labour Party meeting in the Albert Hall a few days earlier. MacDonald apologised but claimed that there would have been a riot if he had tried to stop it. ●

THE "TELEVISOR"

SUCCESSFUL TEST OF NEW APPARATUS

(*The Times*, 28 January 1926)

This rather low-key headline on page nine of the London *Times* was the first report of one of the biggest life-changing inventions of the 20th century.

The reporter told how he, along with members of the Royal Institution and other visitors, were invited to a laboratory in an upper room in Frith Street, Soho, London, on Tuesday, 26 January, where they saw 'a demonstration of apparatus invented by Mr J. L. Baird, who claims to have solved the problem of television'.

Here they were shown a 'transmitting machine', consisting of a large wooden revolving disc containing lenses. The holes were arranged in a spiral, and as the disc turned it scanned the scene in front of it. Behind the disc was a revolving shutter and a light-sensitive cell.

Baird first demonstrated with the head of a ventriloquist's dummy placed in front of the transmitter, which reappeared on a receiver in the same room and then on a receiver in another room. When he moved the head, they could see the movements on the receiver screen. Baird then did the same with a human face.

FAINT, BLURRED IMAGE

The *Times* reporter stated, 'The image as transmitted was faint and often blurred, but substantiated a claim that through the "Televisor" as Mr Baird has named his apparatus, it is possible to transmit and reproduce instantly the details of movement, and such things as the play of expression on the face.'

Born in Helensburgh, Scotland on 14 August 1888, Baird suffered from poor health most of his life, something that spurred him on to experiment with electrical gadgets and communications. He once created a mini telephone exchange in his bedroom that allowed him to talk directly to friends living nearby.

Baird studied at the West of Scotland Technical College and the University of Glasgow, although he never completed his degree course as it was interrupted by the outbreak of World War I. His poor health made him unfit for military service, and he worked as an engineer with the Clyde Valley Electrical Power Company during the war.

Following a short spell in business, Baird moved to the south of England in the hope of improving his health, settling on the coast in Hastings where he concentrated on developing a system for transmitting moving images.

On 2 October 1925, using a ventriloquist's dummy he nick-named Stookie Bill, he transmitted a 30-line vertically scanned greyscale image at five pictures per second. Excited, he went downstairs and fetched 20-year-old office worker, William Edward Taynton, to see what a human face would look like. Taynton became the first person to be televised in a full tonal range.

DAILY EXPRESS LUNATIC

Baird later took his machine to the *Daily Express* in order to get publicity but the editor was alarmed when he heard he was in the building and shouted to his newsroom, 'For God's sake, go down to reception and get rid of a lunatic who's down there. He says he's got a machine for seeing by wireless! Watch him – he may have a razor on him!'

Following the successful public demonstration in Frith Street, the Baird Television Development Company Ltd was formed.

In 1927, he sent a live 30-line television signal 438 miles (730km) from London to Glasgow along telephone cables. A year later, his company transmitted pictures of a man and a woman to an astonished gathering watching in New York.

COLOUR TELEVISION

Baird also invented an early colour TV system and made the first television programmes for the British Broadcasting Corporation (BBC) in 1929. His broadcast system for the BBC included sound, but never had more than 240 lines – almost the limit of his mechanical system.

Baird's electromechanical system was eventually superseded by purely electronic systems.

Although the development of television was the result of work by many inventors, each with an integral part to play, Baird was the first person in the world to demonstrate a practical working television system and to bring it to the attention of the world. ●

SEEK CONGRESSIONAL MEDAL OF HONOR FOR LINDBERGH

(*Stamford Advocate*, 23 May 1927)

THE FIRST SOLO FLIGHT across the Atlantic turned 25-year-old American aviator Charles Lindbergh into an instant hero and celebrity of the day.

Born in Detroit, Michigan, on 4 February 1902, Lindbergh spent much of his first 18 years on his family's farm in Minnesota and was fascinated by the occasional aeroplane that flew over the fields. It was to become a lifelong passion and, when he was 20, he joined a flying school, learning first about the mechanics before making his first flight as a pilot.

Four years later he enrolled at a U.S. Army flying school at San Antonio, Texas, and graduated first in his class.

In 1926, he became the first airmail pilot between Chicago, Illinois, and St Louis, Missouri. And it was during this time that he determined to take part in an exciting challenge that had been laid down by New York hotel businessman Raymond Orteig in 1919, offering $25,000 for the first non-stop flight between New York and Paris.

SPIRIT OF ST LOUIS

Lindbergh persuaded a group of St Louis businessmen to back his venture and then helped design and supervise the building of a plane that would soar him into the history books. The result was a single-engine monoplane called the *Spirit of St Louis*.

He was thought by many to have little chance of success as other contenders opted for multi-engine planes and at least one other crew member aboard.

On 20 May 1927, he took four sandwiches, two containers of water, a compass and map aboard the *Spirit of St Louis* and then gunned her down a dirt-track runway in Roosevelt Field, Long Island, and, at 7.52am, took to the air.

Along the way he encountered some sleet, which made him consider turning back but he soon put such notions out of his mind and continued on his epic flight.

Lindbergh later described how he flew low over the coast of Europe to call out to a fisherman on his boat, 'Which way is Ireland?' but that the man did not understand him.

LE BOURGET FIELD

On the evening of 21 May he crossed the coast of France, followed the Seine River to Paris and touched down at Le Bourget Field at 10:22pm (local time). The 3,600-mile journey had taken thirty-three and a half hours.

A jubilant crowd rushed forward to welcome him and were delighted when he thrust his face out of the window and asked, 'Where am I?'

As he opened the door, he was lifted onto the shoulders of officials who carried him away from the enthusiastic crowd who all wanted to shake his hand, pat his back or simply touch him.

Despite his long journey, Lindbergh insisted he did not feel tired and happily conducted a press conference standing up.

His achievement excited the world. It was the heroic, daredevil, adventurous stuff that boy's dreams are made of. The following morning he waved to crowds gathered below him as he stood on the balcony of the American Embassy.

In the days that followed, his fame grew and grew. The President of France, Gaston Doumergue, pinned the Legion of Honor upon his lapel. When he returned home to America aboard the USS *Memphis*, a convoy of warships and aircraft escorted him up the river to Washington where President Coolidge bestowed him with the Distinguished Flying Cross.

MEDAL OF VALOR

New York City gave him the largest tickertape parade ever, with about four million people lining the parade route. The Mayor pinned New York's Medal of Valor upon him.

Lindbergh's achievement inspired others to take an interest in aviation not only in his homeland but around the world.

He embarked on a sponsored, three-month nationwide tour in the *Spirit of St Louis*, touching down in 49 states, visiting 92 cities and giving 147 speeches.

On 21 March 1929, President Coolidge presented him with the nation's highest military decoration, the Congressional Medal of Honor.

Throughout the rest of his life, Lindbergh acted as an adviser to America on aviation. He taught American fighter pilots how to get increased range from their planes, was appointed a Brigadier General in the Air Force Reserves and made many goodwill visits around the world. •

GREATEST CRASH IN WALL STREET'S HISTORY

(*Daily Mail*, 25 October 1929)

THE FEEL GOOD factor of the 'Roaring Twenties' was to end abruptly at the end of the decade with a shocking collapse of share prices on New York's Wall Street stock market. As investors lost huge sums of money, confidence in the economy was shattered and it was to usher in the 'Great Depression' of the thirties.

In the 1920s the United States was enjoying a boom time of prosperity and easy money was to be made on the stock market. Potential investors didn't even need to have much money up front. Such was the confidence in the economy that banks were willing to lend more than two-thirds of the face value of the stocks, which the investor could later sell at a profit before paying the loan.

All was well so long as the price continued to rise and few saw any reason to doubt that it would. But if the unthinkable were to happen, and the bubble burst, then huge losses would be incurred.

There seemed no reason, however, for investors to suspect

that any kind of downturn in the economy was anywhere in sight. A much-respected economist and financial guru of the time, Irving Fisher, proclaimed that 'Stock prices have reached what looks like a permanently high plateau.' Many believed that share prices would simply continue to rise indefinitely.

FLORIDA DISASTER IGNORED

Yet there had been some signs that the economy was not as rock steady as was believed when land prices in Florida collapsed in 1926. Florida had been enjoying a property boom, with building projects forging ahead in a state that was being promoted as a tropical paradise. Speculators snapped up tracts of land and investors funded new developments, fuelling a rapid rise in property prices.

The rapid rise, unfortunately, proved to be a huge discouragement to potential buyers and the devastating 1926 Miami hurricane, which left almost 400 dead and caused damage estimated at $100 million ($1.3 billion in today's terms), left many investors' projects quite literally in ruins.

The Florida experience, and the fact that farm produce prices were being driven steadily lower due to over-production, should have served as a warning that there was no firm foundation for the soaring price of stocks and shares. Nevertheless, the stock market hit an all-time high on 3 September 1929, before it dropped sharply, only to rise and drop again.

INVESTORS IN PANIC

Many dismissed it as a blip. The market had dropped before and recovered in rude health. But when it declined sharply again on 4 October, some began to get jittery. And as it continued to decline, panic started rising. There was an avalanche of selling on 21 October as frightened investors who had pumped so much of their money into the stock market began to sell their shares at any price. On 24 October – a day that was to become known as 'Black Thursday' – 12,894,650 shares were sold, overwhelming the Exchange as it struggled to keep up with transactions.

There was panic on the Exchange floor, too, as traders screamed and shouted and watched in despair at collapsing prices.

That evening, five of the country's bankers issued a statement saying that due to the heavy selling of shares, many were now under-priced. But still, people were desperate to sell.

WORLD FINANCIAL CRISIS

Over the weekend the events were covered by newspapers across the United States, fuelling further fear and panic. And on 28 October, 'Black Monday', more investors decided to get out of the market. The following day, 'Black Tuesday', around 16 million shares were traded. The market had lost over $30 billion in the space of two days.

America had loaned huge sums of money to European countries and, following the Wall Street Crash, they suddenly recalled the loans, which had a big impact on the European economy, causing a general world financial crisis.

Lack of money led to mass unemployment in America and Europe as businessmen could no longer borrow sufficient amounts to run their companies. The Roaring Twenties had skidded to an abrupt halt as the world economy entered the 'Great Depression' of the thirties. •

GHANDI SEIZED BY BRITISH

FOR INDEFINITE DETENTION; TROOPS POSTED FOR CRISIS

(*New York Times*, 5 May 1930)

MOHANDAS 'MAHATMA' GANDHI was arrested and imprisoned by the British authorities in India for his campaign of civil disobedience, which he called satyagraha (insistence on truth).

His incarceration caused widespread international publicity as did the violent beatings that British-led Indian police and troops perpetrated on peaceful protesters.

Known as 'Mahatma' (great soul), Gandhi was the leader of the Indian nationalist movement against British rule, and his policy of non-violence frustrated and ultimately embarrassed the colonial power.

Born on 2 October 1869 in Porbandar, Gujarat, he attended university and went to London to train as a barrister.

In 1893, he accepted a job at a law firm in Durban, South Africa. Appalled by the treatment of Indian immigrants in the country, he campaigned for their rights and was sent to prison many times during his 20-year stay.

RETURN TO INDIA

In 1915, he returned to India and four years later he led a protest against the Rowlatt Act, which allowed the British to imprison for a maximum of two years, without trial, any person suspected of terrorism living in the Raj.

Gandhi's continuing campaign of peaceful non-cooperation with the British included the boycotting of British goods, which led to arrests of thousands. In 1922, Gandhi was sentenced to six years' imprisonment but was released after two years.

After a quiet period he began his biggest and most audacious satyagraha campaign in 1930 with a protest against the tax on salt.

Britain's Salt Acts prohibited Indians from collecting or selling salt and they were compelled to buy it from the British who levied a heavy tax on the commodity.

On 12 March 1930, Gandhi set off from Sabarmati near Ahmedabad with 78 followers on a 241-mile march to the coastal town of Dandi.

ILLEGAL SALT

As they passed through one village after another he stopped to talk to local people and many joined the march so that by the time they arrived on 5 April their ranks had grown to many thousands. The following day, Gandhi walked down to the sea, raised a lump of muddy salt and declared, 'With this, I am shaking the foundations of the British Empire.'

He then boiled it in seawater, producing illegal salt, and encouraged the others to copy his example. In the days that followed, thousands more did likewise in coastal cities such as Bombay and Karachi.

Civil disobedience broke out all across India, soon involving millions of Indians, and British authorities arrested more than 60,000 people.

Gandhi himself was arrested and imprisoned on 5 May en route with his followers to protest at the Dharasana Salt Works in Gujarat, 25 miles south of Dandi.

Shortly after midnight, while Gandhi was fast asleep, two Indian officers and thirty heavily-armed policemen arrested him. But the march continued under the leadership of a female poet and activist named Sarojini Naidu. It was to result in the 2,500 marchers being ruthlessly beaten by policemen at the Salt Works on 21 May.

The protesters refused to retaliate and the incident gained widespread international coverage in newspapers.

BRITISH FORCED TO NEGOTIATE

In January 1931, Gandhi was released from prison. Faced with mass disobedience across India, along with international criticism and condemnation for their unfairness and brutality in dealing with dissenters, the British government was compelled to negotiate with Gandhi.

At a meeting with Lord Irwin, the Viceroy of India, Gandhi agreed to call off the satyagraha in exchange for an equal negotiating role at a London conference on India's future. In August, Gandhi travelled to the conference as the sole representative of the nationalist Indian National Congress.

India's independence was finally granted on 14 August 1947, under the guidance of the last Viceroy, Lord Louis Mountbatten, when the country was split and the new dominion of Pakistan came into being.

Gandhi was one of many opposed to the partition of India and it caused great bloodshed amongst those who were cut off by the newly imposed boundaries. Nearly one million people died in the violence that ensued between Hindus and Muslims.

Gandhi went on a hunger strike, saying he would not eat until the violence stopped but his efforts to achieve reconciliation between Hindus and Muslims were to lead to his death.

On the way to a prayer meeting on 30 January 1948, he was shot dead by a fellow Hindu named Nathuram Godse, who felt that he had betrayed the Hindu cause. •

HITLER MADE CHANCELLOR OF GERMANY

(*New York Times*, 31 January 1933)

THE NAZIS' RISE to power caused concern throughout Europe after their nationalistic leader, Adolf Hitler, was elected Chancellor of Germany.

German resentment and anger over the Treaty of Versailles, which they had been forced to sign in 1919, continued to run deep. The loss of land, heavy financial compensation, the stripping of her army and her exclusion from the League of Nations was humiliating.

The governing democratic Weimar Republic was seen as weak and the bleak economic climate added to the misery and feeling of hopelessness at the country ever recovering.

Hitler had made an earlier attempt to sieze power. The Nazi Party had started out as a small party in Bavaria called the German Worker's Party, which was opposed to the Treaty of Versailles and communism. Hitler's enthusiasm and flare for rhetoric saw him quickly rise to leadership.

THE NAZIS EMERGE

The party was renamed the National and Socialist German Workers Party and, with inflation running high, the Nazis, as they were known, attempted a political *coup d'etat* in November 1923. They had plotted to seize control of Munich and then stage a march on Berlin, but it was a disastrous undertaking. The police opened fire on the marchers, they dispersed and Hitler was arrested. Two days later he was given a five-year prison sentence.

In the event, he only served two years. He took the time whilst inside to write *Mein Kampf.* On his release, the economy was picking up and most Germans felt he had little to offer them. But then came the Wall Street Crash of 1929, followed by the Great Depression.

The rise in unemployment, fears of a communist uprising and the continuing heavy load of wartime reparation put the German economy in crisis. Disillusioned by the Weimar, Hitler's extremist but patriotic ideas found an audience.

PERSECUTION OF JEWS

In such a climate, he became ever more popular. A charismatic and inspiring public speaker, people responded to his talk of tearing up the Treaty of Versailles, rearmament and territorial expansion. It was intoxicating stuff after years of brooding resentment and misery. And he even managed to pass on his anti-Semitism by attributing some of the blame for Germany's economic plight to the greed of Jews, talking of his nation's Aryan 'master race'.

He said what many wanted to hear – higher prices for farmers' produce, construction jobs for the unemployed, help for small businesses – and he encouraged people to boycott Jewish-owned shops. The Nazis became ever more menacing and the feared stormtroopers would stand outside these shops, painting slogans on the windows and scaring off potential customers. Jewish professionals such as doctors, lawyers and local government officials were forced to give up their jobs.

Once he became Chancellor, his stormtroopers crushed any opposition or dissent as he sought to control the influential institutions – economy, education, business – and his propaganda machine went into overdrive under Dr Joseph Goebbels.

MILITARY EXPANSION

Young people were encouraged to join Nazi Party organisations such as the Hitler Youth, for boys, and the League of German Maidens, for girls. Trade unions were banned and replaced by the German Labour Front. Education was controlled by the state, and newspapers, radio, cinema and the theatre placed under Nazi control. Books were heavily censored or burnt if they did not fit Nazi ideology.

Hitler increased the size of the German army to 550,000 by 1936, and to 850,000 by 1938. A further 900,000 men were trained as reserves and he embarked on the making of a modern air force and navy.

Unemployment figures fell rapidly, mainly due to the increase in the number of men in the armed forces and public-works schemes constructing municipal buildings, motorways and bridges.

Under Hitler, Germany was fast becoming a mighty nation once more and he was eager to claim new territory. ●

EDWARD VIII ABDICATES

KING RENOUNCES CROWN FOR LOVE

(*London Herald*, 13 December 1936)

A CONSTITUTIONAL CRISIS in 1936 shocked the British public when the King walked away from the throne to marry the woman he loved. Edward's decision to abdicate rather than live without his beloved Wallis was to change the course of British history.

As a divorcee and a Catholic, Wallis Simpson was not constitutionally suitable for King Edward VIII on both counts: the monarch is nominal head of the Church of England which did not allow divorcees to re-marry.

Edward first met Baltimore-born Wallis at a house party on 10 January 1931. He was then Prince of Wales and she was married to businessman Ernest Simpson, following her divorce from navy pilot Earl Winfield Spencer.

She made little impression on the Prince then but they bumped into each other again in May and in January 1932 he dined at the Simpsons' London flat, staying until 4.00am. At the end of the month, the Simpsons were invited to spend a weekend at Edward's country retreat, Fort Belvedere in Berkshire.

SUNSHINE HOLIDAYS

Things took a more serious turn when, in August 1934, Edward took a party, including Wallis Simpson, on holiday to Biarritz, followed by a cruise along the Spanish and

Portuguese coasts. Notably, Ernest Simpson was not among them. That November, Wallis attended a party at Buckingham Palace in honour of the Duke of Kent.

Edward succeeded his father, George V, on 20 January 1936, becoming King Edward VIII. In July, Ernest Simpson moved out of the couple's home and the following month Wallis joined the King and other guests for a cruise along the Yugoslav, Greek and Turkish coasts. Photographs of the pair together appeared in the American and continental press but British newspaper editors turned a blind eye to the gossip and speculation, as did the British establishment. And nothing appeared in the press.

But the situation could not be ignored much longer. In October, after the King had begun renting a house for Wallis in Regent's Park, Prime Minister Stanley Baldwin confronted him over the relationship, asking him if he could be more discrete and to try to persuade Wallis to put off her plans to divorce her husband. But he failed in his endeavour and on 16 November the King sent for Baldwin and told him he wanted to marry Mrs Simpson.

KING THREATENS ABDICATION

Baldwin insisted that the British public would not accept her as Queen and he was shocked when the King replied that he was prepared to abdicate if the government opposed his marriage.

The King later suggested that Parliament bring in new legislation that would enable him to have a 'morganatic marriage' in which he would still be King but she, as a 'commoner', would not be Queen. But when this was rejected, Baldwin told him he had three choices: to finish his relationship with Mrs Simpson, to marry against the advice of his ministers who would then resign, or to abdicate.

On 3 December, the story broke in the British press and the tone was widely disapproving. The general feeling in the country was that she was more in love with status than with Edward. Wallis went to France to escape the furore. Then, on 9 December, the King informed the government of his decision to abdicate.

'After long and anxious consideration I have determined to renounce the throne, to which I succeeded on the death of my father, and I am now communicating this, my final and irrevocable decision.'

HISTORIC BROADCAST

He was to be succeeded by his younger brother, Albert George 'Bertie', the Duke of York. The following day, Edward signed the Instrument of Abdication and on 11 December he made an historic broadcast to the nation.

'At long last I am able to say a few words of my own. I have never wanted to withhold anything, but until now it has not been constitutionally possible for me to speak. A few hours ago I discharged my last duty as King and Emperor, and now that I have been succeeded by my brother, the Duke of York, my first words must be to declare my allegiance to him. This I do with all my heart.

'You all know the reasons which have impelled me to renounce the throne. But I want you to understand that in making up my mind I did not forget the country or the Empire, which, as Prince of Wales, and lately as King, I have for 25 years tried to serve. But you must believe me when I tell you that I have found it impossible to carry the heavy burden of responsibility and to discharge my duties as King as I would wish to do without the help and support of the woman I love.'

Bertie was crowned King George VI on 12 May 1937 and his wife, Elizabeth Bowes-Lyon (later, the Queen Mother), Queen Elizabeth.

Their two young daughters, Princesses Elizabeth and Margaret became first and second in line to the throne. And on 3 June 1937, Edward, now the Duke of Windsor, married Wallis Simpson in France. •

OWENS COMPLETES TRIPLE AS 5 OLYMPIC MARKS FALL

(*New York Times*, 6 August 1936)

ADOLF HITLER'S NOTION of a superior Aryan race took a battering at the 1936 Olympics in Berlin when black American athlete Jesse Owens was the star of the show, winning four gold medals.

Berlin had been chosen to host the event by the International Olympic Committee before the Nazis had risen to power. Some countries talked of boycotting the event but none did. In fact, more countries entered than ever before.

It was Nazi Propaganda Minister Joseph Goebbels who had pushed for the games, persuading Hitler that it would be a great showcase for a resurgent Germany with her athletes showing their superiority.

An impressive Olympic sports complex stretching 325 acres was built about five miles from West Berlin with the centrepiece being a huge stadium that could seat 110,000 spectators.

FINEST OLYMPIC FACILITIES

The Olympic Village of 140 buildings contained a post office and a bank. There were stewards on hand who could speak various languages and the training facilities included a 400-metre track and a full-sized indoor swimming pool. These were the best facilities that

Olympic athletes had ever seen.

But there was an international outcry over the exclusion of Jewish athletes from Germany's team. Some of those excluded were top tennis player Daniel Prenn, boxing champion Erich Seelig and four-time Word Record holder in track and field events Lilli Henoch. The Nazis also disqualified athletes of Romani origin, including another boxing champion, Johann Trollmann.

In a move to appease critics, the Nazis put Jewish fencing star, Helene Mayer, who had won gold at the 1928 Olympics, into their team.

BERLIN SANITISED BY NAZIS

In the weeks leading to the start of the Games, the streets were 'swept' of 'undesirables' and the many 'Jews Not Welcome' signs taken down from restaurants, hotels and other public places.

When visitors from around the world descended on Berlin for the opening ceremony on 1 August, they walked through streets that were gleaming clean and marvelled at the size and spectacle of the imposing sports complexes where Olympic flags flew alongside the swastika.

The main stadium was packed to capacity and the impressive airship Hindenburg flew low over the stadium trailing the Olympic flag. When Hitler and his entourage walked in, the *Deutschland Über Alles* national anthem was sung. As the teams paraded, there was speculation about who would and wouldn't give the Nazi salute to Hitler as they passed by his seat. Some athletes did and others did not, but there was some confusion because the Olympic salute with right arm held out sideways was not dissimilar.

The climax of the opening ceremony was the arrival of the Olympic torch, which had been carried, by relay, from Olympia, Greece – the first time this had been done, something that was to become a regular feature at future Games.

CONTEST BEGINS

The following day, the competition began with the track and field events. Jesse Owens, 23, had broken three world records and tied a fourth the previous year at an athletics meeting in Michigan.

During the course of that opening Olympic week he outsprinted and out-jumped everyone to win four gold medals in the 100m, 200m, long jump and as a member of the 4x100m relay team.

There was much mention in the foreign press of Hitler being furious at Owens's success. But Owens himself never felt any resentment. He later recalled Hitler standing up and waving to him when he glanced up at him in his box seat.

In the end, the Olympics were a triumph for Germany both on and off the track. They came first with 33 gold medals, followed by the U.S. with 24 and Hungary with 10.

The Games had been the most impressive to date with superb facilities and organisation. It was the first time that the Olympics had been televised and they were preserved on film by Hitler's favourite director, Leni Riefenstahl. Her four-hour film, *Olympia*, was released in two parts, beginning in April 1938.

The next Olympics, in 1940, were scheduled for Tokyo, but Hitler's plans for far greater victories meant that there would be no more Olympic Games until after World War II, in 1948. ●

HINDENBURG BURNS IN LAKEHURST CRASH;

21 KNOWN DEAD, 12 MISSING; 64 ESCAPE

(*New York Times*, 7 May 1937)

THE MAJESTIC Hindenburg airship – the biggest in the world – offered a speedy alternative to transatlantic crossing by liner. But when disaster struck, the horrifying pictures and news footage shocked the world, shattering confidence in airships and ending their golden era.

The mighty LZ 29 Hindenburg was the pride of the German Zeppelin passenger-carrying airship fleet. At 245m (804 feet) in length the Hindenburg was more than three times as long as a modern Boeing 747 Jumbo Jet and over twice the 747's overall height.

The airship could not, however, compete with the 747's passenger capacity, accommodating just 72 guests as opposed to more than 400 in a Jumbo. Hindenburg passengers, however, travelled in great style.

Passenger cabins were cramped, with an upper and lower bunk, a folding wash basin and a collapsible writing table but for most of the voyage passengers would be expected to use the lounge, restaurant, reading room or promenade areas (where there were large, sloping windows looking down at an angle), all in the belly of the great silver-skinned beast. While the public areas were not as luxurious as the finest ocean liners of the time, the lounge did have its own, custom-built baby grand piano, made mainly from aluminium and covered with pigskin. Unlike a modern airliner, therefore, there was plenty of space for passengers to move around aboard the Hindenburg.

INAUGURAL FLIGHTS

It began its first transatlantic services in 1936 and the airship's inaugural flight for the 1937 season had attracted much attention from the media, who had gathered at Lakehurst Naval Air Station, New Jersey, to watch the Hindenburg arrive from Frankfurt.

The previous year, the Hindenburg had completed ten successful trips with a full capacity of 72 passengers but for this first flight of 1937 it was only half full with 36 passengers and 61 crew.

Around 7:00pm local time, on 6 May, at an altitude of 650 feet (200m), the Hindenburg approached Lakehurst and, 18 minutes later, it began to drop water ballast from the stern to level out. After this was accomplished, two mooring lines were dropped from the bow, which were to be secured to the mooring winch. The port line was connected but before the other could be secured, witnesses on the ground saw flames from the top and side of the airship. On board, some people had heard a muffled explosion just moments earlier.

The flames rapidly spread and within 34 seconds the Hindenburg was engulfed.

MIRACULOUS SURVIVORS

With little time to react, some passengers leapt to their deaths from the blazing airship when it was still some 300 feet in the air. Others managed to jump to safety when it was lower or were rescued from the burning wreck after it had hit the ground. Of the 97 people on board, 35 died along with a member of the ground crew.

Because there were so many news teams at Lakehurst, the full horror of the incident was captured on both moving and still images. Some commentators described the Hindenburg crash as being 'the *Titanic* of the sky'.

Nobody is sure where the fire started or what caused it. Initially, there were those, including the Captain, Max Pruss, who thought it was sabotage and various passengers and crew members came under suspicion. But subsequent enquiries by both German and American investigators showed no evidence of any sabotage.

Another suggestion was that engine failure had caused sparks to ignite either the airship's outer skin or leaking hydrogen, the highly flammable gas used as a lifting agent.

One of the more popular theories is that the fire was caused by static electricity, which built up in the airship after it had passed through a storm. But there is much debate about whether it caused hydrogen or the outer skin to ignite.

The tragedy killed off the air-ship era and two years later Pan American Airlines provided a much faster means of travel as they inaugurated the world's first transatlantic aeroplane passenger service. •

BRITAIN'S FIRST DAY OF WAR

CHURCHILL IS NEW NAVY CHIEF

(*Daily Mirror*, 4 September 1939)

AFTER EFFORTS to appease German Chancellor Adolf Hitler failed to quell his ambition, British Prime Minister Neville Chamberlain finally gave in to the inevitable and declared war on Germany.

This historic newspaper had the dramatic opening sentence, 'Britain and Germany have been at war since 11 o'clock yesterday morning.' It went on to say that a war cabinet of nine had been set up and that Winston Churchill, who had been First Lord of the Admiralty during WWI, was returning to that post.

The paper also contained what were to become famous speeches by Chamberlain and King George VI.

In his broadcast at 11.15am on 3 September, the PM, in a clipped English accent, announced, 'I am speaking to you from the Cabinet Room at 10 Downing Street. This morning the British Ambassador in Berlin handed the German Government a final note stating that unless we heard from them by eleven o'clock that they were prepared at once to withdraw their troops from Poland a state of war would exist between us.

'I have to tell you that no such undertaking has been received and that consequently this country is at war with Germany.'

THE KING'S SPEECH

That evening the King had his own personal battle to overcome – a crippling stutter – to make his broadcast to the nation. 'In this grave hour, perhaps the most fateful in our history, I send to every household of my people, both at home and overseas, this message, spoken with the same depth of feeling for each one of you as if I were able to cross your threshold and speak to you myself.

'For the second time in the lives of most of us we are at war. Over and over again we have tried to find a peaceful way out of the differences between ourselves and those who are now our enemies. But it has been in vain. We have been forced into a conflict…'

It was a stirring yet measured speech urging the nation to stand 'calm and firm and united' and he did not underestimate the difficulty of the undertaking.

'The task will be hard. There may be dark days ahead and war can no longer be confined to the battlefield. But we can only do the right as we see the right, and reverently commit our cause to God.'

With the harrowing World War I having ended only 21 years earlier,

the British had no appetite for another war, but Hitler's aggressive expansion in Europe could not be ignored.

After being defeated in WWI, Germany was forced to accept a humiliating agreement under the Treaty of Versailles that reduced her territory, imposed huge reparations and put limits on the size of her army.

EXPANSION CAMPAIGN

A growing feeling of resentment in the country inspired the charismatic Nazi Party leader Adolf Hitler and, in 1933, he had been appointed Chancellor of Germany. He set about re-armament and embarked on a campaign of expansion in Europe, annexing Austria and part of Czechoslovakia.

The British and French objected but conceded the territories to Hitler so long as he promised no further expansion. But Hitler was encouraged by their weak response and went on to take over the remainder of Czechoslovakia. With his eyes next on Poland, Britain and France guaranteed their support to the Poles. So when Germany invaded Poland on 1 September, Britain committed herself and her colonial countries to war. A few hours later, France did likewise. It was to become a global conflict.

Churchill had been among the first to recognise the growing threat of Hitler and many were pleased to see him at the heart of the war cabinet – although others criticised him as a 'warmonger'.

In the spring of 1940, Chamberlain came under mounting pressure to resign. He finally gave way and Churchill became Prime Minister on 10 May. ●

175 NAZI PLANES DOWN

RAF TRIUMPHS IN BIGGEST AIR BATTLES OF WAR

(*Daily Herald*, 16 September 1940)

ON 18 JUNE 1940, British Prime Minister Winston Churchill gave a speech in the House of Commons saying, 'The Battle of France is over. The Battle of Britain is about to begin.'

Four days later, France surrendered to Germany and Hitler turned his attention towards Britain.

A fleet of invasion barges was assembled in French, Belgian and Dutch ports, with German troops practising embarkation and landing drills on adjacent beaches. Hitler and his military chiefs identified landing sites along the south coast of England and laid detailed plans about how each objective would be captured, how paratroops would be deployed inland to encircle the coastal defences, exactly which German units would be allocated to each stretch of coastline and precisely how far inland they expected to push in the hours and days following the landings.

The Germans also drew up lists of influential people in major towns across Britain who would immediately be arrested. Some were earmarked for execution. Hitler even went as far as to choose Senate House in Bloomsbury, the administrative centre of the University of London but then being used as Britain's Ministry of Information, as his London headquarters.

RAF TO BE DESTROYED

Before any invasion could be launched, however, Hitler knew that he had to gain air superiority. The invasion, codenamed 'Operation Sea Lion' called for vast minefields to be laid at sea, sealing off the English Channel to stop Royal Navy ships from decimating the invasion fleet. Some Royal Navy vessels were bound to get through, but the Luftwaffe would hold them at bay.

In order that the German aircraft could operate freely, and to ensure that the invasion fleet was not bombed out of existence by the British, Hitler required that the RAF be destroyed. He instructed Herman Goering, the head of the Luftwaffe, that the RAF must be 'beaten down to such an extent that it can no longer muster any power of attack worth mentioning against the German crossing.'

'Operation Sea Lion' was planned to take place in mid-September 1940.

The Luftwaffe's principal weapons were its Messerschmitt 109 fighters along with a variety of bombers and hybrid fighter-bombers.

The RAF's 700 or so Spitfire and Hurricane fighters were hugely outnumbered, but the Germans' numerical superiority was countered by the fact that they had the disadvantage of having to fly further, operating at the limit of their fighter aircraft's range. Britain also had the advantage of an excellent radar early-warning system, an effective fighter plane in the Spitfire and the remarkable ability to be able to manufacture more planes at an astonishing rate.

The battle began in mid-July, with the Luftwaffe attacking shipping in the English Channel as well as coastal towns and defences. From 12 August attacks were made directly on RAF airfields and radar bases and there were intense battles. By the end of the month the Germans had lost more than 600 aircraft and the RAF about half that number.

RAF BOMBS BERLIN

At the beginning of September, Britain took the offensive and infuriated Hitler by launching air attacks on some of Germany's industrial areas – and Berlin itself. In retaliation, Hitler ordered the bombing of London and other major British cities from 7 September. It was the beginning of 'the Blitz'.

On 15 September more than 1,000 enemy aircraft flew in and

carried out a day-and-night attack on London. It became known as 'Battle of Britain Day'. The RAF battled them in the skies above the capital and as they flew over the south coast.

At the end of the day, the RAF announced that they had shot down 175 enemy aircraft and the newspapers duly trumpeted the triumph. It did wonders for the morale of civilians who had to shelter on a daily basis during the Blitz. But it was far from the truth. In reality the Germans had lost 56 planes to the RAF's 27. But it was a decisive moment in the conflict between the two countries. Hitler had failed to gain air superiority and postponed his plans to invade Britain. On 17 September, he focused on the invasion of Russia, although the Luftwaffe continued to bomb Britain until the end of the war.

INVASION CANCELLED

In mid-October, Hitler ordered his invasion fleet to be dispersed. Britain had successfully defended herself in battle and had gained the upper hand. It was a huge boost to the nation and was considered to be Hitler's first major defeat – a crucial turning point in the war.

It is estimated that between 10 July and the end of October, the Luftwaffe lost 1,887 planes to the RAF's 1,023. Nearly 500 British pilots and aircrew had been killed and thousands of civilians died during the bombings.

In one of his most memorable speeches, Churchill saluted the achievement of the RAF with the words, 'Never in the field of human conflict was so much owed by so many to so few.' •

JAPAN, U.S. AT WAR

104 DIE IN HAWAII RAID; 2 U.S. TRANSPORTS SUNK

(*Seattle Post-Intelligencer*, 8 December 1941)

A SURPRISE ATTACK by Japan on the U.S. Pacific Fleet at Pearl Harbor, on Oahu, the third largest and chief island of Hawaii, on 7 December 1941, shocked America to the core.

At 7.55am the first of two waves of Japanese aircraft – fighters and bombers – were launched from six aircraft carriers and opened fire on the base. A second wave followed at 9.00am, pounding the fleet for an hour. Within two hours, five battleships had been sunk, another 16 damaged and 188 aircraft destroyed. Over 2,400 Americans were killed, another 1,178 injured, but under 100 Japanese had died.

The U.S., which had followed a policy of isolationism during the war, was stunned and incensed by the action. It came during a time when Japanese officials in Washington were negotiating with U.S. Secretary of State Cordell Hull on lifting U.S. sanctions imposed after continuing Japanese aggression against China.

U.S. DECLARES WAR

The following day, the United States declared war on Japan. In a speech to Congress, President Roosevelt called the attack on Pearl Harbor, 'a day that will live in infamy'. Within an hour of the speech, Congress passed a formal declaration of war against Japan and officially brought the U.S. into World War II.

On 11 December, Germany and Italy declared war on the U.S. and America immediately reciprocated.

Adolf Hitler made his announcement at the Reichstag in Berlin, saying he had tried to avoid direct conflict with the U.S. but under the Tripartite Agreement, Germany was obliged to join with Italy to defend her ally.

Following the Pearl Harbor attack, there were queues of volunteers at U.S. armed forces recruiting stations, all eager to fight for their country.

The background to the attack could be traced back to a decade earlier when, in 1931, Japan embarked on a policy of expansion, moving in to Manchuria in northern China and exploiting the resources there.

JAPANESE AGGRESSION

Having gained confidence from the occupation, Japan became more aggressive and expanded further into Indochina. The U.S., which had territories in the area, imposed trade sanctions on Japan in 1939. Then, on 27 September 1940, Japan signed the Tripartite Agreement with Germany and Italy, becoming a formal member of the Axis alliance fighting the European war.

Early in 1941, a concerned Roosevelt moved the Pacific Fleet from San Diego to Hawaii in a show of power to try to discourage further Japanese expansion in the Far East. In July, he stopped oil exports to Japan, but this only had the effect of encouraging Japan to invade the oil-rich Dutch East Indies in January 1942.

Hostility between Japan and the U.S. was growing. Japan had ambitions to invade more territories in Southeast Asia belonging to the U.S., Britain and the Netherlands. Fearful that the U.S. might step in to try to prevent them, Japan had begun planning a strike on the Pacific Fleet in early 1941.

OFFICIAL INVESTIGATIONS

There was much bewilderment as to why the U.S. had been so taken by surprise by the attack. Six wartime and one post-war investigation revealed a lack of coordination and communication between Washington and Oahu and an underestimation of Japan's aerial strength.

As a result, Lieutenant General Short, Commander for the defence of military installations in Hawaii, was relieved of his post on 17 December 1941. So too was Navy Commander Admiral Kimmel.

A commission headed by U.S. Supreme Court Associate Justice Owen J. Roberts, known as the Roberts Commission, was held soon after the attack on Pearl Harbor. It accused the two men of being unprepared and said that they did not take seriously enough an earlier warning from Washington that there might be an air attack at Pearl Harbor.

A later report in 1945 was more fairly balanced. It stated, 'The underlying cause of this error of judgement was General Short's confidence that Japan would not then attack Pearl Harbor. In fairness to him it must be borne in mind that this belief was shared in by almost everyone concerned including his superior officers in the War Department in Washington. He was undoubtedly influenced in such a belief by the then prevailing psychology which completely underestimated the Japanese military capabilities and particularly the advance which they had made in the use of aircraft.' ●

VE-DAY – IT'S ALL OVER

ALL QUIET TILL 9PM – THEN THE LONDON CROWDS WENT MAD IN THE WEST END

(*Daily Mail*, 8 May 1945)

IT WAS THE NEWS that the world had been waiting for. After six long years of fighting, suffering and hardship, Germany had finally surrendered and the war in Europe had ended.

It had happened on 7 May 1945 but was not to be officially announced until a day later. However, as news spread, Londoners could not contain their joy any longer. And that evening, around 9pm, celebrations broke out in the capital.

The *Daily Mail* reported how, 'Bonfires blazed from Piccadilly to Wapping. The sky once lit by the glare of the blitz shone red with the Victory glow.'

It described people linking arms singing, dancing and waving flags. Favourite cockney wartime songs were sung at the tops of their voices – 'Roll out the Barrel', 'Tipperary', 'Bless 'em All' and 'Pack Up Your Troubles'.

They needed to let their hair down after being blitzed and then facing the fear of the dreaded German V1 'Doodlebug' missiles which flew over from 1944. They also had to endure food rationing. If ever there was a time to party, this was it.

Since the beginning of the year, the end had been in sight following a series of capitulations. The German forces in Italy surrendered on 2 May and then in Northern Germany, Denmark and the Netherlands.

SURRENDER DOCUMENT SIGNED

The final document of unconditional surrender was signed at General Dwight Eisenhower's headquarters in Rheims at 2.41pm on 7 May 1945. But it was the following day that would be declared 'Victory in Europe' (VE) Day and back in Britain people sat by their radios at 3.00pm to hear Churchill announce that the war with Germany over.

In Trafalgar Square a large crowd gathered to hear Churchill's voice relayed over loudspeakers. Despite the jubilation there was an extraordinary hush when he began talking.

In a broadcast from the Cabinet Room at Number 10 Downing Street, Churchill paid tribute to Russia and the allies.

'Today, perhaps, we shall think mostly of ourselves. Tomorrow we shall pay a particular tribute to our Russian comrades, whose prowess in the field has been one of the grand contributions to the general victory.'

He went on to say, 'After gallant France had been struck down we, from this Island and from our united Empire, maintained the struggle single-handed for a whole year until we were joined by the military might of Soviet Russia, and later by the overwhelming power and resources of the United States of America.

'Finally almost the whole world was combined against the evil-doers, who are now prostrate before us. Our gratitude to our splendid Allies goes forth from all our hearts in this Island and throughout the British Empire.

JAPAN'S TREACHERY AND GREED

'We may allow ourselves a brief period of rejoicing; but let us not forget for a moment the toil and efforts that lie ahead. Japan, with all her treachery and greed, remains unsubdued. The injury she has inflicted on Great Britain, the United States, and other countries, and her detestable cruelties, call for justice and retribution. We must now devote all our strength and resources to the completion of our task, both at home and abroad.'

Shortly after Churchill's speech, King George VI, Queen Elizabeth and Princesses Elizabeth and Margaret came out onto the balcony at Buckingham Palace to acknowledge the cheering throng. When the Royal Family made a further appearance at 5.30pm they were accompanied by Churchill and a huge cheer went up.

That evening, at 9.00pm, King George VI made a speech to the nation and empire. 'Today we give thanks to Almighty God for a great deliverance. Speaking from our Empire's oldest capital city, war-battered but never for one moment daunted or dismayed – speaking from London, I ask you to join with me in that act of thanksgiving.

'Germany, the enemy who drove all Europe into war, has been finally overcome.' •

FIRST ATOMIC BOMB BROPPED ON JAPAN;

MISSILE IS EQUAL TO 20,000 TONS OF TNT; TRUMAN WARNS FOE OF A 'RAIN OF RUIN'

(New York Times, 6 August 1945)

IT WAS A TERRIFYING new bomb of massive destruction, killing thousands of Japanese civilians, that was the final act in ending World War II.

Germany had surrendered to the Allies on 7 May 1945 but the war was dragging on in the Far East with Japan determined to continue fighting.

The U.S., Britain and China had called for Japan to surrender in the Potsdam Declaration of 26 July 1945. It carried the threat that if they did not do so it would result in 'the inevitable and complete destruction of the Japanese armed forces and just as inevitably the utter devastation of the Japanese homeland'. But this was rejected.

Angered that, despite intense bombing of Japanese cities, America was sustaining heavy casualties in fighting at Iwo Jima and Okinawa, U.S. President Harry S. Truman gave the order to drop the ultimate weapon – the atom bomb.

Since 1939, American, British and Canadian scientists had been working in the U.S. on harnessing the power of the atom for military purposes. This top-secret work was known as the Manhattan Project and was later put under control of General Leslie Groves of the U.S. Army Corps of Engineers. The race was on because it was known that Germany was also working on an atomic bomb.

A special laboratory was also set up near Santa Fe under the direction of physicist Dr J. Robert Oppenheimer. The first test of the atomic bomb took place on 16 July 1945, in a remote desert section of New Mexico. Oppenheimer and other eminent scientists, who had gathered to witness it, were said to have been nervous about just what they were unleashing on the world.

ENOLA GAY TAKES OFF

Following the successful testing, a B-29 aircraft, nicknamed Enola Gay after the mother of the pilot of the plane, Colonel Paul Tibbets, took to the air on the morning of 6 August 1945. It was carrying the atom bomb and was accompanied by two other B-29s as it made its way on a six-hour flight to Japan.

The city of Hiroshima had been targeted because it contained a military-supplies depot and was an assembly area for troops. But it was also a heavily populated civilian area. When the bomb was dropped, it devastated an area of five square miles (13 square kilometres). Around 40,000–70,000 people were killed outright and a further 100,000 would die of radiation poisoning over the next five years.

President Harry S. Truman announced the news from the cruiser, USS *Augusta*, in the mid-Atlantic, saying that the device was more than 2,000 times more powerful than the largest bomb used to date.

A RAIN OF RUIN

His statement carried the warning of more to come. 'It was to spare the Japanese people from utter destruction that the ultimatum of 26 July, was issued at Potsdam. Their leaders promptly rejected that ultimatum. If they do not now accept our terms, they may expect a rain of ruin from the air the like of which has never been seen on this earth.'

Truman added, 'What has been done is the greatest achievement of organised science in history. We are now prepared to obliterate more rapidly and completely every productive enterprise the Japanese have above ground in any city. We shall destroy Japan's power to make war.'

U.S. Secretary of War, Henry L. Stimson said that this new weapon 'should prove a tremendous aid in the shortening of the war against Japan'. And in a prophetic note, he remarked, 'The scientists are confident that over a period of many years atomic bombs may well be developed which will be very much more powerful than the atomic bombs now at hand.'

But despite the devastation, Japan refused to give up the fight. And so on the morning of 9 August, a second atomic bomb headed for the city of Nagasaki, one of the largest sea ports in southern Japan, which produced ships and military equipment.

The bomb killed another estimated 40–70,000 instantly and the following day the Japanese government presented a letter of protest to the government of the U.S. via the government of Switzerland. Then, on 12 August, Emperor Hirohito finally gave the order to surrender. In his declaration to his people he said, 'The enemy now possesses a new and terrible weapon with the power to destroy many innocent lives and do incalculable damage. Should we continue to fight, not only would it result in an ultimate collapse and obliteration of the Japanese nation, but also it would lead to the total extinction of human civilization.' •

STATE OF ISRAEL IS BORN

(*Palestine Post*, 14 May 1948)

THE STATE OF ISRAEL was proclaimed on 14 May 1948 in Tel Aviv – the first Jewish state in 2,000 years.

In a ceremony at the Tel Aviv Art Museum, Jewish Agency Chairman David Ben-Gurion, who was to become Israel's first premier, pronounced the words 'We hereby proclaim the establishment of the Jewish state in Palestine, to be called Israel' to applause from the crowd that had gathered.

There had been much fighting over the years leading to this moment and it resumed the very next day as Arab armies from the neighbouring countries of Jordan, Egypt, Lebanon, Syria and Iraq invaded Israel but were resisted.

Britain had taken over Palestine after the collapse of the Ottoman Empire during the Great War and, in 1917, the 'Balfour Declaration' stated that Britain intended to establish a Jewish homeland in Palestine.

BRITISH RULE EXTENDED

But because of Arab opposition and continued fighting in the region, British rule continued throughout the 1920s and 1930s.

In 1947, the British government announced it would withdraw from

Palestine, stating it was unable to arrive at a solution acceptable to both Arabs and Jews. The newly created United Nations approved the Partition Plan for Palestine on 29 November, which would divide the country into two states – one Arab and one Jewish. The Jews were to possess more than half of Palestine, although they made up less than half of Palestine's population.

There was fierce objection from Palestinian Arabs and, aided by supportive Arab nations, they fought against the Jews, determined to claim territory, but the Jews managed to protect the land that had been agreed as theirs and Partition went ahead.

The fighting continued for a year until a ceasefire was declared and temporary borders, known as the Green Line, were established. Jordan annexed what became known as the West Bank and East Jerusalem, and Egypt had control of the Gaza Strip.

SUEZ CANAL CLOSED

In 1950, Egypt closed the Suez Canal to Israeli shipping and armed clashes took place along Israel's borders. On 26 July 1956, President Nasser of Egypt nationalised the Anglo-French Suez Canal Company, declaring that the revenue from the canal would finance the building of a dam at Aswan.

Israel joined a secret alliance with Britain and France to free the Canal from Egypt and in November an Anglo-French aerial and ground assault began on Cairo. In April 1957 the canal was fully reopened to shipping

But conflict between the two sides has continued to break out. In May 1967, a number of Arab states began to mobilise their forces, which led Israel to make a pre-emptive strike on 5 June against Egypt, Jordan, Syria and Iraq.

SIX-DAY WAR

The battle that ensued became known as the Six-Day War. It resulted in Israel increasing its borders, capturing the Sinai Peninsula, the Gaza Strip, the West Bank, the Golan Heights and old Jerusalem.

The Six-Day War, named by Chief of the Israeli Defence Force and future Prime Minister Yitzhak Rabin after the biblical days of creation, may not have been a long, drawn-out affair, but it was brutal and bloody. The Israelis lost almost 1,000 personnel, while the Egyptians are estimated to have had over ten times that number killed, wounded or missing in action. Jordan is thought to have suffered as many as 6,000 fatalities while there were 1,000 Syrian deaths, with many more wounded.

In 1979, Israel and Egypt signed an historic peace agreement in which Israel returned the Sinai. And in 1993, Israel and the Palestine Liberation Organization (PLO) signed a major peace accord, in which they agreed the gradual implementation of Palestinian self-government in the West Bank and Gaza Strip.

But fighting between Israelis and Palestinians resumed in Israel and the occupied territories and tension and resentment remain. ●

MAO HEADS PEIPING REGIME

(*New York Times*, 1 October 1949)

MODERN DAY CHINA was born on 1 October 1949 when Mao Tse-tung (Zedong) proclaimed the founding of the People's Republic of China.

The day before, he had been elected Party Chairman of the new communist regime after they had finally defeated the Nationalists to seize power.

The *New York Times* reported on the historic moment, referring to the capital of Beijing as Peiping, as it was known by many at the time. The paper also mentioned that Western powers were worried about this new development, which meant that the Soviet Union had a new Eastern ally.

Mao was born on 26 December 1893 into a peasant family in Shaoshan, in Hunan province, central China. After training as a teacher, he travelled to Beijing and worked as a library assistant where he read Marxist literature. Influenced by Lenin and the Russian Revolution, he became a founder member of the Chinese Communist Party (CCP) in 1921 and set up a branch in Hunan.

MAO IN RETREAT

In 1923, the Kuomintang nationalist party allied with the CCP to defeat the warlords who controlled much of northern China. But four years later the Kuomintang leader Chiang Kai-shek launched an attack on the Communists and Mao and his colleagues retreated to southeast China.

In October 1934, with the Kuomintang army circling the Communists' base in Jiangxi province, Mao led his men on a mammoth journey across difficult terrain to the northwest on an escape route said to have been 8,000 miles (12,500km) long and to have taken 370 days.

Named the 'Long March' it gained Mao enormous respect and symbolised the determination and struggle of the Communists to reach their goal.

During eight years of war with Japan, from 1937 to 1945, there was an uneasy alliance between the Communists and Kuomintang, but shortly after the end of World War II, civil war broke out between them.

It ended in victory for the Communists and Mao proudly announcing the founding of the People's Republic of China.

STATE OWNERSHIP

Mao set out to reshape China and was initially aided by the Soviet Union. Industry came under state ownership and farmers were organised into collectives. Those who objected were ruthlessly dealt with.

But as relationships with the Soviet Union began to cool he attempted to introduce a more 'Chinese' form of communism in 1958, with what he called the 'Great Leap Forward'. This involved a drive for increased agricultural and industrial production with huge communes running their own collective farms and factories.

Each family received a share of the profits and also had a small private plot of land. But three years of floods and bad harvests severely damaged levels of production, leading to famine and the deaths of millions. In 1962 it came to an end and the country resorted to a more traditional form of economic production. Mao's position was weakened but he was determined to forge ahead with reform.

THE 'CULTURAL REVOLUTION'

After having publicly criticised the Soviet Leader Nikita Khrushchev for backing down over the Cuban Missile Crisis, Mao launched the 'Cultural Revolution' in 1966, to distance China from the Soviet model of communism and to purge political opponents whose views were too conservative. He warned the Red Guard and students that the revolution was in danger and that they must stop the emergence of a privileged class, which he said had happened in the Soviet Union.

Some of his writings at this time were gathered in a handbook called *Quotations of Chairman Mao Tse-tung*, and widely distributed to Chinese citizens.

The purges resulted in violence and death as opposition was crushed. Mao remained in charge of the nation until his death in 1976. •

TRUMAN ORDERS U.S. AIR, NAVY UNITS TO FIGHT IN AID OF KOREA

(New York Times, 27 June 1950)

PRESIDENT TRUMAN ordered the Air Force and Navy into the Korean War following a call from the United Nations Security Council for member nations to help South Korea repel an invasion from the North.

In the aftermath of World War II the Allies replaced Japan as the colonial power of Korea. Seven days before the end of the war, the Soviet Union had seized the moment by entering Korea. Now, at the Allied summit meetings, it was agreed to divide Korea at the 38th parallel, with the USSR in charge north of this line, and the U.S. in the south. This was to be a short-term measure until the return of Korean independence.

The Soviets backed a Stalinist regime in the north under Kim Il-sung and created the North Korean Peoples' Army, equipped with Russian tanks and artillery. In the south, elections were held and Syngman Rhee was made President.

Both occupying forces withdrew from Korea by 1949. A well-equipped and trained army of around 135,000 in the north contrasted sharply with little more than a constabulary force in the south of 98,000.

Emboldened by its military superiority, the north crossed over the 38th parallel in the early hours of 25 June 1950.

A unified Korea was the goal of both sides but one wanted a communist country and the other a democracy.

U.S. FORCED TO RETREAT

U.S. troops were hurriedly sent from bases in Japan but, caught off-guard, they were compelled to retreat. President Truman called on the newly formed United Nations Security Council for support and the council passed a resolution which called on all members to help repel the invasion.

Fourteen nations agreed to help, committing a force of some 300,000. The bulk of the troops were American, with Britain, Canada and Australia all making significant contributions.

By 25 September, the U.N. force had recaptured Seoul and reclaimed the rest of the territory but Truman saw the chance to unify Korea under a single, pro-Western government and ordered the American General Douglas MacArthur, Commander of the U.N. forces in Korea, to pursue the northern invaders across the 38th parallel and deep into their own territory.

They pushed on towards China, ignoring warnings that China would enter the war if the troops invaded North Korea.

On 15 October, a confident MacArthur told Truman that it would all be over by Christmas, but ten days later the Chinese army, which had been secretly massing at the border with Korea, attacked the U.N. troops. They beat a hasty retreat and by the New Year were fighting to hold a line to the south of Seoul.

After a few more months of fighting they were able to push the enemy back to the area of the 38th parallel. With the situation at 'stalemate' the U.N. pushed for a ceasefire.

MACARTHUR DISMISSED

MacArthur wanted to extend the fight against the Chinese and 'communism' and openly criticised Truman for his orders to contain the fighting to Korea. Truman then sacked MacArthur as commander of the U.N. forces in Korea and of U.S. forces in the Far East. He was replaced by General Matthew Ridgeway

The two sides held peace talks in April 1951 but they dragged on for two years. One of the main sticking points was the repatriation of prisoners. Tens of thousands of communist prisoners were held in camps on Koje Island off the coast of South Korea. While the north demanded that all prisoners be returned, there were many in the camp who didn't want to go back. Eventually it was agreed to offer asylum to the latter. Prisoners from both sides were returned when an armistice was signed on 27 July 1953. •

THE CROWNING GLORY: EVEREST IS CLIMBED

(*News Chronicle*, 2 June 1953)

THE NEWS THAT a British expedition was the first to reach the summit of Mount Everest – the highest point in the world – didn't reach newspapers until a few days after the event. But it was perfect timing, coming on the day before the coronation of Queen Elizabeth II.

The expedition, led by Colonel John Hunt, set off for the Himalayas in February. Hunt had named two two-man teams for the final assault on the summit – Tom Bourdillon and Charles Evans; and Edmund Hillary and Tenzing Norgay.

Hillary was a New Zealander who found a love of mountaineering on a school trip to Mount Ruapehu, south of Auckland, when he was 16.

After spending two years as a navigator in the Royal New Zealand Air Force, he joined an alpine club to take on all the national peaks. In search of bigger challenges, he travelled to the Himalayas and then set his sights on becoming the first man to climb Mount Everest.

Tenzing was a Sherpa mountaineer from Nepal, who had been part of several other mountaineering teams that had attempted, but failed, to conquer Everest.

CHANCE OF GLORY

Hunt's team set up its final camp at 25,900 feet (7,890m) and Bourdillon and Evans had their chance of glory when they set off for the summit on 26 May. But they had to turn back 300 feet

(91m) from the top, when Evans's oxygen system failed. Now it was down to Hillary and Tenzing.

After a gruelling climb up the southern face, they reached the top of the world at 11.30am on 29 May.

The two men hugged each other with joy and Hillary took a now-famous photograph of Tenzing holding his pick aloft. But no pictures were taken of himself.

Tenzing buried sweets and a pencil given to him by his daughter as a Buddhist offering to the gods. Hillary left a cross that had been entrusted to him by John Hunt.

OXYGEN RUNNING OUT

They remained on the summit for just 15 minutes because they were low on oxygen, before making their descent. Snow had covered much of their tracks, which made retracing their route more difficult.

The first person they met was teammate, George Low, who had climbed up to meet them with hot soup. Hillary greeted him with the down-to-earth victorious phrase, 'Well, George, we knocked the bastard off.'

Hunt initially mistook Hillary and Tenzing's exhausted appearance for one of defeat but after hearing of their success, the team hugged each other in celebration.

Hillary later described the peak, which is 29,028 feet (8,847m) above sea level, as 'a symmetrical, beautiful snow cone summit'.

He was knighted, along with Hunt, on return, by the new young Queen, and Tenzing was awarded the George Medal.

AFTER EVEREST

After the ascent, Hillary led a number of expeditions to the South Pole but shunned the celebrity spotlight to devote his life to helping the Sherpas of Nepal's Khumbu region. He set up a trust to help build hospitals, schools and bridges. In 1985, he was made New Zealand's High Commissioner to India and lived in Delhi.

He spoke out about what he considered to be the commercialisation of Everest and climbers who left rubbish behind and ignored others in distress as they passed them en route to the summit. He was made an honorary Nepalese citizen in 2003 and died in 2008.

Tenzing received many honours and continued to work in his beloved mountains as a guide. He went on to become head of field training at the Himalayan Mountaineering Institute in Darjeeling and established Tenzing Norgay Adventures, a trekking and guiding company, in 1978. When he died in 1986 at the age of 71, the company was taken over by his son, Jamling, who climbed Everest ten years after his father's death and, along with Peter Hillary, the son of Edmund Hillary, he was part of an expedition to climb the mountain again in 2002, on the 50th anniversary of their fathers' conquest.

Peter Hillary was part of the team for the assault on the summit and, after their successful attempt, he put in a call to his father using a satellite phone, something that would have been almost beyond imagination in 1952. •

WHY YOU ARE YOU

NEARER SECRET OF LIFE

(*News Chronicle*, 15 May 1953)

THE DISCOVERY OF the secret of life was greeted with a subdued reception. Despite later being described by some as the most significant contribution to science since Darwin's theory of evolution, it took a while for people to become aware of what had happened.

The unravelling of the structure of deoxyribonucleic acid (DNA) – the material that makes up genes which pass hereditary characteristics from one parent to another – was made by biologists Francis Crick and James Watson on 28 February 1953 at their laboratory in Cambridge.

PUB ANNOUNCEMENT

Later that day, a euphoric Crick walked into the local public house, The Eagle, and announced that he and his colleague 'had found the secret of life.'

It may have sounded like an outrageous boast from a pub bore but it was true. The pair had discovered the elusive 'double helix' structure of DNA in which two strands coil around each other, both consisting of complementary elements that fit together and when uncoiled can produce two copies of the original. It confirmed theories that it carried life's hereditary information.

Crick, who was born near Northampton, studied physics at University College, London, and then biology at Cambridge University.

By 1949 he was working at the Medical Research Council unit at the Cavendish Laboratory in Cambridge under the general direction of Lawrence Bragg, who had won the Nobel Prize for Physics in 1915 at the age of 25.

In 1951 an American student from Chicago, James Watson, who at 23 was twelve years Crick's junior, arrived and they enjoyed a shared passion for studying the structure of DNA.

X-RAY STUDIES

The pair worked together using some key information that had been obtained by Maurice Wilkins and Rosalind Franklin, both working at King's College, London, who had been using X-ray diffraction to study DNA.

This helped them to finally crack the 'double helix' structure and Bragg proudly made the announcement at a conference in Belgium on 8 April 1953. It went unreported by the press.

Crick and Watson's findings were published in the scientific journal *Nature* on 25 April 1953. Their comment, 'This structure has novel features which are of considerable biological interest,' has become famous as one of science's most famous understatements.

Bragg then gave a talk at Guy's Hospital Medical School in London on 14 May, which resulted in an article by Ritchie Calder, science editor of the *News Chronicle*, the following day. It was the only British newspaper to carry a report on the ground-breaking discovery.

In 1962, Crick, Watson and Wilkins all won the Nobel Prize. Rosalind Franklin had died of cancer four years earlier, aged just 37, and so missed out on receiving the Prize for her crucial work in the discovery of DNA.

CREDIT TO OTHERS

Like most scientific discoveries, it is the work of many others who have led the way or contributed to the understanding of the subject that makes the achievement possible.

Back in 1868, almost a century before the Nobel Prize was awarded to Watson, Crick and Wilkins, a young Swiss physician named Friedrich Miescher, isolated something no one had ever seen before from the nuclei of cells. He called the compound 'nuclein' which is today called nucleic acid – the 'NA' in DNA.

In the late 1940s, the scientific community were aware that DNA was most likely the molecule of life, but breaking down the structure of it proved to be beyond them. After Crick and Watson found the answer, it provided a launching pad for a rapid advance in molecular biology that led to genetic engineering, stem cell research and DNA fingerprinting. •

RUTH ELLIS TO HANG

THE ONLY VERDICT, SAYS JUDGE – 'JEALOUSY NO DEFENCE'

(*Evening News*, 21 June 1955)

THE TRIAL OF Ruth Ellis, who shot dead her lover, was a controversial and landmark case as she became the last woman in England to be hanged.

The story had all the ingredients of a movie. Platinum-blonde Ellis, 28, was a former model from Wales who became a nightclub hostess after moving to London. At the age of 17 she had become pregnant by a Canadian soldier and gave birth to a son. She brought him up as a single parent for a while until he went to live with her mother.

In early 1950, she became pregnant by one of the customers at the nightclub where she worked but had the pregnancy terminated. Later that year she married another customer of the club who proved to be a jealous and violent alcoholic, who was convinced she was having an affair. After she gave birth to a daughter in 1951, he refused to acknowledge that he was the father and they separated shortly afterwards.

GLAMOUR GIRL

In 1953 she became a manager of another London nightclub and attracted a number of celebrity friends. Her glamorous looks and vivacious personality also caught the eye of promising racing driver, David Blakely, who moved into her flat above the club. She became pregnant for a fourth time but aborted the child.

She then began seeing a former WWII RAF pilot, Desmond Cussens. When she was sacked as manager of the club she moved in with him at his home in Oxford Street. But her tempestuous relationship with Blakely continued, causing increasing jealousy and anger between the two men.

On Easter Sunday, 10 April 1955, she went in search of Blakely and found his car parked outside a pub called The Magadala in Hampstead, north London. At around 9.30pm he emerged with his friend Clive Gunnell. She called to him but he ignored her and carried on walking towards his car. She then took a gun from her handbag and fired at him. It missed and he started to run. She ran after him and hit him with her second shot. He collapsed on the pavement and she fired three more bullets into him.

'I AM GUILTY'

In a state of shock, she asked Gunnell to call the police and was shortly arrested by an off-duty policeman who heard her say, 'I am guilty. I'm a little confused.' She was taken to Hampstead police station where she made a detailed confession to the police and was charged with murder.

Her trial at the Old Bailey opened on 20 June and the jury took just 14 minutes to find her guilty of murder. Mr Justice Havers sentenced her to death.

The case received much publicity in the press and there was a groundswell of sympathy for her from those who felt that she had been ill-treated by the men in her life and that the law should be more lenient towards what many considered to be a 'crime of passion'. Thousands signed petitions asking for the death penalty to be lifted in her case.

SINGING AND CHANTING

At midday on 12 July 1955, the day before her execution, Ellis made a statement to her solicitor in the condemned cell saying that the gun had been provided by Cussen and that he had driven her to the murder scene. But the Home Office refused to act on this and there was to be no reprieve.

The night before she was due to be hanged at Holloway Prison, a crowd of 500 formed outside the gates singing and chanting for her. Some broke through police cordons to bang on the prison doors, calling for Ellis to pray with them.

The following morning, the executioner, Albert Pierrepoint, went about his duties and she was hanged at 9.00am.

The case sparked debate about British criminal justice and the death penalty. Two years later, Parliament changed the law to allow a defence of diminished responsibility. The death penalty in the U.K. was suspended in 1965 and permanently removed in 1970.

Ruth Ellis's family continued to campaign for her murder conviction to be reduced to manslaughter on the grounds of provocation. At the Court of Appeal in September 2003, they argued that she was suffering 'battered woman syndrome' and that she had suffered a miscarriage just 10 days before the killing after David Blakely had punched her in the stomach.

The Court rejected the appeal, saying that it could only rule on the conviction based on the law as it stood in 1955. Diminished responsibility did not then exist and she had been properly convicted of murder. •

FIRST BLOWS BY NAVY AND R.A.F

CRUISER SINKS AN EGYPTIAN FRIGATE

(*Guardian*, 1 November 1956)

THE ATTACK BY BRITAIN and France on Egypt, part of which became known as the 'Suez Crisis', was a worldwide political disaster and the last gasp of the British Empire.

Construction on the canal began on 25 April 1859 after former French diplomat, Ferdinand de Lesseps, persuaded the Viceroy of Egypt, Mohamed Said, to allow a shipping canal through the 100 miles of desert between Africa and Asia. The Universal Company of the Suez Maritime Canal was set up but Britain, suspicious of France, declined the offer of shares in the company. And so Egypt acquired 44% of the shares.

The canal opened in November 1869 and, during the first year of its existence, some three-quarters of the vessels using it were British.

Said had been succeeded after his death in 1867 by his nephew, Ismail. When he fell into debt he offered his country's shares in the canal for sale. The British Prime Minister, Benjamin Disraeli, bought Egypt's shareholding for £4 million.

ACCESS TO OIL

Not only did the waterway provide Britain with a quicker route to her empire but, as oil became an increasingly important commodity at the beginning of the twentieth century, it also meant quicker access to the oilfields of the Persian Gulf.

Britain and France defended the Suez Canal through both World Wars and, despite Egypt being declared an independent state in 1936, there continued to be a heavy British presence in the country. In 1951, when Nahas Pasha became leader of the recently elected nationalist Wafd party, there was a backlash with attacks on the British garrison. Fighting continued on and off between the sides as relationships deteriorated.

In 1954, Colonel Gamel Abdul Nasser came to power, intent on ending British occupation, on building up Egyptian forces for an attack on Israel and on constructing a high dam at Aswan to irrigate the Nile valley.

CANAL NATIONALISED

It was agreed on 19 October 1954 that British troops were to be withdrawn from Egypt by June 1956 but could return if the canal was threatened by anyone. On 26 July 1956, President Nasser nationalised the Anglo-French Suez Canal Company to finance his dam.

Britain and France were alarmed, while America and Israel were concerned that Egypt was looking to the Soviet Union for arms. A secret meeting was held between Britain, France and Israel in which it was agreed that Israel should attack Egypt, thereby providing a pretext for an Anglo-French invasion of Suez.

Israeli troops began an invasion on 29 October 1956. The next day, Britain and France issued ultimatums to both sides to stop the fighting immediately. Two days later the two colonial powers launched an aerial bombardment on military airfields. Troops were parachuted in and overpowered the defence. Arab countries expressed their readiness to come to the aid of Egypt should she ask for it.

CEASEFIRE IMPOSED

The canal was almost back under Anglo-French control when a ceasefire was called on 6 November, after pressure from the United Nations.

The U.S. President, Dwight D. Eisenhower, was furious at being left out of the loop. In a TV broadcast he said that the 'armed attack' by Britain had been launched 'in error'. He added, 'We do not accept the use of force as a wise or proper instrument to settle international disputes.'

In Britain there was considerable outrage too over Britain's military offensive, with petitions to Downing Street and a mass demonstration in London's Trafalgar Square in which protestors carried banners proclaiming 'LAW not WAR!'.

The Labour Party said that Britain's attack was 'in clear violation of the United Nations charter'.

Under world pressure, Britain, France and Israel withdrew their forces and a U.N. peacekeeping force was sent in to supervise the ceasefire and to restore order.

British Prime Minister, Anthony Eden, denied any prior knowledge of the planned attack by Israel. The incident marked the end of historical colonial powers Britain and France acting independently of world opinion. Britain's relationship with the Middle East was severely damaged. Harold Macmillan, who succeeded Eden, repaired relationships with America, becoming friends with President John F. Kennedy and persuaded him to let Britain have the Polaris nuclear missile. The two countries have continued to support each other in general terms ever since. ●

SOVIET FIRES EARTH SATELLITE INTO SPACE

IT IS CIRCLING THE GLOBE AT 18,000 M.P.H.; SPHERE TRACED IN FOUR CROSSINGS OVER U.S.

(*New York Times*, October 5 1957)

AT JUST UNDER 23 inches (58cm) in diameter it was the size of a beach ball but it was a scientific marvel, causing fear and wonder in equal measure, which was to make a huge impact around the world.

With the U.S. and Soviet Union in the midst of the Cold War, each was trying to do outdo the other to prove superiority. Although both countries had talked about launching satellites into space, the U.S. was caught napping when the Soviets successfully launched the world's first artificial satellite, Sputnik 1, on 4 October 1957.

Sputnik weighed just under 184 pounds, had four antennae and contained a radio transmitter, batteries and a thermometer. It was a tremendous propaganda coup for the communist system, with Soviet scientists describing it as the first stage in interplanetary travel.

The U.S. only found out about the launch at a reception at the Soviet Embassy that night. The following day's reports in the newspapers caused much unease amongst the American public, who had no real idea what a satellite actually was.

The Russians had been developing rockets with which to launch missiles at the U.S. and, in August 1957, one of their R-7 rockets travelled 6,000 kilometres carrying a simulated H-bomb warhead. Some Americans now feared that Sputnik was either some kind of weapon or was being used to target American cities for atomic-bomb attacks.

SECRET CODE

It was 500 miles up, travelling at 18,000 miles an hour and it circled the globe every 96 minutes, flying over the U.S. seven times a day. The regular 'beeping' sound could be heard by ham-radio enthusiasts and many Americans found it deeply unsettling. In the days after the launch there were several paranoid articles in the newspapers. One asked if the beeping could be some kind of secret code.

At first, President Eisenhower tried to play down Sputnik's launch, claiming that it did not increase his concern about national security and that there would be no change in funding or priority for satellite or missile programs.

But he was criticised for his lack of investment in his country's space programme and for what some considered to be his lack of concern for Americans' safety. General concern increased when the Soviets launched Sputnik 2 on 3 November 1957. At 1100 pounds it was bigger than its predecessor and was carrying a passenger – Laika, the dog.

One near-hysterical U.S. news reporter took a flight of fancy, suggesting the possibility that it had been launched to hit the moon with a hydrogen bomb.

U.S. ROCKET EXPLODES

Meanwhile the U.S. was still to get a satellite off the ground and now it was desperately trying to make up for lost time. Funding was made available for students keen to enrol in aerospace engineering programmes and projects. And the government put pressure on scientists to launch a satellite as soon as possible. A highly publicised launch on 6 December 1957 was a disaster when the rocket carrying the satellite exploded on the launch pad. It was a great embarrassment to the U.S.

Finally they put their first satellite, Explorer, into orbit on 17

March 1958. But they were soon trumped when, fourteen weeks later, the Soviets launched their third and biggest Sputnik yet. It carried more scientific equipment than previous satellites from either country.

On 29 July 1958, Eisenhower signed a bill that created the National Aeronautics and Space Agency (NASA), which ushered in a whole new world of achievement.

Sputnik 1 had shattered American perception that the U.S. was the world's leading scientific and technological superpower. As well as deeply embarrassing them, they were shaken and nervous that their Cold War enemy had shown her superiority.

The race was now on to be the first to get a man into space. •

21 DEAD
7 MANCHESTER UTD
PLAYERS PERISH
IN AIR CRASH

(*Daily Sketch*, 7 February 1958)

THEY WERE THE DREAM TEAM. The 'Busby Babes' –
a nickname derived from their manager's name and
their youth. With an average age of just 24, they were the
most exciting young football players of their generation.

Tragically, these potential world beaters, who were aiming to win the 1st Division Championship for a record-breaking third consecutive time as well as finding glory in Europe, were cut off in their prime when the dream died on 6 February 1958.

There had been speculation that Manchester United might be capable of 'doing the treble' that season – champions of Division 1, the FA Cup and European Cup.

They had beaten Red Star Belgrade 2–1 at their home ground of Old Trafford in January and had flown out to Belgrade for the away leg, which they drew 3–3. It was enough to put United through to the semi-finals.

DIFFICULT LANDING

The following day their British European Airways plane stopped to refuel in Munich on its way home. Snow and ice had made landing tricky but it was even more difficult when they tried to take off again.

Captain Thain aborted take off after noticing an uneven tone in the engines. The passengers, including team, officials and sports journalists, disembarked for refreshments in the terminal building.

The second attempt was also aborted for the same reason, described by Captain Thain to his passengers as a 'slight engine fault', which would need to be checked.

Once more the passengers returned to the departure lounge. Manchester United's star player, left-half Duncan Edwards, sent a telegram to his landlady saying, 'All flights cancelled. Flying home tomorrow. Duncan.' But unexpectedly, they were called back onto the plane, which was ready to leave.

SKID DISASTER

By now, the snow was heavier, causing a layer of slush to build up. The plane gathered speed but was unable to reach the velocity required to get off the ground. It skidded off the end of the runway, ploughed through a fence and struck a nearby house, which tore off the port wing and part of the tail. The starboard side of the fuselage hit a wooden hut.

Inside the aircraft, twenty people were killed outright. Captain Thain got out and shouted to everyone to evacuate before the plane exploded.

Inside, United and Northern Ireland goalkeeper, Harry Gregg, had bumped his head and blood was pouring down his face, but he realised he was alive. He crawled towards a hole in the wreckage and kicked it wider so that he could get out. Gregg saw the Captain shouting and others running away but just then he heard a baby crying.

Heroically he crawled back and found the baby girl under some debris and brought her out where he handed her over to a radio operator. Gregg then went back in and rescued the mother – Vera Lukic, the pregnant wife of a Yugoslavian diplomat.

Outside, he saw his teammates Bobby Charlton and Dennis Viollet hanging half in and half out of the plane, and he dragged them clear by the waistbands of their trousers.

SEVERED ARM

On seeing central defender Jackie Blanchflower with his right arm almost severed, Gregg used his tie to wrap tightly around it.

In the event the plane did not explode and the injured were all rescued and taken to Rechts der Isar Hospital in Munich.

Manager Matt Busby was thought to be the most seriously injured with a punctured lung, fractured ribs and leg injuries. He had blood transfusions and was given the last rites. A hospital spokesman said, 'We do not have much hope of saving him.'

Winger Albert Scanlon was unconscious for three weeks and Duncan Edwards had broken ribs and a fractured right leg. Bobby Charlton suffered minor head injuries.

Seven of Manchester United's talented players had died immediately after the crash – team captain Roger Byrne, Mark Jones, Eddie Colman, Tommy Taylor, Billy Whelan, David Pegg and Geoff Bent.

Also amongst the fatalities were several sports journalists, team officials and plane crew.

The bodies of the deceased were flown home on 7 February and thousands turned out to line the streets for the funerals.

THE LAST RITES

Busby received the last rites for a second time, while Duncan Edwards and the co-pilot Kenneth Rayment were getting worse by the day.

That Saturday, a two-minute silence was observed at football matches around the world. Despite the tragedy, United fielded a team to take on Sheffield Wednesday in a Fifth Round FA Cup tie, which they won 3–0.

Duncan Edwards, United's undoubted star player died from his injuries on 21 February at the age of 21, followed a week later by Kenneth Rayment, which brought the final death toll to 23 of the 44 passengers and crew aboard the flight.

Busby made a miraculous recovery and was sent to Switzerland to recuperate with his wife, Jean.

Meanwhile, under the guidance of assistant manager Jimmy Murphy, United made it to the FA Cup Final on 3 May. Busby, who had returned home, slowly made his way to the bench with the aid of a walking stick to watch them play. They lost 2–0 to Bolton Wanderers.

A few days later, United beat AC Milan 2–1 in the home leg of their European Cup Semi-final. But the following week they were thrashed 4–0 in the away game at the San Siro Stadium, which knocked them out of the Cup.

TITLE CHALLENGE COLLAPSES

United only won one League game after the crash, causing their title challenge to collapse and they fell to ninth place in the League.

The injuries suffered by Jackie Blanchflower and winger Johnny Berry, meant that neither of them would be able to play again.

Matt Busby believed that football should be exciting and his innovative idea to amass a team full of youngsters – many straight from school – that could be honed to play in the attacking, creative style that he wanted, thrilled the public and was the foundation for all that followed.

Manchester United became one of the biggest and best-loved football clubs in the world.

A decade after the Munich Disaster, Busby, the great survivor, led his beloved team to become the first English club to win the European Cup. •

BIRTH CONTROL PILL APPROVED BY COMMISSION

(*Reno Evening Gazette*, 9 May 1960)

A SMALL NEWS ARTICLE at the bottom of the front page of this Nevada newspaper might easily be missed by a reader but it ushered in one of the biggest scientific, social and cultural events of the century.

It reported how the U.S. Food and Drug Administration (FDA) had approved a pill as safe for contraceptive or birth-control use.

The pill was called Envoid, made by G. D. Searle and Co., Chicago. It was the first commercially available oral contraceptive.

The drug had been on the market for several years but only for treatment of female disorders. One of the most influential pioneers behind the invention of the pill was Margaret Sanger, a Catholic nurse and birth-control campaigner who opened America's first birth-control clinic in 1916.

WOMEN'S RIGHTS

Sanger felt that, in order for women to be able to have an equal place in society, they needed to be able to determine when to have children. She was pro-birth control but anti-abortion. After meeting

American biologist Gregory Pincus in 1951, she persuaded him to research the use of hormones in contraception and managed to raise $150,000 backing through the Planned Parenthood Federation of America, which she had helped to set up. When the money ran out, Pincus was financed by Sanger's associate, women's rights activist and philanthropist Katharine McCormick.

Meanwhile, in Mexico City, Austrian-born chemist Carl Djerassi created a progesterone pill while working at a pharmaceutical research company. Although aware that it could be used for contraception, it was intended for menstrual disorders and infertility. But within a decade it would become known as the contraceptive pill.

It was Pincus and Catholic gynaecologist John Rock who went on to fully test, produce and distribute the pill for contraceptive purposes.

Rock had founded a clinic to teach the rhythm method, the only form of birth control accepted by the Catholic Church. Pincus had successfully tested progesterone on rats and, in 1952, Rock was recruited to lead the clinical trials of the new contraceptive pill.

Meanwhile, Polish-born American Frank Colton, chief chemist at the pharmaceutical company Searle, was also developing a synthetic progesterone.

More successful trials followed and, in 1957, the FDA approved the Pill on prescription for women with severe menstrual disorders. There was an upsurge in women claiming such gynaecological problems until, finally, three years later, it was approved for contraceptive use.

TRIALS IN THE U.K.

There was huge demand for it. Trials were conducted in the U.K. in 1960 and in 1961 it was approved for use in Britain, with the Germans having adopted the pill shortly before the Brits and a string of other western countries following closely behind.

In France, contraception was illegal until December 1967, but thereafter the pill swiftly became the most widely used method of birth control. One of the world's most technologically advanced nations, Japan, was one of the last to adopt the pill as a contraceptive, the Japan Medical Association expressing concerns over the effect its long-term use might have on the women who took it. It was not approved for use in Japan until 1999. There was plenty of controversy and opposition, which included health scares and accusations that it promoted promiscuity and a relaxation of moral standards.

But it helped usher in the sexual revolution and gave women control and independence.

The Pill was to become the leading method of birth control used by more than 100 million women around the world. •

THE INNOCENCE OF LADY CHATTERLEY

(*Evening Standard*, 2 November 1960)

THE TRIAL OF Lady Chatterley sounded like a member of the aristocracy was in the dock for a misdemeanour. It referred, of course, to D. H. Lawrence's novel, but in some ways the court hearing was a class divide. And the daily proceedings provided entertaining reading in the newspapers.

In 1959, a new passage had been added to the Obscene Publications Act, which said that a book considered obscene by some but which could be shown to have 'redeeming social merit' might still be published.

D. H. Lawrence's novel, *Lady Chatterley's Lover*, about a passionate affair between the lady of the house and the family gamekeeper, Mellors, had been banned in Britain for decades because of graphic language and descriptions of sex. Only a heavily censored version was available. The full original version had, however, been published in Italy in 1928 and later in France.

ANNIVERSARY EDITION

Now the book was causing a stir again after the publishers, Penguin, decided to take advantage of the new clause in the Obscene Publications Act and printed 200,000 copies of the unexpurgated novel as part of a complete set of the author's work to commemorate the 30th anniversary of his death in 1960.

Penguin sent 12 copies to the Director of Public Prosecutions, who decided that the text did contravene the Obscene Publications Act and brought about a prosecution – the first novel to be tested under the 1959 clause.

The six-day trial at the Old Bailey began on 27 October. The defence lined up 35 eminent witnesses including bishops and leading literary figures. These included Dame Rebecca West, a novelist, travel writer and journalist who had covered the Nuremberg Trials for *The New Yorker* and been appointed DBE in 1949 for her services to literature.

Also in the defence corner was E. M. Forster, the prolific and much-respected author who wrote *A Room with a View, Howards End* and *A Passage to India*. He was joined by Cecil Day-Lewis, the Poet Laureate of the United Kingdom, who also wrote mystery adventure yarns under the pen name Nicholas Blake; and Richard Hoggart, a prominent academic and university professor whose book, *The Uses of Literacy*, was required reading for anyone studying English or the media.

EVERY OBSCENITY NOTED

The prosecution had gone through the book noting every obscenity and given copies of the novel to the jury to read.

In what was to become a famous remark, prosecution counsel Mervyn Griffith-Jones asked the jury, 'Would you approve of your young sons, young daughters – because girls can read as well as boys – reading this book? Is it a book that you would have lying around in your own house? Is it a book that you would even wish your wife or your servants to read?'

There were amused smiles in court as well as disbelief that Griffith-Jones should be so out of touch with the times and assume that the jury of twelve – chosen from ordinary members of the public – would have servants. They were also amazed by his rather sexist notion of females.

Many thought that once these words had come out of his mouth in his opening address, the case was already lost.

The defence team, led by Gerald Gardiner, capitalised on the blunder to show that the prosecution was out of touch and that Penguin represented the common man in the modern world.

PENGUIN'S LONG-TERM BATTLE

In his closing address, Gardiner remarked, 'I do not want to upset the prosecution by suggesting that there are a certain number of people nowadays who as a matter of fact don't have servants. But of course that whole attitude is one which Penguin Books was formed to fight against, which they have always fought against.

'Isn't everybody, whether earning £10 a week or £20 a week, equally interested in the society in which we live, in the problems of human relationships including sexual relationships? In view of the reference made to wives, aren't women equally interested in human relations, including sexual relations?'

After six days, the jury took three hours to acquit Penguin Books of all charges. Most of the newspapers thought the prosecution was silly but avidly reported on it and there were few complaints about the jury's decision. Times were changing and the permissive sixties were on their way.

The court case proved to be wonderful advertising for the novel as all 200,000 copies of it were sold on the first day of publication and two million over the next few months.

It was a watershed moment and other obscenity cases would follow with liberation usually defeating censorship.

PEOPLE APPALLED

But, despite *Lady Chatterley's* victory, there were many people throughout the country – outside of literary or trendy social circles – with strict morals who were appalled by the outcome.

The Home Office received many letters of protest, copies of the book were burned on the streets of Edinburgh and women librarians in South Wales asked permission not to handle it.

In a House of Lords debate, the 6th Earl of Craven made the memorable comment: 'I made a trip on the M1 the other day, on my way to Manchester, and stopped at Forte's restaurant... It was the day that Lady Chatterley's Lover was on sale to the public and there, at every serving counter, sat a snigger of youths. Every one had a copy of the book held up to his face with one hand, while he forked nourishment into his open mouth with the other. They held the seeds of suggestive lust, which was expressed quite blatantly by glance and remark, to the girls serving them. That I saw with my own eyes... Purity is sacrificed on the altar of promiscuity as woolly-headed intellectuals pour their vociferous sewage into the ears of the public.' •

MAN ENTERS SPACE

(*Huntsville Times*, 12 April 1961)

THE RACE TO PUT the first man into space was on. Following Russia's successful launch of the Sputnik satellites in 1957, America was determined to gain the upper hand. They were busy preparing their Mercury capsule but did not realise that the Soviets were secretly forging ahead with their own Vostock space programme.

When they discovered that they had been beaten once again, the country was stunned and embarrassed, while Russia enjoyed her moment of triumph and enjoyed a magnificent propaganda coup.

A big picture of Russian cosmonaut Yuri Gagarin dominated the front page of this Alabama newspaper, as it did many other throughout the world, after he became the first man into space.

The achievement was engineered by the remarkable Sergei Korolev. He had qualified as a pilot and began designing gliders and then rocket engines. In 1933, he successfully launched the first liquid-fuelled rocket in the USSR.

CAPTURED NAZI STORES

After World War II, the Russians captured Nazi stores of V2 rocket components and used them to develop their own missile system. On 21 August 1957, Korolev launched the Soviet R-7 rocket, the world's first intercontinental ballistic missile. This was followed by the world's first satellite,

Sputnik 1, in October, before Korlov then put the first dog, Laika, into space the following month.

Towards the end of 1959, Yuri Gagarin was one of 20 pilots chosen for the Soviet space programme. Slightly built, he was one of the few pilots able to fit into the cramped Vostock 1 capsule and was eventually selected.

On the morning of 12 April 1961, he sat inside the capsule as it was launched from a pad at Baikonur, in Kazakhstan. At 9:07am (local time), the capsule went into orbit around the earth and Yuri Gagarin became the world's first man in space.

One hundred and eight minutes later, after making a single orbit, the 27-year-old cosmonaut parachuted back to Earth.

GAGARIN 'IMMORTAL'

Gagarin became an instant hero. Premier Nikita Khrushchev was elated and telephoned him to say, 'You have brought glory to our homeland. You have shown courage and heroism. You have made yourself immortal.'

Khrushchev compared him to Christopher Columbus, and named him a hero of the Soviet Union.

People gathered in the square and streets of Moscow to celebrate. Streets were named for him in many Soviet cities, monuments were erected, and Government officials pinned medals on his tunic. He was later to travel the world, meeting leaders and royalty as an international celebrity.

Despite America's disappointment, President John F. Kennedy sent congratulations to Moscow with the words, 'The people of the U.S. share with the people of the Soviet Union their satisfaction for the safe flight of the astronaut in man's first venture into space... It is my sincere desire that in the continuing quest for knowledge of outer space our nations can work together to obtain the greatest benefit to mankind.' And he told a press conference that the flight was 'a most impressive scientific accomplishment.'

Responding to American newspaper reporters' criticism of the U.S. space programme, Kennedy admitted, 'We are behind.'

FIRST AMERICAN IN SPACE

Less than a month later, astronaut Alan Shepard became the first American in space. But by now

Kennedy had his mind on what was seen as the ultimate goal – to put a man on the moon. It was a challenge that he could not afford to lose.

On 25 May 1961, just a few weeks after Gagarin's flight, Kennedy made his speech committing the United States to sending a man to the moon and returning him safely before the end of the decade. ●

EAST GERMAN TROOPS SEAL BORDER WITH WEST BERLIN TO BLOCK REFUGEE ESCAPE

(*New York Times*, 14 August 1961)

THE RAPID ACTIVITY shortly after midnight on 13 August 1961 caught Berliners napping. The quiet, almost deserted streets of East Berlin was shattered by the sound of screaming sirens as police and troops in cars, trucks and on motorbikes sped through the city.

Working at speed, troops and construction workers set up barbed-wire fences up to six feet (1.83m) high along the border with West Berlin and by daylight the city had been divided.

Nobody was allowed to cross the border and road and train transport between the two sectors of the city was halted.

Thousands of angry demonstrators quickly gathered on the West Berlin side of the divide. At one crossing point, protesters tried to trample down the barbed wire but were driven back by guards with bayonets.

The following day – a Monday – thousands of East Berliners who arrived for their daily commute to work in the West were told it would no longer be possible.

The momentous incident was the dramatic response by East Germany's Head of State, Walter Ulbricht, to the continuing flow of refugees from East to West Berlin.

PERMANENT STRUCTURE

Within days, troops began replacing the barbed wire with concrete blocks and the wall became a permanent structure. It was officially called the 'Antifaschistischer Schutzwall' or 'Anti-Fascist Protection Rampart'.

It eventually stretched some 100 miles around West Berlin. Consisting of a mixture of concrete nearly 12 feet high, wire fencing and various watch towers, it was to become the most potent symbol of the Cold War – a tangible vision of Churchill's 'Iron Curtain' description of Communist Eastern Europe.

The historical background to this divisive edifice can be traced back to the end of World War II when the victorious Allied powers divided Germany into four zones, each occupied by Britain, the United States, France or the Soviet Union. The same was done with Germany's capital city, Berlin, which was located in the Soviet quarter.

But as relations between the Soviet Union quickly began to disintegrate it developed into an East–West, communism–capitalism divide.

In 1949, West Germany became The Federal Republic and East German the Democratic Republic. The two countries developed very differently. The capitalist west experienced a rapid growth in its economy while those in the east experienced hardship, poor living conditions and restriction of movements. This model was encapsulated on a smaller scale within Berlin with the western sector becoming an 'island' of democracy within Communist East Germany.

ARMED GUARDS

There was a regular flow of people leaving East Berlin for the more prosperous west, an exodus which reached around 1,700 daily. After the Wall went up, people attempted to climb across it, despite armed guards keeping an attentive watch. Many paid with their lives.

Towards the end of the 1980s, the 'Iron Curtain' over Eastern Europe began to lift. In 1989 Hungary opened its border with Austria and thousands of East Germans found a route into West Germany.

With the Communist regime crumbling, a huge crowd attended a pro-democracy demonstration in East Berlin's main square on 4 November of that year and the government of East Germany resigned three days later. Two days after that, thousands gathered at the Berlin Wall protesting to be let through. Some started to hack at the wall and to everyone's amazement, the guards stood back. The euphoric crowd then started to knock it down in earnest. Once it had been breached, they streamed across the border that had cut them off for 28 years and were welcomed with open arms by West Berliners who had clambered onto the concrete wall in front of the Brandenburg Gate to look across.

The barrier had come down at last and East and West greeted each other like long lost friends. On 3 October 1990, the two Germanys merged to form a new united country. ●

WE BLOCKADE CUBA ARMS

(*Daily News*, 23 October 1962)

FOR 14 TENSE DAYS in 1962, the United States and the Soviet Union appeared to be on the brink of a nuclear war.

The front page of this New York newspaper refers to a U.S. naval blockade of Cuba in response to an aggressive move by the Soviets which was the start of what became known as the 'Cuban Missile Crisis.'

In August and September of 1962, U.S. intelligence services gathered evidence of Russian-built MiG-21 fighters and surface-to-air missiles on the Caribbean island of Cuba.

Then, on 14 October 1962, an American U-2 reconnaissance plane photographed long-range Soviet nuclear missiles on Cuba, capable of being launched at the American mainland. There was also an increase in the number of Soviet ships arriving in Cuba.

President John F. Kennedy was prompted into action. He was in a difficult situation at home with elections due to take place for Congress in two months' time. Public-opinion polls showed that his ratings had fallen to their lowest point since he became president.

INVASION OF CUBA PLANNED

An executive committee of the National Security Council was set up and the fourteen members discussed what to do. Several tense meetings followed in which they debated what their response would be. They ranged from taking no action at all to an invasion of Cuba and the overthrow of Fidel Castro.

Eventually, it was decided to put a naval blockade in place around Cuba to prevent the Soviets from bringing in more military supplies. The U.S. also demanded the removal of missiles already there.

Kennedy announced the discovery of the missiles and his response in a televised address to the nation on 22 October. And he warned that any nuclear attack from Cuba would result in 'a full retaliatory response upon the Soviet Union'.

ACT OF AGGRESSION

The U.S. Air Force was put on stand-by for attacks on Cuba and the Soviet Union. Nikita Khrushchev telegrammed Kennedy warning that the United States' 'pirate action' would lead to war. In a second telegram he said that the blockade was 'an act of aggression' and that his country's ships would be instructed to ignore it. The scene was set and now the world waited to see what happened as Soviet ships continued to make their way to Cuba. If they did not turn back or refused to be

searched, a war was likely to begin.

On 24 October, Kennedy was informed that the ships had stopped just before they reached the blockade. An angry Khrushchev sent another telegram to Kennedy accusing him of creating a crisis to gain support for himself and his party. Two days later and the breakthrough came when Khrushchev proposed that the Soviet Union would be willing to remove the missiles in Cuba in exchange for a promise by the United States that they would not invade Cuba. The following day he also demanded that America remove its nuclear bases in Turkey.

SPY PLANE SHOT DOWN

While diplomatic exchanges and demands continued, the U.S. still had to keep track of what was happening at the missile bases being built on Cuba. Their latest information, based partly on photographs taken by the U-2 spy planes, showed that the bases were now operational. Further U-2 flights were scheduled to monitor the situation.

On 28 October, America sustained the only fatality resulting from enemy action during the confrontation when U-2 pilot

Major Rudolf Anderson was shot down over Cuba. The Americans knew that the Cubans did not have the capability to shoot down the high-flying U-2s. Only a Soviet anti-aircraft missile would be able to hit a U-2. They had already decided that, if a U-2 was shot down, they would consider it as an act of aggression on the part of the Russians. They would then have no choice but to strike back at the Soviets.

Fortunately, the Americans decided to change their minds and put the incident down to a regrettable error of judgement. It was later disclosed that the Russians had ordered that their missiles should not be used against the U-2s because they knew that the Americans would be likely to retaliate. The missile that downed the spy plane had been launched on the orders of an over-zealous local commander in Cuba. The incident had brought the world one step closer to all-out nuclear war.

Kennedy publicly agreed not to invade Cuba and privately promised the removal of the nuclear bases in Turkey.

The Cuban Missile Crisis was finally over on 28 October. The 'unthinkable' had been averted and the world began to breathe again.

The event appeared to frighten both sides, who found it difficult to 'lose face' in public by backing down. A result of this was that America and the Soviet Union set up a direct private communications link that became known as the Hot Line.

A Test Ban Treaty was signed between the two countries in August 1963, prohibiting the testing of nuclear weapons in the atmosphere. •

PROFUMO QUITS

(Daily Mail, 6 June 1963)

BRITISH SECRETARY OF STATE for War, John Profumo, resigned from government over a notorious 'sex scandal' after admitting he lied to Parliament about his relationship with good-time girl, Christine Keeler.

The Conservative MP confessed that he had misled the House of Commons in an earlier statement about his relationship with Keeler. Prime Minister Harold Macmillan said that he had no option but to accept his resignation, adding, 'This is a great tragedy for you, your family and your friends.'

Profumo, who was married to the actress Valerie Hobson, had first met Keeler at a pool party in July 1961 at Cliveden, the beautiful Buckinghamshire home owned by Lord Astor. The host was party-loving London osteopath Stephen Ward, whose list of high-profile clients included Lord Astor, Winston Churchill, Ava Gardener and Frank Sinatra. Lord Astor

allowed him the use of a cottage on the Cliveden estate, and at the party he introduced 46-year-old Profumo to 19-year-old Christine Keeler

TOPLESS SHOWGIRL

Ward had a penchant for pretty young women from lower-income backgrounds, whom he introduced to high society. Keeler worked as a topless showgirl at a cabaret club in London's Soho, where she met fellow dancer, Mandy Rice-Davies. It was here that they met Stephen Ward who introduced them to his world of racy parties and celebrity friends.

Both girls got a lot of attention at the Cliveden party, where other guests included Yevgeni Ivanov, the senior naval attaché at the Soviet Embassy. Profumo's first sight of Keeler was as she stepped naked from the pool. Before leaving he asked for her telephone number, which she gave him, and they embarked on an affair. But what he didn't know was that she was also in a relationship with Ivanov.

Rumours about the affair began to circulate because it compromised national security. It was the height of the Cold War and the country was still reeling from the revelations that intelligence officers Guy Burgess and Donald Maclean were Soviet spies. As War Secretary, Profumo would be privy to the most sensitive and secret information regarding the security of the country. What if Keeler was passing on secrets told to her by Profumo to Ivanov?

After MI5 learned of the liaison, Profumo ended the affair but by the time he had, Westminster was buzzing with gossip and word had reached the newspapers.

HOUSE OF COMMONS SHOCK

Profumo sought to distance himself from the Cliveden set but on the evening of 20 March 1963,

the whispers turned into direct confrontations when the Labour MP Barbara Castle stood up in the House of Commons and asked whether the Secretary of State for War had been involved with Christine Keeler.

In the House the following day, Profumo declared that there had been 'no impropriety whatsoever' in his relationship with Keeler. He continued to deny anything improper but events were already spiralling out of control. The previous December a petty criminal and jealous lover of Keeler's went after her and fired shots outside Ward's flat in London, where she had been visiting with Mandy Rice-Davies.

Stephen Ward faced a trial for living off immoral earnings, and newspapers ran lurid stories about a world of decadence and orgies.

FAMOUS RIPOSTE

While giving evidence at Ward's trial, Rice-Davies made what was to become a famous riposte to the prosecuting counsel's statement that Lord Astor denied an affair with her or had even met her. She replied, 'Well, he would, wouldn't he?'

On 5 June 1963, Profumo decided to confess. In his letter

of resignation from Parliament he expressed 'deep remorse' at the embarrassment he had caused his colleagues and his constituents.

Stephen Ward was prosecuted for living off immoral earnings. On the last day of his trial, he killed himself with an overdose of sleeping tablets.

The scandal rocked the Conservative government and was instrumental in the party's defeat by Labour in the 1964 election.

A few days after his resignation, Profumo had arrived at the door of a charitable settlement for the deprived in the East End of London called Toynbee Hall, and asked whether there was anything he could do to help.

He began by cleaning and washing dishes, eventually becoming its chairman and then president. In the last 40 years of his life he was a tireless worker for charity at Toynbee and in 1975 his selfless work was officially recognised when he was appointed CBE on the advice of the Labour Prime Minister Harold Wilson. ●

KENNEDY SLAIN ON DALLAS STREET

(*Dallas Morning News*, 23 November 1963)

S HORTLY AFTER NOON on 22 November 1963, President John F. Kennedy was assassinated as he rode in a motorcade through Dealey Plaza in downtown Dallas, Texas.

The incident was captured on news footage and shown around the world with many barely able to believe their eyes.

The charismatic Kennedy had been preparing his campaign for the next presidential election and was touring Texas to meet and greet the people.

On the morning of 22 November, the presidential party flew from Carswell Air Force Base to Dallas and were greeted on their arrival by a crowd of well-wishers.

The First Lady, Jacqueline Kennedy, dressed in pink, was handed a bouquet of red roses, which she took with her to the waiting limousine – an open-topped Lincoln Continental.

Texas Governor John Connally and his wife, Nellie, were already seated in the car as the Kennedys entered and sat behind them. Vice President Lyndon Johnson and his wife occupied another car in the motorcade.

The procession left the airport and travelled along a ten-mile route to the Trade Mart where the President was scheduled to speak at a luncheon.

SUDDEN GUNFIRE

People lined the route, cheering and waving as the motorcade passed by, and the Kennedys happily waved back. But then all hell broke loose as gunfire suddenly reverberated in the plaza and the President slumped to one side, falling into Jacqueline's arms. He had been shot in the neck and in the head.

Governor Connally was hit in the back, probably by one of the bullets that had passed through the President. Witnesses said that three shots were fired from the window of a building called the Texas School Book Depository.

The security forces leapt into action and all the passengers were told to keep their heads down as the cars sped to Parkland Memorial Hospital just a few minutes away.

Police and Secret Service agents rushed into the School Book Depository building and recovered a rifle with a telescopic sight but the assassin had fled. However, a witness gave police a description of a man he had seen leaving a building a few minutes earlier.

POLICEMAN SHOT DEAD

Patrolman J. D. Tippitt, 38, driving alone in a squad car, stopped to question a man who he thought fitted the description but as he got out of his car, the man shot him dead with a revolver.

The gunman fled and entered a cinema a few blocks away but the cashier phoned police saying that there was a man there who looked suspicious and constantly changed seats.

Police entered the cinema, the lights went up and the killer rose from his seat and aimed his revolver at one police man and pulled the trigger – but the weapon failed to fire.

The police arrested him. His name was Lee Harvey Oswald, a 24-year-old recently hired employee at the Texas School Book Depository.

Meanwhile, the President and Governor Connally were operated on at the Parkland Memorial Hospital. Connally was saved but nothing could be done for the President. A Catholic priest was summoned to administer the last rites, and at 1:00pm John F. Kennedy was pronounced dead.

Vice President Lyndon Johnson was sworn in as the new U.S. leader and on Sunday morning, 24 November, households across the country were glued to their TV sets to catch a glimpse of Oswald being transferred from police headquarters to the county jail. Suddenly a man aimed a pistol and fired at point-blank range. The assailant was identified as Jack Ruby, a local nightclub owner. Oswald died two hours later at Parkland Hospital.

The Warren Report, commissioned to investigate the President's death, concluded he had been killed by shots fired by Lee Harvey Oswald from the Texas School Book Depository building. But conspiracy theories have abounded ever since. Was Oswald a hired hitman and, if so, who hired him? And did Jack Ruby kill Oswald in order to silence him?

Many books and documentaries have been made, aiming to shine more light on the truth behind the assassination. The tragic incident continues to intrigue and fascinate successive generations. •

3,000 FANS GREET BRITISH BEATLES

(*New York Times*, 8 February, 1964)

'**B**EATLEMANIA', which had swept Britain and Europe, surged across the Atlantic after the 'Fab Four' made their first U.S. visit on 7 February 1964.

Their Pan Am plane touched down just after 1.00pm local time at New York's Kennedy Airport to a scene of hysteria as 3,000 fans screamed in excitement, crowding the ground, balconies and roof of the terminal.

When the plane door opened and George Harrison appeared, the exhilaration was a wall of sound. Harrison was followed out by John Lennon, Paul McCartney and Ringo Starr – all looking like they couldn't quite believe what they were seeing and hearing.

Home-made placards were held aloft beseeching them, 'I love you, please stay'. The crowd chanted 'We Want the Beatles' as the mop-haired, be-suited lads from Liverpool made their way down the steps.

POLICE DRAFTED IN

Around 200 photographers and reporters were there to record this momentous event, bigger than any visit by a royal or head of state. And more than 100 policemen were drafted in to keep things under control.

The Beatles' schedule included three appearances on America's biggest variety TV show of the time, *The Ed Sullivan Show*, plus a handful of concert dates. But first they were ushered into the airport for their first U.S. press conference. Such was the noise and commotion that they could barely hear the questions shouted at them.

IRREVERENT HUMOUR

McCartney commented, 'We've never seen a reception like this. It's fantastic.' And Lennon showed some of their typical cheeky, irreverent humour when asked what the appeal of their music was. 'If we knew, we'd form another group and be managers,' he replied.

America had been anticipating their arrival for a few months after reports came through of this musical phenomenon from across the Atlantic.

Time and *Newsweek* were among the first U.S. publications to take notice of the 'Beatlemania' craze and ran articles in mid-November 1963, after the Beatles had the honour of performing before the Queen Mother at the Royal Variety Show in London.

Lennon had got a big laugh from the audience at the prestigious royal event when he had remarked, 'For our last number I'd like to ask for your help. Will the people in the cheaper seats clap your hands, and the rest of you, if you'll just rattle your jewellery.'

In October 1963, Ed Sullivan and his wife were in London, stuck at Heathrow Airport, because of the chaos surrounding a Beatles arrival from Sweden. When he discovered the cause of the delay he took note.

In November and December, 'Beatlemania' began to make short news reports on U.S. TV, and when their single, 'I Want to Hold Your Hand', was first played on radio there by disc jockey Carroll James at Washington's WWDC on 17 December, it shot to the top of the U.S. charts.

On the morning of their impending arrival at Kennedy airport, radio stations were stoking the mounting excitement amongst America's youth by playing Beatles songs.

TV RECORD BREAKERS

Their first performance on the *The Ed Sullivan Show* on 9 February would go down in history as one of the most-watched shows of all time, reaching a record-breaking audience of 73 million.

They performed the songs 'All My Loving', 'Till There Was You', 'She Loves You', 'I Saw Her Standing There' and 'I Want To Hold Your Hand'.

They appeared twice more on the show in subsequent weeks and by the time they left for home, America had been charmed.

The Beatles were the first British band to break into the American market and became an integral part of pop music and popular culture around the world. ●

U.S. FORCES OUT OF VIETNAM;

HANOI FREES THE LAST P.O.W.

(*New York Times*, 29 March 1973)

THE LAST OF THE U.S. troops finally left Vietnam on 29 March 1973, after a long, tiring and bloody conflict, which failed in its objective and made America determined never to repeat the same mistakes again.

American involvement in Vietnam began in the 1950s after communist forces in the north of the country, led by nationalist Ho Chi Minh, successfully defeated the colonial power of France in 1954.

During this Cold War period, America's foreign policy in Asia revolved around the 'domino theory' that if one country fell to communism then surrounding countries would also fall. And so they had sent aid to France and the south Vietnamese, but after the defeat the country was split into communist north and pro-American south.

The split was to cause much suffering as plans eventually to unify the country never materialised. The communists killed thousands of landowners in the north and their farming policies lead to extensive famine. And in the south, the corrupt Saigon government of Ngo Dinh Diem ruthlessly crushed any opposition, killing tens of thousands.

Diem's regime sparked a guerrilla resistance movement of communists in the south known as the Vietcong, who were supported and supplied by communists in the north via a route known as the Ho Chi Minh Trail. This led to an increased involvement by the U.S.

Diem was killed in a coup in 1963 by dissident military officers and eventually General Nguyễn Văn Thiệu took control.

OPERATION ROLLING THUNDER

Following an attack by the North Vietnamese Army (NVA) in August 1964, when they torpedoed a U.S. destroyer in the Gulf of Tonkin, the U.S. launched aerial strikes on the enemy's naval bases. And in February 1965, with the South Vietnamese Army struggling against the Vietcong, the U.S. launched Operation Rolling Thunder, a sustained bombing campaign against targets in North Vietnam.

This was followed in July by the deployment of 100,000 U.S. soldiers. Australia, New Zealand, Korea, the Philippines and Thailand also contributed troops.

But the Vietcong guerrillas proved to be very effective in their tactics. They made good use of jungle cover, which led to the U.S. army spraying a toxic solution called Agent Orange over the jungle, as well as napalm to burn through the thick foliage. And Vietcong guerrillas were often difficult to distinguish from civilians. Even women and children were used to set booby traps. Troops became demoralised trying to fight an enemy they could seldom identify.

By the end of 1967, there were 485,000 U.S. soldiers in Vietnam and they were sustaining a high rate of casualties. Back home, a general feeling of pointlessness and horrific pictures of napalm victims in news footage led to a groundswell of protest about U.S. involvement.

In addition, a concentrated movement by the NVA and Vietcong, known as the Tet Offensive, caught the Americans off guard when they attacked 36 provincial capitals and five major cities, including Saigon, where they penetrated the U.S. embassy compound. They were eventually beaten back but the offensive showed that the enemy was still strong and capable, and any thoughts of U.S. nearing victory quickly receded.

NIXON ELECTED PRESIDENT

Political support for President Johnson waned despite his calling for peace talks. Richard Nixon was elected President in November 1968 and sought to extricate U.S. troops without losing face. The following June, U.S. troops began training and equipping the South Vietnamese Army to be able to look after themselves, and over the next three years more than 500,000 U.S. solders returned home.

Ho Chi Minh died in 1969, but his successor Le Duan continued to fight. A peace deal was finally negotiated in January in which U.S. forces would leave and South Vietnam would have the right to determine its own future. But peace was short-lived after the last U.S. troops left with both the south and north accusing each other of breaking the terms of the truce.

In early March 1975, the NVA mounted an invasion of the south. As they approached Saigon, Thiệu fled to Taiwan and, on 30 April, the tanks rolled in. Thousands of south Vietnamese left the country, fearing reprisals.

Saigon was renamed Ho Chi Minh City on 2 July 1976. Vietnam was reunited as a communist country, the Socialist Republic of Vietnam. •

4 CHILDREN DIE, 160 MISSING IN S. WALES HORROR

(*South Wales Echo*, 21 October 1966)

IT WAS ONE OF THE most poignant of British disasters that caused the small Welsh mining village of Aberfan to be evermore associated with the tragic incident that occurred on 21 October 1966.

At 9.15am of that morning a waste tip of coal began to slide down the mountainside to the village of Aberfan, near Merthyr Tydfil, in South Wales. It was sunny on the higher ground but fog had enveloped the valley and so visibility below was poor.

The tipping gang up the mountain had seen the slide start, but could not raise the alarm because their telephone cable had been repeatedly stolen. But it was later accepted that it would have been too late to escape the impending disaster even if a call had been made.

FARM COTTAGE DESTROYED

Down in the village, nobody saw anything, but everybody heard the rumbling noise getting louder and louder. The waste first destroyed a farm cottage in its path, killing all the occupants, and gained momentum as it headed towards Pantglas Junior School, just below. The children had just returned to their classes after singing 'All Things Bright and Beautiful' at their assembly.

There was little time to move and children and teachers were mostly 'frozen' where they were as the waste hit the school with devastating consequences. After demolishing the school and around 20 houses, the slide came to a rest. A total of 144 people were killed in the Aberfan Disaster, 116 of them school children.

When news of the incident spread, people were so horrified that many rushed there to try to help rescue those trapped. But nobody was rescued alive after 11 on that day and it was nearly a week before all the bodies were recovered.

LOCAL WORRIES ABOUT TIP

At a subsequent enquiry into the incident it was revealed that there had long been local worries over the stability of the tip. The Chairman of the National Coal Board (NCB) claimed that the disaster had been unforeseeable and that the tip moved due to springs that no one had known about surfacing beneath the giant mound of waste.

In fact, concerns had been raised up to three years before about the amount of spoil being dumped on the hillside above the school and the springs were marked on various maps dating back to before the NCB began dumping there. Local villagers remembered playing there when they were young, long before the NCB began dumping operations.

The NCB blamed abnormally high levels of rainfall for causing the coal waste to move, but the enquiry established that there had previously been several minor slips and that a range of NCB personnel, from those working in the tipping gangs to senior management, had known that the tip was not stable.

The Inquiry of Tribunal found that the NCB was wholly to blame for the disaster and should pay compensation for loss and personal injuries. They were ordered to pay grieving families just £500 per child. The report stated, 'The Aberfan Disaster is a terrifying tale of bungling ineptitude by many men charged with tasks for which they were totally unfitted, of failure to heed clear warnings, and of total lack of direction from above. Not villains but decent men, led astray by foolishness or by ignorance or by both in combination, are responsible for what happened at Aberfan.'

NEW REGULATIONS IMPOSED

The enquiry found that there was no legislation in place for dealing with the safety of tips. In future all tips should be treated as civil-engineering structures and that managers and surveyors should as soon as possible be made aware of the rudiments of soil mechanics and ground-water conditions. Provision should be made for regular inspection of all tips by qualified persons

In the wake of the tragedy major changes were made in the way mine waste was managed across Wales and the rest of the U.K. And Aberfan was to become enshrined as an enduring memory of the tragic loss of innocent young lives. ●

MAN WITH A NEW HEART

(*Cape Argus*, 6 December 1967)

C HRISTIAAN BARNARD performed the first human-to-human heart transplant, on 3 December 1967, in Cape Town, South Africa.

For the first few days the patient was reported to be doing well but, sadly, died 18 days later. However, the operation had been successfully carried out and hundreds more heart transplants were to take place all over the world following this medical achievement.

The idea of replacing a heart with another one had fascinated medics, as well as science-fiction writers, for years.

In Moscow during the 1930s and 1950s, Vladimir Demikhov had transplanted a heart into another animal and had managed, rather bizarrely, to graft a second head onto a dog.

HEART TRANSPLANT DOG

In America, fellow transplant pioneers, Norman Shumway and Dick Lower, succeeded in bringing a dog's heart back to life after it had been stopped and stored in saline for one hour. It led to them performing their first successful canine heart transplant. The dog lived for eight days before tissue rejection set in.

Christiaan Barnard, a director of surgical research at Cape Town

University's medical school in South Africa, had become fascinated by this work. His attention had turned towards heart surgery while studying at Minnesota Medical School. Later, he visited Demikhov in Moscow and, on his return to Cape Town, he too grafted a second head onto a dog.

Shumway had been one of his contemporaries at Minnesota, and Barnard closely followed his progress. Barnard was soon able to replace diseased heart valves with artificial ones.

By September 1967, advances in a new anti-rejection drug in kidney transplants encouraged Shumway to announce his intention, once he had the right donor, to perform a human heart transplant.

'WE ARE READY . . .'

Meanwhile, Barnard was eager to beat Shumway in the race. After performing his first kidney transplant, he stated, 'The machinery of the transplant team had functioned perfectly. We are ready to undertake a heart transplant.'

On 14 September 1967, a grocer named Louis Washanksy had been admitted to Groote Schuur Hospital in Cape Town with diabetes and incurable heart disease. Velva Schrire, Groote Schuur's chief cardiologist, recommended him as a potential heart transplant recipient. Barnard then awaited a suitable donor.

On 2 December, 25-year-old Denise Ann Darvall was involved in a fatal car crash. She was admitted to Groote Schuur Hospital and declared brain dead. After her blood type was found to be compatible with Washkansky's, her father gave his permission for the doctors to use her heart for the transplant.

Mr Washkansky had just an 80 per cent chance of surviving the operation but without it he faced certain death.

WASHKANSKY'S HEART REMOVED

The donor heart was removed and kept working via mechanical means while Washkansky's heart was also removed and the process of suturing and cauterising veins and arteries began.

With the new heart beating strongly inside Washkansky, a wide-eyed Barnard looked at his team and said in Afrikaans 'Dit gaan werk! [It's going to work!]'

Thirty hours after the operation, Washkansky was able to speak, but remained in critical condition.

He lived 18 days after the operation before dying of double pneumonia attributed to his suppressed immune system. Despite the setback, the transplanted heart had functioned normally until his death.

Barnard's success turned him into a celebrity but the operation caused controversy on ethical grounds. Nevertheless, over 100 heart transplants were performed around the world in 1968.

In the 1970s, the development of better anti-rejection drugs made transplantation more viable. Dr Barnard continued to perform heart transplant operations, and by the late 1970s many of his patients were living up to five years with their new hearts. ●

MARTIN KING SHOT TO DEATH

(*Daily News*, 5 April 1968)

THE AMERICAN civil rights leader, Dr Martin Luther King, Jr., was shot dead by a single bullet to the neck as he stood on a hotel balcony in Memphis.

An inspiring orator, he had encouraged black people to rebel against injustice by peaceful means but his violent death led to rioting on the streets and accusations of government or FBI involvement in the shooting.

Born in Atlanta, Georgia, on 15 January 1929, King came from a family of ministers. While studying at a theological seminary he learned about Mahatma Gandhi's non-violent civil disobedience campaign that he used successfully against British rule in India. King became convinced that the same methods could be employed by blacks in their civil rights struggle in America.

After his ordination, King took a doctoral degree at Boston University and married Coretta Scott, with whom he was to have four children. In 1955, he became pastor of the Dexter Avenue Baptist Church in Montgomery, Alabama, and it was here that he became actively involved in civil rights.

ROSA PARKS ARRESTED

On 1 December 1955, a 42-year-old black woman named Rosa Parks was arrested after she refused to give up her seat on a bus to a white man, as was expected. This caused anger amongst the black community and King was at the forefront of a campaign to end such inequality. It grew into a mass boycott of buses by black people, which lost the transport companies revenue and received world-wide publicity. During this time, King was amongst many who were arrested and his house was fire-bombed. The boycott lasted for several months until it ended in victory.

His non-violent strategy was the blueprint for similar protests across America's southern states, which included sit-ins that eventually ended segregation in restaurants, public parks, swimming pools, theatres, museums and on beaches.

In 1957, King founded the Southern Christian Leadership Conference to rally his fellow Negro ministers throughout the South and he led several peaceful protest marches.

DREAMS OF FREEDOM

He was a stirring and inspiring speaker with a soulful, lyrical voice, using biblical references and talking of dreams of freedom to great effect in rallying speeches across the country, increasingly becoming the figurehead of the civil rights movement.

He made one of his most famous speeches to a huge crowd that had marched to Washington for 'jobs and freedom' on 28 August 1963. He was the last speaker and captivated his audience with poetic words such as, 'I have a dream that one day on the red hills of Georgia, the sons of former slaves and the sons of former slave owners will be able to sit down together at the table of brotherhood.'

Meanwhile, President John F. Kennedy's Civil Rights bill was still being debated in Congress when he was assassinated in November 1963. The new President, Lyndon Baines Johnson, kept up the pressure and was able to get the legislation passed in 1964, making racial discrimination in public places illegal and requiring employers to provide equal employment opportunities.

In 1964, Martin Luther King was awarded the Nobel Peace Prize. He continued to campaign against the war in Vietnam, which provided him with enemies in high places in America. He also encouraged black people and white people living in poverty to unite and to strive for a fairer society.

SANITATION WORKERS STRIKE

In early 1968, he supported sanitation workers in Memphis –

90 per cent of whom were black – who sere striking against poor working conditions.

Meanwhile, Senator Robert F. Kennedy was running for President, promoting similar policies to King – pro-civil rights and anti-war and -poverty.

On 3 April 1968, King made another famous speech at the Mason Temple, in Memphis, in which he said, 'I would like to live a long life – longevity has its place. But I'm not concerned about that now. I just want to do God's will. And he's allowed me to go up to the mountain. And I've looked over, and I've seen the promised land. I may not get there with you. But I want you to know tonight, that we, as a people, will get to the promised land.'

After the meeting, King and his party went to the Lorraine Motel. The following day he was shot dead on the balcony.

His death was followed by rioting in 125 cities. A convicted armed robber named James Earl Ray, who had escaped from prison, was arrested at London's Heathrow Airport and extradited to America. He pleaded guilty to having shot Martin Luther King and was given a prison sentence of ninety-nine years.

Ray was to later say that he had been framed as part of an FBI plot to kill King, and there are certainly those who believe that he was not acting alone. However, his appeals for a new trial were rejected and he died in prison in 1998. ●

HOW BOBBY WAS SHOT!

(*Chicago Daily News*, 5 June 1968)

FIVE YEARS AFTER his brother, President John F. Kennedy, was assassinated in Dallas, 42-year-old Robert F. Kennedy was shot dead during his campaign to become U.S. President.

Robert Kennedy had put himself forward to be the Democratic Party's nominee for President on 16 March 1968.

After winning the primary in California, he gave a victory speech to his campaign supporters in the Ambassador Hotel's Embassy Room in Los Angeles at around 12.10am on 5 June 1968. In euphoric mood, he was then taken on a shortcut through the hotel kitchen en route to a press conference in the Colonial Room. As he walked along a corridor he took time to shake hands with hotel workers when a gunman rushed towards him repeatedly firing a revolver.

Kennedy was struck three times at point-blank range from behind. One bullet struck behind his right ear from about an inch (2.54 cm) away, the others near his right armpit and in the back of the neck.

SCENE OF CHAOS

Pandemonium broke out. The *Chicago Daily News*'s west coast bureau chief, who was there at the time, described how there was 'screaming and angry confusion' all around him. There was added chaos as reporters and photographers, hearing the shots and screams, rushed in to see what was going on.

As Kennedy slumped to the floor, his security man, Bill Barry, punched the gunman in the face and others forced him against a table and disarmed him before he was led away by police.

After a while, Robert Kennedy's wife, Ethel, who was also at the hotel, was brought in to be with her husband. She knelt beside him and, still conscious, he appeared to recognise her before he was taken away on a stretcher and rushed for emergency treatment at the Central Receiving Hospital. He lost consciousness and medics tried to revive him before he was taken several blocks away to the Hospital of the Good Samaritan for surgery, about 30 minutes later.

GUNMAN IDENTIFIED

As the shocking news of the incident spread, the gunman was identified as 24-year-old Jordanian immigrant Sirhan Bishara Sirhan.

Although Sirhan was born in Jerusalem, he was a Jordanian citizen and emigrated to America with his family when he was 12 years old. They lived for a short time in New York before moving to California.

Sirhan's motive for the murder was patriotic, but his loyalty lay with the Arab nations in the Middle East, not with his adopted country of America. He claimed that he had decided Robert Kennedy must die because the presidential candidate had promised that, as soon as he was elected, he would send fifty fighter aircraft to Israel to help the Israelis defend their borders.

This promise, coupled with the fact that Kennedy had supported Israel during the Six-Day War in which so many Arabs had died, had made Sirhan decide to kill Kennedy on the anniversary of the start of that conflict.

That evening, at 5.30pm, Kennedy's press aide, Frank Mankiewicz, announced that Kennedy's doctors were 'concerned over his continuing failure to show improvement' and that his condition remained 'extremely critical as to life'.

He was pronounced dead at 1.44 am on 6 June, nearly 26 hours after the shooting.

SENTENCED TO DEATH

Sirhan was convicted of murder and sentenced to death but this was commuted to life imprisonment after the California Supreme Court invalidated all pending death sentences imposed in California prior to 1972.

Like his elder brother before him, Robert Kennedy's death has been the focus for 'conspiracy theories' ranging from there having been more than one gunman to CIA involvement.

His body lay in repose at St Patrick's Cathedral in New York for two days before a funeral mass was held on 8 June. He is buried near his brother, John, at Arlington National Cemetery. ●

MAN ON THE MOON

AND THE MESSAGE FROM EARTH: WE'RE BREATHING AGAIN!

(*Daily Mirror*, 21 July 1969)

HAVING STATED HIS intention in a 1961 speech to land a man on the moon by the end of the decade, U.S. President John F. Kennedy's goal was achieved when Neil Armstrong became the first man on the lunar surface on 20 July 1969.

Millions around the world watched enthralled as the space craft, *Columbia*, was launched from Cape Kennedy, Florida, four days earlier. On board were Commander Neil Armstrong, lunar module pilot, Edwin 'Buzz' Aldrin, and command module pilot, Michael Collins.

After establishing an orbit around the Moon, Armstrong and Aldrin crawled into the lunar module *Eagle*, which detached from the command module and was rocket boosted towards the Moon as *Columbia* continued its orbital flight.

TENSION IN HOUSTON

Back on Earth in Mission Control at Houston, Texas, tension was building. And as the *Eagle* neared the Moon's surface, some of the shirt-sleeved flight controllers sat or stood silently at their consoles, barely able to breathe.

There was a moment of panic at 300 feet above the Moon's

surface when Armstrong saw that they were heading towards a large crater and he took over semi-manual control, guiding the *Eagle* to safety.

Armstrong was later to recall, 'The auto-targeting was taking us right into a football-field-sized crater, with a large number of big boulders and rocks.'

Finding a more level place to land, Armstrong lowered the module down onto the rocky surface in the Sea of Tranquility. There was a dramatic pause before he radioed back, 'Houston, Tranquility Base here. The *Eagle* has landed.'

'WE ARE BREATHING AGAIN.'

A relieved Mission Control replied, 'Roger, Tranquility. We copy you on the ground. You got a bunch of guys about to turn blue. We are breathing again. Thanks a lot.'

About six-and-a-half hours later, Armstrong opened the landing craft's hatch, made his way down a ladder and set foot on the Moon, making the comment, 'That's one small step for a man; one giant leap for mankind.'

He described the surface as being like powdered charcoal and he left deep footprints as he walked around. After 19 minutes he was joined by Aldrin. They set up a television camera and jumped across the landscape to test movement, also collecting dust and rock samples. In a patriotic moment, which must have been galling for their Soviet space rivals, they planted the Stars and Stripes flag into the soil and unveiled a plaque bearing President Nixon's signature and an inscription reading, 'Here men from the planet Earth first set foot upon the Moon July 1969 AD. We came in peace for all mankind.'

HISTORIC PHONE CALL

The astronauts then heard from Nixon, who said, 'This certainly has to be the most historic telephone call ever made.' He congratulated them on their achievement, adding with a flourish, 'For one priceless moment in the whole history of man all the people on this Earth are truly one; one in their pride in what you have done and one in our prayers that you will return safely to Earth.'

Armstrong and Aldrin spent 21 hours on the Moon. After rejoining the *Columbia* mothership, all three astronauts returned to Earth on 24 July, splashing down in the Pacific Ocean.

Their leap into the unknown had scientists wondering whether they might have picked up an alien infection and so they were held in quarantine for almost three weeks before being released, waving and cheering to the crowds.

That evening they were guests of honour at a State Dinner in Los Angeles. And they went on to visit 25 countries in a celebratory tour.

The lessons learned paved the way for further space exploration and visits to the moon in years to come, although the dangers inherent in sending men into space would lead to several tragedies and near misses along the way. •

UP, UP AND AWAY!

(*Daily Mirror*, 3 March 1969)

THE SUPERSONIC AIRLINER, Concorde, made a
faultless maiden flight on 2 March 1969.

The *Daily Mirror* splashed with a huge front-page picture of the striking-looking, delta-winged and droop-nosed plane taking off from Toulouse.

Strong winds meant the test flight was in doubt for much of the day. But as it sped down the runway, there was a spontaneous burst of applause from watching reporters and cameramen when the wheels lifted off the ground. Just 27 minutes later, it landed.

The French pilot, André Turcat, commented after landing, 'Finally the big bird flies, and I can say now that it flies pretty well.'

The test flight was a gentle one, reaching 10,000 feet (3,000m), with a top speed of 300mph (480kph), although it was capable of 1,300mph (2,080kph).

It was hoped to start flying commercially in 1973 with an eye to transatlantic flights, cutting the flying time between London and New York from 7 hours 40 minutes to 3 hours 25 minutes.

CONCORDE PARTNERSHIP

Concorde was the result of separate British and French projects to create the world's first passenger-carrying commercial supersonic aircraft. To keep the cost of the enterprise down they joined in 1962 to develop the plane together. The partnership led to the British Aircraft Corporation (later British Aerospace) and Aerospatiale of France building 20 Concordes.

They were powered by four Olympus 593 engines, built jointly by Rolls-Royce and the French Snecma company.

Following its successful maiden flight, Concorde embarked on a sales and demonstration tour on 4 September 1971, completing its first supersonic flight on 1 October 1969. But it had a bumpy ride when it came to securing deals.

Heavy fuel consumption – 5,638 imperial gallons every hour – threatened to make it uneconomical for airlines to buy such a plane at a time when fuel prices had shot up.

SUPERSONIC SERVICE

British Airways bought five Concordes on 28 June 1972, but it wouldn't be until four years later, on 21 January 1976, that it commenced commercial supersonic travel from London to Bahrain, and Air France from Paris to Rio.

On 22 November 1977, Concorde made its first London–New York commercial flight.

It began operating daily flights to America out of London Heathrow and Paris's Charles de Gaulle airports, cruising at around 1350 mph at an altitude of up to 60,000 feet (11 miles). The flight took around three-and-a-half hours

– less than half the normal flying time for other jets.

It set a record time in February 1996 between New York and London taking just 2 hours 52 minutes and 59 seconds.

But the hopes and dreams for Concorde never really took off when it came to demand from paying customers. Then, on 25 July 2000, its previously unblemished safety record was scarred by a horrific crash shortly after taking off from Charles de Gaulle Airport, which killed 113 people.

The fleet of just 20 was grounded while a full investigation took place and £17m was spent on safety improvements. Flights resumed in November 2001 but public confidence had been lost. In April 2003, British Airways and Air France announced the plane would be retired due to falling passenger revenue and rising maintenance costs.

FINAL FLIGHT

Concorde's final commercial flight was on 24 October 2003 from New York to London.

The aircraft was such a symbol of national pride that thousands of spectators turned up at Heathrow to witness Concorde's decommissioning.

At a 2003 auction of Concorde memorabilia and artefacts at the Olympia exhibition centre in Kensington, London , pieces being sold ranged from seats and cutlery to cockpit instruments and even a nose cone.

A number of enthusiasts are working to raise the vast amounts of money required to restore the most complete surviving Concordes in order that the aircraft might one day take to the air again, if only for display flights at air shows.

Despite a number of alternative supersonic airliner design studies having been proposed since the demise of Concorde, including one that could carry 300 passengers at more than five times the speed of sound and reach Sydney from Brussels in less than five hours, the age of supersonic travel is currently suspended. ●

THREE SPACEMEN ARE HOME SAFE

SPLASHDOWN FOUR MILES FROM SHIP

(*Houston Chronicle*, 18 April 1970)

IT WAS TO BE THE third lunar-landing attempt in the U.S. space programme, as Apollo 13 was launched on 11 April 1970.

On board were astronauts Commander James A. Lovell, command module pilot John L. 'Jack' Swigert and Fred W. Haise as lunar module pilot. And, despite a few glitches, things were going so well that, after two days, Joe Kerwin, the capsule communicator back at Mission Control, remarked, 'The spacecraft is in real good shape as far as we are concerned. We're bored to tears down here.'

But he wasn't going to be bored for long, as the mission became the most fraught to date after an explosion on board left the astronauts fighting for survival.

COMFORTABLY WEIGHTLESS

Nine hours later, as the crew finished a 49-minute TV broadcast showing how comfortably they lived and worked in weightlessness, a relaxed Lovell said, 'This is the crew of Apollo 13 wishing everybody there a nice evening, and we're just about ready to close out our inspection of *Aquarius* [the lunar module] and get back for a pleasant evening in *Odyssey* [the command module]. Good night.'

Minutes later, oxygen tank No. 2 blew up in the service module, which damaged No.1 tank, and reserves of oxygen began to leak into space. It left the command module without power or air and short of water. They were about 200,000 miles from Earth.

In words that have since become famous, Swigert calmly reported, 'Houston, we have a problem.'

MISSION ABORTED

The mission was aborted and it was decided that the only chance they had of saving the crew was to shut down the command module entirely to conserve batteries for re-entry into the earth's atmosphere later. In the meantime they would move into the lunar module, which had a separate oxygen supply, and use its engines (that had been intended for the moon landing) to set them on a course that would take them home. But it was fraught with problems. A module equipped for two men for two days would have to sustain three men for four.

It was estimated that the crew would run out of water after about five hours of normal usage, so they rationed themselves to six ounces each per day, which was about one fifth of normal intake, and drank extra fruit juices.

Sleep was almost impossible because of the cold. When the electrical systems were turned off, the spacecraft lost an important source of heat. The temperature dropped to 38 degrees Fahrenheit and condensation formed on all the walls.

SIGHS OF RELIEF

Four hours before landing, the crew jettisoned the damaged service module and, two and a half hours prior to re-entry, it was time to see if the plan of firing the command module back to life would work. When the systems came back on there were sighs of relief on board, in Mission Control and from people following the drama around the world.

An hour later, the lunar module was also jettisoned and Mission Control felt it was losing an 'old friend' as it radioed, 'Farewell, *Aquarius*, and we thank you.'

Re-entry to the earth's atmosphere on an Apollo mission

routinely involved four minutes of radio blackout as a layer of ionized air built up around the command module, blocking communications. Not knowing whether *Odyssey* had sustained any damage, the radio blackout brought heightened tension to Mission Control, especially when the silence continued for 33 seconds longer than expected.

But the radio crackled back into life as the command module parachuted out of the sky to splash down safely in the South Pacific on 17 April at 1.07pm local time (7.07pm BST).

Within minutes, helicopters were on the scene and the astronauts were airlifted onto the recovery ship, *Iwo Jima*, where they spent the night before flying to Samoa to be reunited with their families. •

THE DEATH STEPS

(*Daily Record*, 4 January 1971)

THE TRADITIONAL New Year derby football match between historic rivals Celtic and Rangers on 2 January 1971 had failed to live up to expectations on the pitch.

On a drizzly, overcast day, the mist hanging over the Rangers ground, Ibrox Stadium in Glasgow, summed up the mood of the spectators who were feeling downcast at having had little to cheer about during a rather dull game.

But just a minute from the end, it suddenly flared into life when Jimmy Johnstone scored for Celtic. A huge roar went up and that seemed to be that... until Rangers equalised during injury time with a goal by Colin Stein. This time it was the Rangers fans who roared their approval and, as the final whistle blew, they turned to make their way out of the stadium with spirits considerably lifted.

Those heading towards the Stairway 13 exit felt the usual squeeze of a crowd leaving the stadium. They had become used to it at big games. But as they made their way down the steep steps, people felt themselves being pushed forward and many were lifted off their feet. The momentum of the crowd made it impossible to stop or push back and the crush squeezed the life out of those trapped.

CLAMBERING TO SAFETY

Some managed to clamber over the fences at the sides of the stairs. Others helped push people over to safety.

Meanwhile, the players had left the pitch, unaware of what was happening. The Celtic team were on their coach within 15 minutes of the end when their manager, Jock Stein, heard that there had been an accident. He told the driver to take the players back to their home ground while he and his backroom staff returned to help out.

Ambulances were called and bodies were lined along the side of the pitch. Others were taken to the changing rooms.

Sixty-six people died, a third of whom were aged 16 or under, and 145 were injured. It was the worst tragedy in the history of Scottish football and united both rival teams and their supporters in their grief.

PUBLIC ENQUIRY

Initial reports suggested the tragedy had been caused by supporters rushing back up the stairs after the late Rangers' goal and colliding with those leaving the stadium. But a public inquiry discounted this theory, concluding that the deaths were the result of the crush of fans pouring down Stairway 13.

A police officer told the inquiry that bodies were 'like a pack of cards that had been thrown forward, the lower ones were horizontal, others were semi-upright and the last were upright'. Many had died standing up.

THE DEATH STEPS

The Glasgow-based *Daily Record* carried a huge picture of the stairway, alongside which they ran the grim, stark headline, 'The Death Steps'.

Rangers' manager Willie Waddell vowed to make Ibrox a stadium that was both safe and comfortable. He championed a major redevelopment of the ground, visiting Dortmund where the brand new, state-of-the-art Westfalenstadion (now called Signal Iduna Park) was opened in time for the 1974 World Cup matches.

Once plans for redesigning, refurbishing and rebuilding Ibrox were approved, the work took three years and led to most of the stadium being replaced by all-seater grandstands. The capacity of the ground was reduced to 44,000 (80,000 had attended the match on the day of the disaster) and the new Ibrox was opened with a special 'Old Firm' derby match on 19 September 1981.

Sadly, there were several more disasters to come at football stadia across Britain before all of the major grounds were given a proper safety overhaul. •

13 KILLED AS PARATROOPS BREAK RIOT

(*Guardian*, 31 January 1972)

THE SHOOTING OF 13 civilians by British troops in the Bogside area of Northern Ireland on 30 January 1972 became known as 'Bloody Sunday' and was greatly to increase hostilities for decades to come.

In the late 1960s, the Catholic minority in Northern Ireland began organising protest marches against what they saw as unfair treatment by the Protestant-dominated authorities over issues such as housing allocation and voting rights.

Increasingly violent clashes between the two sides and the Royal Ulster Constabulary led to the British Army moving in to try to restore order. But the fighting escalated, and the troops came under repeated attack from bottle- and brick-throwing Catholics. Clashes between the Army and the Provisional IRA led to deaths and injuries on both sides.

In the face of this, internment without trial was introduced and all marches and parades banned. However, the Northern Ireland Civil Rights Association organised a protest march in Derry to protest against internment and the authorities decided to allow the march to proceed in the nationalist areas of the city, but to stop it from reaching Guildhall Square, as intended, in order to prevent a clash.

The 1st Battalion, the Parachute Regiment was drafted in to Derry to arrest any unruly rioters on the day of the march. Barricades were set up, and the march, consisting of around 10,000 people, was redirected to Free Derry Corner. But a splinter group broke off from the main procession and tried to push back the barricade to get to the Guildhall. They threw heavy stones at the Army, who responded with a water cannon, tear gas and rubber bullets.

VIOLENCE ESCALATES

As the violence escalated, a civil rights organiser began to walk through the crowd, telling them through a megaphone that a meeting was starting at Free Derry Corner.

Shortly after, armoured cars appeared in William Street and roared into Rossville Street, causing several thousand people to run away.

Paratroopers from the 1st Battalion piled out of their vehicles and rushed towards the crowd. Then they opened fire with their rifles. Thirteen civil rights marchers were shot dead and others were wounded. A further person later died from his injuries sustained on the day.

The Army's official explanation for the killings, backed by the Home Secretary the following day in the House of Commons, was that their troops had fired in response to a number of snipers who had opened up on them from nearby buildings.

But there were many witnesses, including journalists, who maintained that the soldiers fired indiscriminately into an unarmed crowd.

PARATROOPERS 'RECKLESS'

In April, an inquiry by Lord Widgery reported that the paratroopers' firing had 'bordered on the reckless'. But it concluded that the soldiers had been fired upon first and some of the victims had handled weapons. The Catholic community rejected these findings, calling it a 'whitewash' and began the long campaign for another inquiry.

It finally came in 1998, under Lord Sackville, and after another long wait of twelve years, the Sackville Report, on 15 June 2010, found that none of those killed or injured were 'posing a threat or causing death or serious injury', despite soldiers' claims; they did not fire in response to attacks or threats; members of the official IRA did fire some shots but paratroopers shot first.

Prime Minister David Cameron made a formal apology on behalf of the United Kingdom, calling the shootings 'unjustified', saying that he found the report 'shocking' and that he was 'deeply sorry.'

In the aftermath of 'Bloody Sunday' there was a resurgence of violent opposition to the British presence in Northern Ireland. Many Catholics, angry and resentful, joined the IRA and other militant groups. And Protestant unionists recruited members into rival organisations such as the Ulster Defence Association and Ulster Volunteer Force.

'The Troubles', as these years of hatred and fighting were labelled, were to result in many more deaths. •

NIXON RESIGNS

(*Washington Post*, 9 August 1974)

IN THE EARLY HOURS of 17 June 1972, five men were arrested for burgling the headquarters of the Democratic Party in the Watergate complex in Washington, after a security guard had contacted the police when he noticed tape covering the latches on several doors in the complex, allowing them to close but remain unlocked.

The incident was to lead to the revelation of corruption and lies at the highest political level and to prosecutions and the eventual resignation of the President of the United States.

The five intruders had with them photographic equipment and bugging devices. Intrigued by the story, two young reporters on the *Washington Post*, Carl Bernstein and Bob Woodward, investigated further.

The following day saw the first of a series of their sensational reports, which revealed that one of the burglars was on the payroll of President Nixon's re-election committee.

SECRET IDENTITY

The two journalists' findings were corroborated by a top ranking official source – a contact of Woodward's that they nicknamed 'Deep Throat'. They agreed to keep his identity a secret, and it wasn't until 2005, 33 years later, that he was revealed to be FBI Director, Mark Felt.

Meanwhile, the FBI stepped up its investigation, and many of their findings found their way into the pages of the *Washington Post*. But despite it becoming clear that the burglars were working for Nixon's re-election team by spying on their rival Democrats in an attempt to sabotage their campaign for the Presidency, Nixon was re-elected by a landslide on 7 November 1972.

He continued to deny any prior knowledge of the burglary or of organising a 'cover-up' operation but, by the summer of 1973, the Watergate Affair – as it had become known – had blown up into a national scandal and was the subject of two official investigations.

NIXON INVOLVED

A White House aide revealed that Nixon was instrumental in being part of the cover-up operation. Then, in July 1973, another aide disclosed that the President recorded all of his phone calls in the Oval Office.

Nixon was ordered to hand over the tapes, but a lengthy legal battle ensued after the White House cited 'executive privilege' that the President is entitled to candid and confidential advice from aides.

But the pressure on him mounted when, in March 1974, the special prosecutor indicted former Attorney General John Mitchell, former aides Haldeman and Ehrlichman, and four other staffers for conspiracy, obstruction of justice and perjury in connection with the Watergate burglary.

The Supreme Court eventually ordered the White House to hand over the tapes to the special prosecutor on 24 July 1974. Three days later, the House Judiciary Committee sensationally recommended the President of the United States be impeached and removed from office.

One of the tapes – dubbed by the press as 'the smoking gun' – showed that, despite his denials, he had played a leading role in the cover-up from the start. Nixon lost what remaining support he had and his closest aides told him he had to resign or face the almost certain prospect of impeachment.

PRESIDENT RESIGNS

On 8 August 1974, Nixon announced his resignation as President in a televised address from the Oval Office in which he still failed to admit his guilt.

'By taking this action,' he said, 'I hope that I will have hastened the start of the process of healing which is so desperately needed in America.'

Following his short speech, he shook hands with his successor, Vice President Gerald Ford, on the White House lawn, clambered into a waiting helicopter with his wife, Pat, and daughters, Julie and Tricia, and flew off.

Gerald Ford was sworn into office on 9 August 1974, declaring, 'Our long national nightmare is over.' One month later, he granted Nixon a full pardon for any offences he might have committed as Present, saving him from possible prosecution. ●

KING ELVIS DEAD

(*Sun*, 16 August 1977)

'THE KING OF ROCK 'N' ROLL' was found dead on his
bathroom floor at his Graceland home in Memphis,
Tennessee, following a heart attack.

For years his health had been
deteriorating due to a reliance on
prescription drugs and a fondness
for junk food. But his sudden death
at 42 came as a shock to his millions
of fans around the world.

Elvis had changed the face
of popular music with his high-
energy performances of such songs
as 'Hound Dog' and 'Blue Suede
Shoes'. The wide range of genres
he performed encapsulated, rock
'n' roll, blues, gospel, country and
western, pop and ballad.

Born into a poor family,
on 8 January 1935, in Tupelo,
Mississippi, he was heavily
influenced by local gospel choirs.
After entering various talent
contests, his special quality was

noticed and, under the guidance of
his manager, Colonel Tom Parker,
he was to become a worldwide icon.

He took the music industry by
storm during the fifties with hits like
'Heartbreak Hotel', and 'All Shook
Up'. His unique body movements,
good looks and gleaming smile
had teenage girls going wild. But
many of the older generation
were appalled by his grinding hip
movements which earned him the
nickname of 'Elvis the Pelvis'.

A series of network-TV
appearances raised his profile,
although on some he was only
shown from the waist up. But
despite the controversy, every TV
show he appeared on was a ratings
winner. Elvis had brought rock 'n'

roll to the masses and the masses loved him.

FILM DEBUT

In November 1956, he made his film debut in *Love Me Tender*, and many similar light-hearted musicals followed throughout the sixties. All were panned by critics but that didn't stop his fans from watching them and they made a healthy box office profit.

While Elvis's movies played all over the world, the King himself never did. Apart from a few appearances in Canada in the 1950s, Elvis never took to the stage outside the United States.

Some say that he was keen to tour abroad. He spent two years in Germany when he was in the army doing national service and enjoyed visiting Paris while he was on leave. He would like to have seen more of Europe, but it was not to be.

There were rumours that Colonel Parker quashed any proposed foreign tour plans because, despite having served in the U.S. Army, Parker was an illegal immigrant (he was born Andreas van Kuijk in Holland) and if he left America, he might not be allowed back. Others believed that there were serious security issues at venues big enough to take the

millions of fans who would want to see their idol.

The films, however, were to be the closest any foreign audience ever got to the King, who kept his feet firmly on U.S. soil.

On 1 May 1967, he married Priscilla Beaulieu with whom he had his only child, Lisa Marie, born a year later. He divorced Priscilla in 1973.

LAS VEGAS ACT

During the 1970s he became a resident act in Las Vegas and then made a series of concert tours. But he was looking far from the sexy, lean and energetic Elvis that had rocked the world. Now he was something of a showbiz caricature with a puffy face, an expanding waistline and wearing white, rhinestone-studded jump suits. In more than one concert he appeared remote, and mumbled and slurred his way through his hits.

On the evening of 16 August 1977, he was scheduled to fly out of Memphis to begin another tour. That afternoon his new girlfriend, Ginger Alden, found him lying out on his bathroom floor.

Attempts to revive him failed, and death was officially pronounced at 3:30pm at Baptist Memorial

Hospital. The official report stated that he died of heart failure.

OPEN CASKET

Thousands gathered to file past Elvis Presley's body, which lay, state-funeral-like in an open casket at Graceland the day after his death. And a huge turn-out of around 80,000 people lined the processional route for his funeral from his home to Forest Hill Cemetery where he was buried next to his mother on Thursday, 18 August.

Following an attempt to steal his body later that month, Elvis and his mother were reburied in Graceland's Meditation Garden.

Graceland was opened to the public in 1982 and it regularly continues to attract over half a million visitors each year.

Within a few days of his death, his last single, 'Way Down', topped the U.S. and U.K. pop charts.

U.S. President Jimmy Carter said of Elvis, 'His music and his personality, fusing the styles of white country and black rhythm and blues, permanently changed the face of American popular culture.' •

TEST TUBE MOTHER HAS GIRL

(*Guardian*, 26 July 1978)

A **PICTURE OF A new-born baby, eyes screwed up against the light and yawning, dominated the world's front pages. Not a remarkable picture in itself but the birth of Louise Brown introduced a new era of human reproduction.**

She was the world's first 'test tube baby' conceived by in vitro fertilization (IVF).

Her parents, Lesley and John Brown, had been trying to conceive for nine years but without success because of blocked fallopian tubes.

In 1976, Lesley was referred to Oxford-born gynaecologist Dr Patrick Steptoe, who worked at Oldham General Hospital. He recommended that she try a new experimental procedure that would bypass the fallopian tubes.

Steptoe had been experimenting with laparoscopic (or keyhole) surgery in retrieving an egg from an ovary. Meanwhile, Manchester-born biologist Dr Robert Edwards had realised the potential of IVF as a treatment for infertility since the late 1950s and knew from the work of others that it was possible to take an egg from an animal, like a mouse or a rabbit, and fertilise it with sperm in a test tube. He became focused on trying to do the same thing with a human egg.

After reading about Steptoe's work, he contacted him and the two began working together in 1968 to try to accomplish human in vitro fertilization.

After their pioneering work was rejected for funding by the Medical Research Council, they had to find a private benefactor in order to set up their clinic just outside Cambridge.

ETHICAL DEBATE

Their research became the subject of an ethical debate, with several religious leaders and even some scientists calling for it to be stopped. The pair responded by setting up an ethics committee where they worked at their Bourn Hall Clinic.

After more than 100 attempts, which all led to short-lived pregnancies, they eventually found a successful technique. And when the Browns contacted them, they were ready.

Lesley, 32, had a mature egg removed by Steptoe via laparoscopy, and Edwards cultured it in the laboratory where it was fertilized by John's sperm. A few days later a developing embryo was placed by Steptoe into Lesley's uterus.

It was a success. Louise Joy Brown was delivered by planned Caesarean section at Oldham General Hospital at 11.47pm on 25 July 1978. She weighed 5 pounds 12 ounces.

IVF treatment quickly spread around the world, giving hope to infertile couples. Louise Brown's younger sister, Natalie, was also conceived through IVF, four years later, and became the world's fortieth IVF baby.

Louise married nightclub doorman Wesley Mullinder in 2004, with Dr Edwards attending their wedding. Their son, Cameron, conceived naturally, was born on 20 December 2006.

Edwards and Steptoe continued working together at their clinic – the world's first IVF centre – teaching other doctors haw to carry out the procedure. Steptoe died in 1988. Edwards was awarded the Nobel Prize for medicine in 2010.

Millions of babies around the world have since been born by IVF. Edwards and Steptoe's achievements attracted many other researchers to the field of fertility treatment and advances continue to be made on the foundation of their success. •

MRS THATCHER TAKES OVER

(*Daily Telegraph*, 5 May 1979)

MARGARET THATCHER became the first female Prime Minister of Britain and the first woman to be voted into such high office in the western world on 3 May 1979. Her forceful leadership won her as many critics as supporters but she was to remain in place for 11 years, winning three successive general elections.

In January 1975, when the Labour Party was in power, Thatcher challenged Edward Heath for the leadership of the Conservative Party and, on, 4 February she defeated him by 130 votes to 119, to become the first woman leader of a major political party in Britain.

The Labour government at that time faced difficult economic circumstances, with inflation and unemployment soaring. Harold Wilson was succeeded as PM by Jim Callaghan but, despite Callaghan denying there was any crisis, things failed to improve. Public spending cuts caused unease amongst the workforce, which led to strikes during a period known as the 'Winter of Discontent'.

Callaghan lost a vote of confidence and announced that there would be a general election on 3 May 1979.

Margaret Thatcher firmly blamed the government for the

Winter of Discontent during her campaigning and said that the Conservatives would cut income tax, reduce public expenditure, make it easier for people to buy their own homes and curb the power of the unions.

CONSERVATIVE VICTORY

The Conservatives soared ahead in the public opinion polls and won the election with 43.9 per cent of the vote.

On the steps of Number 10 Downing Street, she quoted St Francis of Assisi: 'Where there is discord, may we bring harmony. Where there is error, may we bring truth. Where there is doubt, may we bring faith. And where there is despair, may we bring hope.'

Britain's new Prime Minister was born in Grantham, Lincolnshire, in 1925. The daughter of local grocer and Mayor of Grantham, Alfred Roberts, Margaret Hilda Roberts and her older sister, Muriel, were brought up in a flat above one of their father's two shops.

Having won a grammar school scholarship to Kesteven and Grantham Girls' School, Margaret went on to study chemistry at Oxford in 1943, graduating with a Second Class Honours degree in 1947.

Like her father, she became heavily involved in politics and was President of the Oxford University Conservative Association. She worked as a research chemist for a time before marrying businessman Denis Thatcher and balancing a budding political career with studying law. She qualified as a barrister in 1953.

Also in 1953, Thatcher gave birth to twins, Carol and Mark, politics taking a back seat for a short while before she returned to the fray as the Conservative candidate for Finchley. Having previously stood in Dartford and Orpington, she was at last successful in the 1959 election. Her career progressed through various ministerial positions until she became leader of the Conservative party in 1975.

In the years following the Conservative election victory in 1977, Thatcher changed the face of the country by curbing union powers, privatising nationalised industries and allowing people to buy their council houses. She became an influential world figure who developed good relationships with U.S. President Ronald Reagan and President of the Soviet Union, Mikhail Gorbachev. The Soviet media nicknamed her the 'Iron Lady'.

In Europe, she fought strongly to renegotiate Britain's contribution to the European Economic budget. But as unemployment rose above 3 million in the early 1980s, she lost a great deal of support. However, that was to change with the Falkland Islands conflict in 1982, which united Britain as the country fought and succeeded in removing Argentine troops from the British overseas territory.

POLL TAX RIOTS

In 1984, she faced down the miners in their bitter strike and she attracted widespread anger and resentment for the introduction of the Community Charge – commonly known as the Poll Tax – which caused public demonstrations and several riots throughout the country in the late eighties and early nineties.

But it was her strident Euro-sceptic stance that was to lead to her downfall as she fell out with several of her party colleagues.

Thatcher was challenged for the leadership of the Conservative Party by backbench MP Sir Anthony Meyer in the 1989 leadership election. She overwhelmingly defeated him but, with public opinion polls now showing that Labour had established a considerable lead over the Conservatives, the rumblings of discontent amongst the party grew ever louder.

On 1 November 1990, Geoffrey Howe, the last remaining member of Thatcher's original 1979 Cabinet, resigned from his position as Deputy Prime Minister over her refusal to agree to a timetable for Britain to join the European single currency. It was a fatal blow for Thatcher.

The following day, Michael Heseltine mounted a challenge for the leadership of the Conservative Party. Opinion polls had indicated that he would give the Conservatives a national lead over Labour and many within Thatcher's Cabinet thought he would win but, true to her 'Iron Lady' persona, she was not going without a fight.

She won the first round of the contest but the majority was not enough to prevent a second round. After consultation with her Cabinet colleagues she announced her resignation on 22 November and was replaced by her Chancellor, John Major.

To the surprise of many, the Iron Lady shed a tear as she left Downing Street. Soon afterwards, she entered the House of Lords as Baroness Thatcher of Kesteven.

Major oversaw an upturn in Conservative support in the 17 months leading up to the 1992 general election, which they won before being toppled by Labour in 1997 when Tony Blair became Prime Minister. •

BOMB ON BOAT KILLS LORD MOUNTBATTEN

(*Irish Times*, 28 August 1979)

LORD LOUIS MOUNTBATTEN, second cousin to Queen Elizabeth II and beloved great uncle of Prince Charles, was murdered, along with three others, by a bomb planted by the Provisional Irish Republican Army while he was on a boating holiday in Sligo, Republic of Ireland.

One of the earl's grandsons, Nicholas, 14, and Paul Maxwell, 15, a local lad employed as crew member, also died in the explosion. Nicholas's grandmother, the Dowager Lady Brabourne, 82, was fatally injured and died the following day.

Nicolas's twin, Timothy, his mother Lady Brabourne (the earl's daughter, Patricia) and her husband, Lord Brabourne, were injured.

Just hours later, 18 British Army soldiers were killed in an ambush in Warrenpoint, Northern Ireland.

Mountbatten, 79, was enjoying his annual summer family holiday in his castle at Mullaghmore, County Sligo, and on the morning of 27 August 1979, they boarded a boat, *Shadow V*, in the harbour, intent on spending the day fishing.

BOMB ON BOARD

But overnight, IRA member Thomas McMahon had planted a 50lb (23kg) bomb aboard and when the boat was 100 yards out, en route for Donegal Bay, it was detonated.

The boat was blown to pieces, and all seven occupants were hurled into the water. Nearby fishermen rushed to the rescue.

McMahon, 31, had been detained in the area by police on suspicion of driving a stolen car two hours before the bomb went off.

Five hours later, 18 British soldiers were killed in two bomb attacks near their base in Warrenpoint, County Down. The first bomb, weighing half a ton, was planted under some hay on a flatbed lorry beside a dual carriageway on the Irish border 44 miles (71km) from Belfast.

It exploded, killing six soldiers of the 2nd Battalion, Parachute Regiment as they travelled past in a lorry at the end of a three-vehicle army convoy.

SECOND BOMB DETONATED

Members of the Queen's Own Highlanders flew in by helicopter from their base at Bessbrook, County Armagh, to take the injured away to hospital. But just after the helicopter took off, a second bomb weighing 800lbs (363kg), concealed in milk pails near the gate house, was detonated, thirty minutes after the first, killing twelve more soldiers – ten from the Parachute Regiment and two Highlanders.

The following day, the IRA admitted carrying out the attacks on both the Mountbatten family and the soldiers. McMahon was convicted of the three boat murders.

Lord Mountbatten was given a state funeral. A navy man, through and through, in World War II he had commanded the destroyer, HMS *Kelly*, which was sunk by German dive bombers off Crete with the loss of 130 men.

In 1942, Winston Churchill appointed him Chief of Combined Operations, and then Supreme Allied Commander for Southeast Asia the following year, conducting the campaign against Japan that led to the recapture of Burma.

VICEROY OF INDIA

In March 1947, he became last viceroy of India with a mandate to oversee the British withdrawal, leading to partition and the independence of two nations, India and Pakistan.

He was created Viscount in 1946 and Earl Mountbatten of Burma the following year. He was later made First Sea Lord and Chief of Defence Staff.

Mountbatten had enjoyed a close relationship with Prince Charles and had been responsible for bringing together the Prince's parents. He had arranged the visit of King George VI and Queen Elizabeth to Dartmouth Royal Naval College on 22 July 1939, making sure to include the young Princesses, Elizabeth and Margaret, in the invitation. They were looked after by his naval cadet nephew, Prince Philip of Greece.

His close association with the Royal Family made him a much-loved and admired figure amongst its members. •

POLAND YIELDS ON INDEPENDENT TRADE UNIONS

(*Washington Post*, 31 August 1980)

THE UNLIKELY FIGURE of a stocky, working-class shipyard electrician was the impetus behind the collapse of the communist regime in Poland. He was later to find himself as President of a new government.

The summer of 1980 saw a series of strikes in Poland in protest at soaring prices and the slow growth of wages. There was anger and resentment towards the government and, in the Lenin shipyard in Gdansk, activist Lech Walesa encouraged workers to strike to underline their demand for higher pay and for the establishment of independent trade unions.

The workers were reluctant to do so at first, fearing reprisals, until popular crane operator Anna Walentynowicz was sacked for her militant behaviour.

This was the nudge they needed to declare a strike on 14 August 1980. A committee was set up and, with a new-found sense of unity and power, they set out 21 demands, including the right to have an independent trade union and the right to strike. They also secured Walentinowicz's swift reinstatement and she joined the committee.

The strike damaged both the economy and the government's image. It became international news and it was finally agreed to recognise the right of independent trades unions – the first in any Eastern Bloc country – with a deal signed on 31 August.

The following month, Solidarity was formed, the workers' first independent trade union, led by Walesa, who was hailed as a working-class hero. It was seen as the start of a movement for political freedom and improved economic conditions in Poland but things soon took a grim turn once more.

MARTIAL LAW

On 11 February 1981, General Wojciech Jaruzelski was appointed Prime Minister, replacing Stanislaw Kania. And on 12 December he imposed martial law.

Solidarity was banned, its leaders were arrested overnight and more than 2,000 workers were dismissed. Full censorship and a six-day working week were re-imposed and the coal mines were placed under military control.

The dream seemed to have ended abruptly. By late 1982, the government was confident that control had been restored and Walesa was released from prison but prevented from returning to work as he was investigated for alleged tax irregularities. He was also barred from

speaking at rallies. But he remained an influential figure and in 1983 was awarded the Nobel Peace Prize.

Meanwhile, the economy was in a bigger mess than ever. The government increased food prices by 40 per cent in February 1988 and, in May, Walesa organised a series of strikes in protest. As support for Solidarity swelled once more, a second wave of widespread strikes took place in August. The government then decided that it was time to negotiate properly with Solidarity.

SOLIDARITY LEGALISED

The trade union was formally legalised again in 1989 and allowed to campaign as a political party in the upcoming elections on 4 June. Meanwhile, the government announced a new economic plan and promised more freedom.

Solidarity had little financial support with which to campaign and polls predicted the party would be defeated in Poland's first free elections. But in the event they won a landslide victory.

The party changed its name to the Citizens' Parliamentary Club, with Walesa as President and, on 25 August, Tadeusz Mazowiecki, a Catholic newspaper editor and Solidarity adviser, became the first non-communist Prime Minister in Eastern Europe for nearly 40 years.

Walesa credited Pope John Paul II for giving him, and others, the confidence to rise up against communism. As Polish Archbishop Karol Wojtyla, he was elected Pope in 1978, and the following year returned to his homeland where millions turned out to greet him.

Walesa met the Pope on several occasions and was amongst many Poles inspired by him. 'Before his pontificate, the world was divided into blocs. Nobody knew how to get rid of communism,' said Walesa. 'In Warsaw in 1979, he simply said, "Do not be afraid."'

After five years as President, Walesa was defeated in an election by the ex-communist minister Aleksander Kwasniewski, in 1995. ●

JOHN LENNON SHOT DEAD

(*Liverpool Echo*, 9 December 1980)

' **J**OHN LENNON, leader of the legendary Liverpool pop group, The Beatles, was shot dead in New York today by a crazed gunman,' reported the *Liverpool Echo* – the newspaper that had tracked the rise of their local lads throughout the 'Beatlemania' years of the 1960s.

The shocking event was mirrored in newspaper headlines around the world. The killing had occurred at 11.00pm local time in New York, outside Lennon's apartment in the Dakota Building in Manhattan. The news reached the U.K. in the early hours of the following day.

Lennon, 40, was shot four times in the back by Mark Chapman. He was rushed to St Luke's Roosevelt Hospital Center in a police car but was pronounced dead on arrival.

After years out of the limelight, Lennon had returned to recording again and had recently released an album called *Double Fantasy* and a single, 'Starting Over'.

Earlier in the fateful day of his murder, he and his wife, Yoko, walked out of their apartment to a waiting car, which was to take them to a recording studio. He was used to being stopped by fans asking for his autograph and so happily obliged 25-year-old Mark

Chapman in signing his copy of *Double Fantasy*.

Chapman, a security guard from Honolulu, Hawaii, had a history of depression and mental illness. He was obsessed with Lennon but had come to hate him for what he saw as his hypocrisy in preaching about peace and the simple things in life whilst enjoying a wealthy and privileged lifestyle.

DEMONS TOLD HIM TO KILL

Chapman was also obsessed with J. D. Salinger's classic novel, *The Catcher in the Rye*, and strongly identified with the protagonist, disillusioned teenager Holden Caulfield. Chapman later claimed to hear 'demons' in his head telling him to kill John Lennon.

In late October 1980, he bought a gun and flew to New York with the intention of doing so but changed his mind after watching the film *Ordinary People*, in which Timothy Hutton plays a suicidal teenager caught up in the midst of a dysfunctional family.

Coming to his senses, he went home but, on 6 December, he returned to New York, with murder once more on his mind.

He began staking out the Dakota Building but, after Lennon graciously gave him his autograph, Chapman was taken aback by his kindness and then tried to battle against the demons in his head.

When the Lennons returned from the recording studio at 10.50pm, Chapman shot him in the back four times. Bleeding profusely, Lennon staggered up five steps to the Dakota reception area and fell to the floor. The concierge rushed to his aid and called the police. Outside, the doorman shook the gun from Chapman's hand and kicked it across the pavement but Chapman was not struggling. He calmly sat down and started reading his favourite book, *The Catcher in the Rye*.

FIRST NEWS REPORTS

The first report of Lennon's death was during the middle of a televised football game on ABC's *Monday Night Football*, which was announced by sports broadcaster Howard Cosell.

Chapman pleaded guilty to murdering John Lennon and received a life prison sentence. He later explained that, as well as hearing demons in his head, he also thought that killing Lennon would make him as famous as his hero.

The death of John Lennon brought worldwide mourning. On 14 December, millions responded to Yoko's request for a ten-minute silence in memory of her husband. Over 200,000 people gathered in Central Park, across the road from the Dakota Building, where John and Yoko liked to walk.

And in Lennon's home town of Liverpool, around 30,000 sang his songs, such as 'Give Peace a Chance' and 'Imagine' in front of St George's Hall.

Sales of his records, both as a solo artist and as a Beatle, soared.

A 2.5-acre memorial was set up in Central Park called 'Strawberry Fields', after the title of the classic Beatles song. Annually, on Lennon's birthday, 9 October, and on the anniversary of his death, visitors and fans from all over the globe flock to Strawberry Fields to pay homage to him. ●

POPE SHOT

(*New York Post*, 14 May 1981)

ST PETER'S SQUARE in Vatican City was full of cheering and waving people with smiles on their faces as Pope John Paul II slowly made his way through the crowd, standing in a specially designed open jeep so that he could see and be seen.

He was reaching out to touch some people – especially the children – when shots rang out and he slumped into his seat, blood staining his white cassock.

Two bullets had struck him in the stomach, another in his right arm and a fourth hit his little finger.

There was a moment's shocked silence before people started screaming and crying and the Pope was driven at speed to the confines of the Vatican, with police and bodyguards running along, keeping the crowd back.

The Pope was taken by ambulance to nearby Gemelli Hospital, with Vatican Radio appealing to the world to pray for his survival.

Police instantly arrested the gunman who had fired a 9mm pistol some 15 feet away at around 5.15pm local time on 13 May 1981. He turned out to be a Turkish citizen named Mehmet Ali Agca, a former member of a far-right terrorist group known as the Grey Wolves, who had been jailed for the killing of a Turkish human rights journalist named Abdi Ipecki in February 1979 but had escaped and was on the run.

As he was led away from St Peter's Square he kept repeating, 'I couldn't care less about life.' In his pocket was found a note on which he had written, 'I, Agca, have killed the Pope so that the world may know of the thousands of victims of imperialism.'

EMERGENCY OPERATION

Meanwhile, surgeons performed a five-hour operation on the Pope. None of the shots had damaged vital organs and his life was not in danger.

The hospital director, Professor Luigi Candia, said one bullet passed through the Pope's body and a section of his intestine was removed.

In St Peter's Square, hundreds had remained behind, praying and singing hymns for the Pope's survival. When loudspeakers from Vatican Radio announced that he was out of danger, a cheer went up and they started to drift home.

The Pope came out of hospital two weeks later. He was re-admitted on 21 June with a lung infection but eventually made a full recovery.

Mehmet Ali Agca was sentenced to life imprisonment in July 1981 for the shooting. There were all sorts of conspiracy theories with a central core that Agca was not working alone. One of the most prominent suggestions was that

he was working for the Soviet and Bulgarian intelligence services who were angered by the Pope's support of the Solidarity movement in his home country of Poland and its commitment to shaking off the Communist regime imposed by Moscow.

POPE FORGIVES GUNMAN

Two days after Christmas, in 1983, John Paul II visited Agca in prison and forgave him. They spoke privately for 20 minutes and the Pope later said, 'What we talked about will have to remain a secret between him and me. I spoke to him as a brother whom I have pardoned and who has my complete trust.'

In June 2000, with the agreement of the Pope, Agca was released after serving 19 years.

On his return to Turkey he was re-arrested and compelled to serve the rest of his sentence for the killing of Abdi Ipekç in 1979. He was released in January 2006.

The Pope, who had always in his life felt a strong attachment to Mary, Mother of Christ, later credited her for saving his life.

'Could I forget that the event in St Peter's Square took place on the day and at the hour when the first appearance of the Mother of Christ to the poor little peasants has been remembered for over sixty years at Fátima, Portugal? For in everything that happened to me on that very day, I felt that extraordinary motherly protection and care, which turned out to be stronger than the deadly bullet.' •

RARE CANCER SEEN IN 41 HOMOSEXUALS

(*New York Times*, 3 July 1981)

THE *NEW YORK TIMES* was the first newspaper to carry a report on a disease that alerted the world to the biggest health concern in generations.

The article told how doctors in New York and California had diagnosed amongst homosexual men 41 cases of 'a rare and often rapidly fatal form of cancer'. The disease usually first appeared in violet-coloured spots on the body and eight of the victims died less than 24 months after the diagnosis was made. 'The cause of the outbreak is unknown.'

Doctors had been perplexed by the increase in the incidence of Pneumocystis carinii pneumonia (PCP) and of the cancer, Kaposi's sarcoma (KS). Neither were new diseases but the outbreak amongst young male homosexuals prompted an investigation.

When the Centers for Disease Control and Prevention in America reported the new outbreak they called it GRID (Gay-Related Immune Deficiency). But as it spread into the heterosexual community and particularly amongst drug addicts and people who received blood transfusions, it became known as AIDS (Acquired Immune Deficiency Syndrome).

RESEARCH CONTROVERSY

Throughout 1982 there was a marked rise of cases in Europe and Africa. Medical scientists around the world investigated what was causing the disease and there was to be some controversy over who identified the virus first.

In France, Dr Montagnier and Professor Barre-Sinoussi of the Institut Pasteur in Paris, isolated a retrovirus that they felt was related to AIDS, in 1983. But a year later, scientist, Dr Robert Gallo of the National Cancer Institute, National Institutes of Health, in Bethesda, USA, also isolated a retrovirus that he too claimed was responsible for AIDS.

It was later discovered that both had discovered the same thing, which an international committee of scientists later named Human Immunodeficiency Virus (HIV).

IMMUNE SYSTEM DESTROYED

The virus infects and gradually destroys the cells in the body that combat infections, leaving the body susceptible to diseases. Without treatment, the immune system will become too weak and a person with HIV may develop diseases that their body will be unable to fight. They are then said to have AIDS.

The most common ways in which HIV is spreading throughout the world is through sexual contact. Other ways include the sharing of needles and by transmission from infected mothers to their babies during pregnancy, birth or breastfeeding.

Tens of millions of people have died of AIDS around the world since 1981 and many more are infected with HIV – the majority living in Africa.

The death of movie star Rock Hudson from AIDS, in 1985, brought the disease even more into the public conscience.

Scientists continue to look for a cure but advancement in new drug therapies means that they are now able to stop HIV from reproducing and allow immune systems to recover. •

GOTCHA

(*The Sun*, 4 May 1982)

THIS MEMORABLE and controversial headline in the *Sun* newspaper during the Falklands conflict inspired nationalist pride in some and appalled others for being jingoistic and insensitive.

It referred to the sinking of the Argentine cruiser *Belgrano*, on 2 May 1982, by torpedoes fired from the Royal Navy submarine, HMS *Conqueror*, resulting in the loss of 323 crew. Controversially, the *Belgrano* was outside of the 200-mile exclusion zone that Britain had imposed around the Falkland Islands and reportedly heading away.

But in a television interview with David Frost, British Prime Minister Margaret Thatcher claimed that the ship was sunk because 'it was a danger to our boys'.

The conflict between the two countries began with an incident on 19 March of that year which took Britain and the Falkland Islanders by surprise. A group of scrap-metal workmen, accompanied by a military presence, landed on South Georgia Island and hoisted an Argentine flag. Within a week the Argentine leadership decided to invade and reclaim the islands.

There had been long historical friction and resentment over possession of the islands, which lie some 290 miles to the east of Argentina. The Argentines had settled there in 1826 but a British expedition took control of the territory in 1832 and declared sovereignty the following year.

ARGENTINE ECONOMIC CRISIS

But Argentina, which has always referred to the Falklands as the Malvinas, has never accepted British sovereignty and has yearned for their 'return'. During the 1970s and 1980s, Argentina was facing an economic crisis and there was widespread dissatisfaction with the military junta that had been governing the country since 1976.

In a move to restore popularity, President General Leopoldo Galtieri, hatched an ambitious plan to reclaim the Malvinas. After the raising of the flag on one of the smaller islands, South Georgia, Argentina sent a fleet of ships and troops to the Falklands. When they were spotted near South Georgia, British Foreign Secretary Lord Carrington said that a diplomatic solution was being pursued.

ENEMY INVASION

On 2 April, the Argentine troops landed on the Falklands and easily brushed aside the resistance from a small base of Royal Marines before Governor Rex Hunt ordered them to surrender. There were enthusiastic public celebrations in Buenos Aires.

Many people in Britain had either never heard of the Falklands or had no idea where they were or that they were a U.K. colony, 8,000 miles away in the South Atlantic. The Argentine junta believed that Britain would not physically defend

the islands but, to their surprise, on 5 April, Britain sent a task force of 28,000 troops and over 100 ships to fight for them.

On 22 April, the task force arrived in the area and a 200-mile exclusion zone was set around the islands. Three days later, a small commando force re-took South Georgia, and Margaret Thatcher called on the nation to 'Rejoice at that news.'

On 1 May, British planes attacked enemy planes at Port Stanley airport. And in the days that followed, several ships were sunk and planes shot down on both sides. These included the sinking of the British destroyer HMS *Sheffield*, on 4 May, with the loss of 20 men, two days after the hit on the *Belgrano*.

The first major British troop landing was at San Carlos on 21 May and, from here, attacks were made on Goose Green and the capital of Port Stanley.

FALKLANDS D-DAY

On 28 May, British troops defeated the Argentines at Darwin and Goose Green and 1,400 prisoners were taken. Now the British were free to march towards Port Stanley, which was liberated on 14 June when

Commander Mario Menendez signed a surrender document – 9,800 Argentine troops laid down their arms. Britain formally declared an end to hostilities on 20 June.

Although sometimes referred to as the 'Falklands War', neither side officially declared war and so it is regarded as a 'conflict' in which 649 Argentines died and 255 British, plus three Falkland Islanders.

The praise and respect that Argentina's military junta had sought and briefly gained quickly evaporated. By contrast, Margaret Thatcher received a tremendous boost in popularity as the British celebrated their victory in regaining a remote colonial island of which many in Britain had previously been completely unaware. •

MURDER

(*Daily Mirror*, 13 October 1984)

A single emotive word, unusually placed vertically down the right-hand side of the front page of the *Daily Mirror*, alongside the subdued face of Margaret Thatcher and the wrecked façade of a hotel.

But Mrs Thatcher, then British Prime Minister, was one of the lucky ones who escaped with her life when an IRA bomb exploded in the Brighton Grand Hotel on 12 October 1984. Inside were members of the Conservative Party, the British government of the time, who had gathered to attend their annual party conference in the seaside town.

The bomb had been planted three weeks earlier by IRA 'operative' Patrick Magee, who checked into Room 629 under the alias of 'Roy Walsh' and concealed the device beneath the bath. He used the timer from a TV video recorder to prime it.

It detonated at 2.54am, crumbling the front of the hotel on the top floors and sending masonry crashing down below. Most were sleeping but Mrs Thatcher was still working in her first-floor suite, finishing off her speech for the next day's conference. At 2.50am, her private secretary entered to hand her an official paper to read and five minutes later there was an explosion.

'I KNEW IT WAS A BOMB'

She was later to recall, 'A loud thud shook the room. There were a few seconds' silence and then there was a second, slightly different noise, in fact created by falling masonry. I knew immediately that it was a bomb.

'Denis [her husband] put his head around the bedroom door, saw that I was alright and went back inside to dress.'

Mrs Thatcher and her husband were entirely unscathed but there were obvious fears that there would be further attempts on the Prime Minister's life. Once Mrs Thatcher had changed her clothes, her security team whisked them both out of the hotel's rear exit, taking them directly to the safety of Brighton police station. They were then transferred to Sussex Police Headquarters at Lewes, spending the rest of the night there.

Back in Brighton, guests who were evacuated or had fled from the hotel mingled in confusion on the sea front, most wearing only their dressing gowns and pyjamas, some shocked, dazed and coated in plaster dust. Five people died in the blast and 34 were injured. The fatal casualties were Anthony Berry, MP, Roberta Wakeham (wife of Chief Whip John Wakeham) north-west area chairman Eric Taylor, Muriel Maclean (wife of Scottish chairman Donald Maclean) and Jeanne Shattock (wife of the president of the south-west Conservative association).

NORMAN TEBBIT RESCUED

Memorable TV news pictures showed Norman Tebbit, President of the Board of Trade, being dug out of the rubble and, in considerable pain, being carried away on a stretcher. His wife, Margaret, who had been trapped alongside him, was paralysed by her injuries.

Within a few hours of the blast, the IRA issued a statement claiming responsibility, adding, 'Mrs Thatcher will now realise that Britain cannot occupy our country and torture our prisoners and shoot our people in their own streets and get away with it. Today we were unlucky, but remember we only have to be lucky once. You will have to be lucky always.'

At Mrs Thatcher's insistence, the conference opened on schedule, less than seven hours after the blast, at 9.30am. She walked onto the conference platform to a thunderous ovation.

'THIS ATTACK HAS FAILED'

In her redrafted speech she briefly alluded to the incident before carrying on as normal. 'The bomb attack was an attempt not only to disrupt and terminate our conference, it was an attempt to cripple Her Majesty's democratically elected government,' she said. 'That is the scale of the outage in which we have all shared. And the fact that we are gathered here now, shocked but composed and determined, is a sign not only that this attack has failed, but that all attempts to destroy democracy by terrorism will fail.'

Magee was caught after finger prints on a hotel registration card assigned to 'Roy Walsh' were a match for those of Magee's in police records, dating back to a time when he was arrested as a juvenile. He was sentenced to 35 years but released in 1999, under the Good Friday Agreement. ●

WORLDBEATER!

(*Sunday Mirror*, 14 July 1985)

The world's biggest rock festival, organised by Bob Geldof to raise money for famine relief in Africa, kicked off at Wembley Stadium with a rousing rendition of 'Rocking All Over the World' by Status Quo.

Described as the 'Woodstock of the eighties', Live Aid was a truly global event and a remarkable achievement of organisation from arranging and sound checking the acts to satellite link ups and screening the event around the world.

At the same time as the Wembley concert was taking place, another was happening in the U.S., at the JFK stadium in Philadelphia. There were also small ones in African countries and the likes of Austria, Norway and Yugoslavia.

An estimated final figure for the money raised from the concerts was £150 million. Astonishingly, for such a mammoth undertaking, Live Aid was arranged in just ten weeks.

The background to the event can be traced back to some harrowing BBC TV news footage of the African famine. Geldof, lead singer of the Boomtown Rats, was so moved by what he saw that he got together with singer Midge Ure from Ultravox to help raise money for the crisis. They co-wrote a song called 'Do They Know It's Christmas' and persuaded some top British singers of the day to record it, under the name of Band Aid. They included Boy George, Sting, George Michael and Paul Young.

CHART TOPPER

The song was rush-released, on 7 December 1984, in time for the Christmas market and became the fastest-selling single ever, hitting the top of the charts both in the U.K. and U.S. and raising £8m. It inspired American pop artists to do something similar. with a song written by

Michael Jackson and Lionel Ritchie called 'We Are The World' featuring both singers on vocals, along with the likes of Bob Dylan, Cyndi Lauper, Harry Belafonte, Paul Simon and Bruce Springsteen.

Surprised by how much money was raised, Geldof set his sights on a huge, famine-busting concert. And in his typical forthright, determined style, played a hands-on part in gathering together the cream of the British music industry to perform and in persuading TV networks around the world to screen the event.

On 13 July 1985, a packed crowd of 72,000 at Wembley Stadium heard a voice over the sound system announce, 'It's twelve noon in London, seven AM in Philadelphia, and around the world it's time for Live Aid.'

ROYAL PATRONS

With Prince Charles and Princess Diana in attendance, music 'royalty' included Queen, David Bowie, Elton John, Dire Straits, George Michael and Paul McCartney. U2 cemented their reputation as stadium rockers and Freddie Mercury had the audience in the palm of his hand. David Bowie

and Mick Jagger sang together in an amusing video performance of 'Dancing in the Street'.

In Philadelphia the 100,000-strong stadium crowd watched top acts including Madonna, The Who, Crosby, Stills and Nash, Hall and Oates, and Led Zeppelin. Mick Jagger and Tina Turner duetted on 'It's Only Rock and Roll' and Phil Collins managed to play at both concerts by crossing the Atlantic on Concorde.

GELDOF SWEARS ON AIR

Throughout the day there was footage of the African famine and televised appeals for people to donate money. At one point, Bob Geldof was so passionate that he swore on live television. News footage of starving African children accompanied by the haunting song 'Drive' by Cars, contained the emotive line, 'You can't go on, thinking there's nothing wrong.'

Prior to the concert, there had been strong rumours that it would feature a reunion of surviving Beatles, Paul, John and Ringo. But this proved to be no more than a rumour. Headline act Paul McCartney sang on his own at the piano but, unfortunately the first two minutes of 'Let It Be' were beset by microphone problems.

After a long day in which 52 acts had been on and off stage at Wembley, David Bowie led the ensemble in the final song, 'Do They Know It's Christmas'. Six hours later, the U.S. concert ended with 'We Are the World'.

The mammoth event was televised to over 1.5 billion people in 160 countries and really made individuals feel that they could help change the world. Bob Geldof was given an honorary knighthood in 1986. ●

EXPLOSION STUNS NATION

(*Florida Today*, 29 January 1986)

THE WORST ACCIDENT in the history of the American space programme was watched live on TV by millions around the world in shock and disbelief.

The graceful shuttle, *Challenger*, launched at 11.38am local time on 28 January 1986, on its tenth mission into space.

The crew of seven was led by Commander Dick Scobee, 46, and one of the astronauts had received worldwide publicity as she was chosen to be the first school teacher in space.

Christa McAuliffe, 37, was picked from among 10,000 entries for a competition to find a teacher to be sent into space so as to encourage children across the country to take a keen interest in space and science education and learn from the shuttle. She was due to give two lectures from space, which would be broadcast on TV to schools.

EXPLOSION HORROR

On the day of the launch, children in classrooms across the country were avidly watching with mounting excitement as, after a delay, *Challenger* took to the skies. But just a minute later, the thrilling spectacle turned to horror as the shuttle exploded above Cape Canaveral, Florida.

There was a moment's stunned silence at the airbase where a crowd, including the astronaut's families, had gathered to watch the take-off. Amongst them was Christa McAuliffe's husband, Steve, and her nine- and six-year-old children. The eerie silence was shared by around 1,200 adults and children watching on a giant television screen erected at the New Hampshire school where Christa McAullife taught. People at home around the world watching on TV shared the shock. Nobody was quite sure – or could quite believe – what had happened.

MISSION CONTROL STUNNED

Even Stephen A. Nesbitt of Mission Control took a moment to react. His voice was heard to report that there had been 'a major malfunction'. Shortly after, he added, 'We have no downlink,' referring to the loss of communication with *Challenger*. This was followed by, 'We have a report from the flight dynamics officer that the vehicle has exploded. The flight director confirms that.'

All seven of the crew aboard were killed. That evening, President Ronald Reagan made a televised address to a stunned nation in which he talked of the bravery and inspirational qualities of the astronauts and vowed that the space programme would continue.

'There will be more shuttle flights, more shuttle crews, more volunteers, more teachers... nothing ends here. Our hopes and journeys continue,' he said. He ended, 'We will never forget them, nor the last time we saw them this morning as they prepared for their journey and waved goodbye and slipped the surly bonds of earth to touch the face of God.'

OPERATIONS SUSPENDED

NASA immediately suspended operations of the shuttle indefinitely until the findings of a board of inquiry. The report, when it arrived in May, stated that the accident had been caused by a leak through a faulty seal or 'O-ring' in one of the solid rocket boosters, which had caused the hydrogen fuel to explode.

The flight was the twenty-fifth by the fleet of shuttles since 1981, and NASA had gained confidence at being able to send reusable manned craft into orbit and bring them back again.

The schedule for 1986 was the most ambitious in the history of the shuttle programme with 15 flights planned. But in the wake of the disaster there were no further manned flights until September 1988 when NASA resumed shuttle missions with the launch of *Discovery*.

But tragedy struck once again, on 1 February 2003, when the *Columbia* shuttle disintegrated over Texas as it was attempting re-entry, leaving another seven crew members dead. The heat shield that protects the shuttle from the searing temperatures of re-entry was fatally damaged on lift-off by a piece of insulating foam that broke away from an external fuel tank.

Two years later, President George Bush announced that he would be cancelling the space shuttle programme. •

NUCLEAR NIGHTMARE IS HERE

(*Daily Express*, 30 April 1986)

THE WORST NUCLEAR power plant explosion that had ever occurred shot radioactive debris up to 1km (3,300ft) into the air and was blown by the wind for hundreds of miles. Yet the Soviet authorities tried to keep it a secret.

In the early hours of 26 April 1986, engineers at the Chernobyl nuclear power station in the Soviet republic of Ukraine were carrying out an electrical power test at reactor number four. They were taking advantage of a planned shutdown of the reactor for routine maintenance but, at 1.24am local time, an uncontrollable power surge occurred, sparking two explosions which destroyed the reactor and sent a plume of more than 50 tons of deadly radioactive material into the air.

It was carried by air currents for miles around with some of it blown as far as Western Europe.

One worker was killed instantly by the explosions and another died a few hours later in hospital as a result of his injuries. A team of 14 firemen arrived minutes later to battle the fires and were later joined by dozens more. All received high doses of radiation.

RADIATION DEATHS

Twenty-eight rescue workers and plant staff would die of acute radiation syndrome in the coming weeks and dozens more suffered radiation burns.

Soviet leader Mikhail Gorbachev who had won praise for his glasnost policy of greater Soviet openness, tried to cover the incident up and it took two days before the authorities confirmed the incident – and that was only after monitoring stations in Sweden, Finland and Norway began reporting sudden high discharges of radioactivity in the atmosphere.

The first sign was when workers arriving at the Forsmark nuclear power station, 60 miles north of Stockholm, set off warnings during a routine radioactivity check. Believing there to be a leak at their own power station, 600 workers were sent home. After similar high radioactive readings at other power plants in Scandinavia, attention focused on the Soviet Union. But when they were contacted, the authorities denied any knowledge of an accident.

ACCIDENT CONFIRMED

The admission, when it came, was low-key. Tucked away on the Soviet news television bulletin on the evening of 28 April, after the farm reports, a statement said, 'An accident has occurred at the Chernobyl nuclear power plant and one of the reactors was damaged. Measures are being taken to eliminate the consequences of the accident. Aid is being given to those affected. A government commission has been set up.'

To try to contain the fire, Chernobyl's managers pumped water into the reactor core but when this proved unsuccessful they turned to dumping boron carbide and a total of 4,000 tons of lead, sand and clay on the facility via helicopters. By May, an input of nitrogen into the reactor cooled it down.

Subsequent international reports blamed the poor design, a lack of safety culture at the plant and errors by operators.

RADIOACTIVE DEBRIS

Because the reactor was not housed in a reinforced concrete shell, as is standard practice in most countries, it allowed large amounts of radioactive debris to escape.

The building of such a shelter then took place and was completed by October, preventing further leakage from reactor number four and allowing the other reactors to continue producing power.

Estimates of those who died or have been subjected to radiation poisoning from the explosions vary wildly but it has been reported that there were fewer than 50 deaths, mostly workers at the plant, but up to 9,000 could eventually die due to radiation exposure.

Radioactive fallout from the disaster caused a pine forest downwind of Chernobyl to die. Wildlife and livestock across Europe were also badly affected, with unusually high instances of birth defects amongst animals even as far away as Britain, where slaughter restrictions remained in place for years for sheep that may have fed on hillsides contaminated by the fallout.

The city of Pripyat, established mainly to house workers at Chernobyl, had a population of around 50,000 by the time of the disaster. It was completely evacuated and remains a ghost town within the exclusion zone around the nuclear plant.

Further afield, in areas where the fallout cloud is known to have caused some contamination, there were increased numbers of human birth defects and unusually high figures for certain cancers which have been associated with the catastrophe.

Chernobyl continued to produce electricity for another 14 years, until international pressure forced its closure in December 2000. •

HUNDREDS DIE AS JUMBO JET PLUNGES INTO VILLAGE

(*Independent*, 22 December 1988)

A JUMBO JET EXPLODED over Lockerbie, Scotland, killing all 259 passengers and crew aboard and 11 people on the ground.

It turned into a murder investigation when evidence was found of a bomb having been concealed inside a cassette player packed in a suitcase. The incident caused a huge international furore, which rumbled on for 11 years before anyone was brought to trial.

The Pan Am flight 103 from Frankfurt to New York, via London, on 21 December 1988, was carrying a large proportion of Americans – 189 in total – many of whom were students or military personnel looking forward to returning home for Christmas.

EXPLOSION OVER LOCKERBIE

As it cruised at 31,000 above the town of Lockerbie in the Dumfries and Galloway region of south-west Scotland, the quiet normality of life below was to be shattered just after 7.00pm local time when the plane exploded.

A Semtex bomb aboard was activated with a timer, which blew

the plane to pieces. Plane debris and dead bodies fell to the ground, scattering over an area of 845 square miles. The fuel it was carrying caused fireballs that set houses, trees and cars alight. Twenty-one of Lockerbie's houses were completely destroyed and 11 residents died.

An eyewitness remarked, 'There was a terrible explosion and the whole sky lit up. It was virtually raining fire – it was just liquid fire.'

BOMB TIMER TRACED

During the investigation, pieces of a circuit board belonging to the bomb's timer device was traced to its Swiss manufacturer and fragments of clothing that were said to have been inside the suitcase led to a tailor in Malta. Both ultimately led to the identity of a Libyan intelligence officer and head of security for Libyan Arab Airlines (LAA), Abdelbaset Ali Mohmed al-Megrahi. His co-conspirator was named as al-Amin Khalifa Fhimah, the LAA station manager at Luqu airport, Malta.

Investigators claimed that the booby-trapped suitcase had been loaded onto the plane at Frankfurt from an earlier flight from Malta.

Both men were formally charged with murder in November 1991

and a warrant for their arrest was issued. But Libya's leader, Colonel Gaddafi, refused to hand the men over, saying that they would be tried in their own country.

Britain and the U.S. obtained a U.N. Security Council Resolution in January 1992 ordering Libya to surrender the Lockerbie suspects. When the demand was refused a threatened worldwide ban on air travel and arms sales came into effect.

LIBYAN ASSETS FROZEN

A year later, tightened sanctions were imposed, including the freezing of Libyan assets in foreign banks and an embargo on oil industry-related equipment.

It wasn't until 5 April 1999 that Libya finally handed over the accused for trial at a military base called Camp Zeist, in the Netherlands, where Scottish judges presided over the court proceedings. U.N. sanctions against Libya were suspended as agreed.

The trial finally got underway on 3 May 2000. Eight months later, on 31 January 2001, Megrahi was convicted of mass murder and sentenced to life imprisonment. His co-accused, Al-Amin Khalifa

Fahimah, was found not guilty and freed.

But Megrahi spent just eight-and-a-half years in Scotland's Greenock Prison. On 20 August 2009, the Scottish authorities released him on compassionate grounds after he was diagnosed as suffering from terminal prostate cancer. He was allowed to fly back to Libya to be with his family. ●

OUR DAY OF TEARS

(*Sunday Echo*, 16 April 1989)

A N FA CUP SEMI-FINAL clash between Nottingham Forest and Liverpool ended in tragedy just minutes after the kick-off – the worst disaster, to date, in British football history.

The match was at Sheffield Wednesday's ground, Hillsborough, on Saturday, 15 April 1989. For some years, football in Britain had been blighted by hooliganism amongst the fans. Fighting, pitch invasions and the throwing of objects at players had led to segregation and fences erected between spectators and the pitch.

The policy of keeping opposing supporters apart meant that Nottingham Forest fans were placed in the 'stands' at the Spion Kop End of the ground and the Liverpool contingent in the Leppings Lane End of the stadium. These terraces were divided into a series of 'pens' by iron railings.

TRAFFIC DELAYS

With the kick-off at 3.00pm, many Liverpool fans arrived with little time to spare – heavy road traffic had been reported – and a large crowd formed at the turnstiles. They became anxious at the slow process of entering the ground and, concerned that they would miss the start of the match, began pressing forward.

With many fans still desperate to enter, worried police asked for the exit Gate C to be opened and around 2,000 people passed through, the majority making their way in to the already overcrowded central 'pens' of the Leppings Lane end.

Gate A was opened a few minutes later, followed by Gate B. It resulted in a rush as those at the front were pushed forward, pressing into the fence to accommodate those who had just arrived.

CROWD SURGES FORWARD

Four minutes into the game, Liverpool player Peter Beardsley took a shot that hit the crossbar at the Leppings Lane end of the ground. It caused the standing crowd to surge forward in excitement, crushing people into the fence.

A few managed to clamber over and onto the pitch and, for a moment, it looked like another pitch invasion. A police officer saw what was happening and ran onto the pitch to tell the referee to stop the game.

For those packed ever more tightly against the fences, however, there was little that could be done. Many of the fatalities were due to compressive asphyxia. They were crushed so tightly that they simply could not expand their chests enough to breathe.

Police and match officials attempted to help those trapped clamber over the fence and others were pulled to safety by fellow supporters in the seating areas above.

But the police, the stadium stewards and the ambulance crews in attendance for the match were overwhelmed by the number of injured.

Fans attempted CPR on friends whom they had managed to drag to safety on a pitch that began to look like a battlefield. For many, the lifesaving attempts simply came too late.

BODIES ON PITCH

Bodies were laid out on the pitch – many of them teenagers and children. Fans assisted the injured by tearing down advertising boards and using them as stretchers.

A total of 96 people were crushed to death and around 766 others injured. Liverpool's *Sunday Echo* newspaper carried the following day's headline, 'Our Day of Tears'.

Lord Justice Taylor was appointed to conduct an inquiry into the disaster. The report found that the main cause was the failure of police crowd control. One of the key elements was the failure to close off the tunnel leading to overcrowded 'pens' once Gate C had been opened.

Following the inquiry, new safety measures were introduced at major football grounds around Britain. Fencing was torn down and standing terraces made way for all-seater venues. ●

CRACKDOWN IN BEIJING

TROOPS ATTACK AND CRUSH BEIJING PROTEST

(*New York Times*, 4 June 1989)

AN ATTACK ON protestors by Chinese troops in the centre of the capital of Beijing shocked the world with its brutality and resulted in many deaths and injuries.

The protests began after the death of former General Secretary of the Chinese Communist Party (CCP), Hu Yaobang, who had gained many enemies amongst the party for his liberal policies including the introduction of a free market and more transparency of government.

Following a series of student protests across China in 1987, Hu was blamed for the incidents and was forced to resign as party General Secretary, although he was allowed to retain a seat in the Politburo.

On the eve of Hu's funeral on 15 April 1989, a crowd of students converged on Tiananmen Square to commemorate him and demand that his contribution to the country be reappraised. It grew into a crowd of around 100,000, who called for Hu's reforming liberalisation to continue.

THOUSANDS GATHER IN SQUARE

Over the following days more and more people joined the students to campaign for political reform and calling for the resignations of repressive party leaders. On 22 April, tens of thousands gathered outside the Great Hall of the People in Tiananmen Square as Hu's memorial service was held. They delivered a petition of demands and insisted on a meeting with Premier Li Peng but it was rejected.

Worried authorities placed armed troops on the outskirts of the crowd. Protests also broke out in cities throughout China, including Shanghai and Wuhan. They were mostly peaceful, although some things were hurled at buildings and there were some clashes with troops.

On 15 May, Soviet leader Mikhail Gorbachev arrived in Beijing for the first Sino-Soviet summit in 30 years. His visit was seen as a formal end to years of hostility between the two communist nations. But large protests forced the cancellation of plans to welcome him in Tiananmen Square, which was a huge embarrassment for the government.

MARTIAL LAW DECLARED

Five days later, martial law was declared in several districts in Beijing as troops moved ominously towards the city centre.

What had begun as a relatively small protest had grown to around one million in numbers by its seventh week with people from all walks of life arriving to support the movement.

Many were chanting 'General strike!' and TV footage was shown all around the world from Western news teams who had been invited in to cover Gorbachev's visit. They were now ideally placed to film what was happening. With the crowd refusing to disperse, the government sent in troops and tanks, which fired indiscriminately, mowing down anyone in their way.

UNARMED CIVILIANS SHOT

The noise of gunfire filled the air. Ordinary, unarmed civilians were stunned that their own army was shooting at them. As people fell dead or injured, they were either carried to hospital or taken there on bicycle rickshaws. Ambulances arrived but were turned away by the troops and two drivers were shot and injured.

A defiant crowd shouted 'Fascists!', 'Stop killing!' and 'Down with the government!'

Precise figures of casualties may never be known but it has been estimated that hundreds were killed and thousands injured.

It was dubbed the 'Tiananmen Square massacre', although most of the bloodshed happened in the surrounding streets.

The savagery of the attack on 4 June caused an international outcry. Meanwhile, the CCP conducted widespread arrests of protestors, banned the foreign press from the country and sacked those in the government thought to be too sympathetic to democratic reform. ●

MANDELA GOES FREE TODAY

(*City Press*, 11 February 1990)

AFTER 27 YEARS in prison, Nelson Mandela was released on 11 February 1990 and the televised moment was televised live around the world.

Four years later, the man who had long campaigned against apartheid and the white government of the National Party in his homeland was elected as the country's first black president.

The South African newspaper, *City Press*, splashed 'Mandela Goes Free Today' on the morning of his release and it was held aloft by many ecstatic supporters who celebrated in the streets.

Mandela had joined the African National Congress (ANC) in 1943 and when the Afrikaner-dominated National Party came to power in 1948, he actively campaigned against the party for its support of the apartheid policy of racial segregation

He qualified as a lawyer in 1952 and opened a law practice in Johannesburg with his partner, Oliver Tambo. In 1958, he married Winnie Madikizela, who was later to take an active role in the campaign to free her husband from prison.

ANC OUTLAWED

Mandela became vice-president of the ANC and, after it was outlawed in 1960, he went underground but was eventually arrested and charged with sabotage and attempting to violently overthrow the government.

In the winter of 1964, he was sentenced to life in prison and spent

18 years on Robben Island before being transferred to Pollsmoor Prison on the mainland in 1982.

In 1980, Oliver Tambo, who was in exile, and Winnie Mandela, launched an international campaign to release Nelson Mandela. Many countries tightened sanctions on South Africa and there was growing pressure for Mandela to be released.

MANDELA REFUSES RELEASE

In February 1985, he refused President P. W. Botha's offer for early release because of the condition that he should reject violence as a political weapon.

At a rally at the Jabulani Stadium, Nelson's 25-year-old daughter, Zindzi, read out his response. Zindzi's mother, Winnie, was restricted under a government banning order but attended the rally in disguise. Zindzi's address became known as the 'My Father Says . . .' speech.

The words that inspired a renewed vigour in the campaign against apartheid were, 'What freedom am I being offered while the organisation of the people remains banned? Only free men can negotiate. A prisoner cannot enter into contracts.'

On 2 February 1990, President F. W. de Klerk, who had succeeded Botha as leader of the National Party the previous year, lifted the ban on the ANC, and Mandela, at the age of 71, was released from prison nine days later.

Celebrations erupted throughout the country. Mandela had been moved to Victor Verster Prison in 1988 and, as he walked through the gates to embrace Winnie, he greeted a waiting crowd with a huge smile and raised fist salute. He then got into a car, which took him to Cape Town where he addressed a huge, joyous gathering.

His opening words were of peace, 'I greet you all in the name of peace, democracy and freedom for all,' he said. 'I stand here before you not as a prophet, but as a humble servant of you, the people.'

ARMED STRUGGLE CONTINUES

But he went on to warn that the armed fight against apartheid must continue.

'Now is the time to intensify the struggle on all fronts. To relax our efforts now would be a mistake, which generations to come will not be able to forgive.'

In 1991, Mandela became president of the ANC and talks took place about forming a new multi-racial democracy for South Africa.

Nelson Mandela and F. W. de Klerk shared the Nobel Peace Prize in 1993 for their efforts to transform South African society.

Mandela's charisma, warmth, beaming smile, humility and seeming lack of bitterness about his long incarceration endeared him to millions around the world.

On 10 May 1994, the ANC won 252 of the 400 seats in the national assembly in the first democratic elections of South Africa's history and Nelson Mandela became the country's first black president. •

CAPITAL SARAJEVO RACKED BY SERB-MUSLIM CIVIL STRIFE

(*Independent*, 7 April 1992)

ON THE DAY THAT the European Community recognised Bosnia as an independent state, Serbian snipers opened fire on a Muslim peace demonstration in the capital city of Sarajevo.

Although there had been much conflict over the years between rival factions, this was regarded as the opening salvo of the Bosnian War.

The multicultural country of Yugoslavia had been created after the Great War by the victorious Western Allies. It comprised several ethnic and religious groups that had been historical rivals, in particular

the Serbs (Orthodox Christians), Croats (Catholics) and ethnic Albanians (Muslims).

During World War II, Yugoslavia was invaded by Nazi Germany and was partitioned. A resistance movement sprang up led by Josip Tito. After Germany's defeat, Tito reunified Yugoslavia, merging together Slovenia, Croatia, Bosnia,

Serbia, Montenegro and Macedonia, along with two self-governing provinces, Kosovo and Vojvodina.

But after Tito's death in 1980, Yugoslavia fell into political and economic chaos as it struggled without his strong leadership.

INDEPENDENCE DECLARED

A new leader arose by the late 1980s, a Serbian named Slobodan Milosevic, who took control of Kosovo. But in June 1991, Slovenia and Croatia both declared their independence from Yugoslavia.

The national army of Yugoslavia, now made up of Serbs controlled by Milosevic, entered Slovenia to subdue the separatists. But with almost no Serbs living there, he withdrew the troops after only ten days of fighting. He then focused on Croatia where a minority of Serbs resided amongst the Catholic population.

During World War II, Croatia had been a pro-Nazi state and Serbs, as well as Jews living there, had been put in concentration camps and killed. In 1991, Serbs living here still felt they were being discriminated against.

Milosevic's forces invaded in July and killed hundreds of Croat men,

burying them in mass graves. By the end of the year a U.S.-brokered ceasefire was agreed between the Serbs and Croats fighting in Croatia.

On 6 April 1992, the U.N. officially recognised the independence of Bosnia, which was a predominantly Muslim country, with Serbs making up 32 per cent of the population.

Milosevic wasted no time in responding. Serbian snipers opened fire from the upper floors of a hotel on a peace gathering below. Bosnian police and Muslim fighters stormed the hotel, firing machine-guns. On the outskirts of the city Muslims exchanged artillery and mortar fire with Serbs in the surrounding hills.

MASS SHOOTINGS

In the weeks, months and years that followed, Bosnian Muslims suffered terribly against the better-armed Serbs led by Radovan Karadzic. There were mass shootings of Muslims and internment in concentration camps reminiscent of the Nazi ones during World War II. There was also reported rape of women as the Serbs sought to eradicate the Muslims in what became known as 'ethnic cleansing'.

With Bosnia in terrible turmoil, the U.N. response was a limited one, with troops deployed to protect the distribution of food and medicine to dispossessed Muslims, but taking no military action.

One of the worst atrocities occurred in Srebrenica when nearly 8,000 men and boys between the ages of twelve and sixty were shot dead. It shocked the world and resulted in a NATO bombing campaign targeting Serbian military positions.

Eventually, Milosevic was ready to talk peace and, in November 1995, he joined Bosnian Muslim President Alija Izetbegovic and Croatian President Franjo Tudjman for peace talks in Dayton, Ohio, U.S.

It was agreed to create two separate entities – a Bosnian-Croat federation and a Bosnian-Serb Republic – each with its own president, government, parliament and police. And an international peacekeeping force was sent in to keep the peace. The agreement also called for democratic elections and stipulated that war criminals would be handed over for prosecution.

Karadzic went into hiding and, on 12 February 2002, Milosevic went on trial charged with 66 counts of genocide and war crimes in Bosnia, Croatia and Kosovo. On 11 March 2006, Milosevic died of a heart attack in his cell in The Hague. There was jubilation in the streets with the news that Karadzic had been arrested in Belgrade on 21 July 2008 after 13 years on the run. •

SCIENTISTS CLONE ADULT SHEEP

TRIUMPH FOR UK RAISES ALARM OVER HUMAN USE

(*Observer*, 23 February 1997)

CLONING – A STAPLE ingredient of science-fiction films and novels – became science fact with the birth of Dolly the Sheep.

Mammals reproduce sexually in a process that involves both a male and female. Cloning is the production of a new, genetically identical individual from a single parent animal.

Scientist Dr Ian Wilmut at the Roslin Institute, near Edinburgh, took a single cell from the udder of an adult sheep, turned it into a viable embryo and implanted it into a surrogate mother. The sheep gave birth to a lamb named Dolly who was genetically identical to the sheep from which the cell was taken.

Although biologists around the world had successfully cloned plants and frogs, this was the first mammal to have been successfully cloned from an adult cell.

MORAL ISSUES

The announcement aroused huge interest as the world's press descended on Roslin to take pictures of Dolly. But there was immediate controversy with ethical and moral issues over whether the procedure would lead to the cloning of humans.

Dolly was born on 5 July 1996 but the announcement was not made until 22 February 1997 when the publication of the result could be fully prepared.

Dolly started her life in a test tube. Once normal development was confirmed at six days, the embryo was transferred into a surrogate mother. An ultrasound after about 45 days confirmed the pregnancy, which proceeded without any problem until the lamb was born.

DNA tests showed that Dolly was identical to the ewe who donated the udder cell but unrelated to the surrogate mother.

NEW HEALTH PRODUCTS

Explaining the reason behind the birth of Dolly, Dr Wilmut stated, 'Apart from showing the biological principle that it is possible to get a cell to begin development again in this way – which has fascinating implications for studies of cancer and suchlike – the initial importance is that we will be able to use this for research in biology and also to make new health care products'.

As the debate about the potential for human cloning rumbled on, Wilmut opposed the notion and called it 'repugnant.'

Despite the spectacular outcome achieved with Dolly, in 2008 Wilmut decided to abandon the technique used to create her. Instead of using embryonic stem cells, Wilmut began working with a procedure developed by Japanese researcher Professor Shinya Yamanaka to generate stem cells from adult skin cells in mice. He hopes this will lead to effective treatments for diseases such as Parkinson's.

DOLLY'S NORMAL LIFE

Dolly was encouraged to lead a normal sheep's life. She was mated with a small Welsh mountain ram and produced six lambs. Later she had arthritisbut then there were fears for something more serious when some of the sheep at Roslin contracted pulmonary adenomatosis. This disease is caused by a virus that induces tumours to grow in the lungs of affected animals. It is incurable and infectious.

A CT scan (computerised tomography) carried out on Friday, 14 February 2003, confirmed the Roslin team's worst fears. Tumours were growing in Dolly's chest. Since a general anaesthetic had been necessary to perform the scan it was decided that it would be best if Dolly did not regain consciousness and an overdose of an anaesthetic agent was administered to end her life.

Her early death raised debate that it may have been due to the cloning process but Roslin scientists stated that they did not think there was a connection with Dolly being a clone and that other sheep on the farm had similar ailments.

Dolly's remains were conserved by taxidermists and she was put on display at the National Museum of Scotland in Edinburgh. ●

DIANA DEAD

6AM SHOCK ISSUE

(*News of the World*, 31 Aug 1997)

THE NEWS WAS so sudden and shocking that people could scarcely believe it. Diana, Princess of Wales, had died in a car crash in Paris in the early hours of Sunday, 31 August 1997. So too had her companion, Dodi Al Fayed, and the driver of the car, Henri Paul.

For the past week there had been pictures in the newspapers of Diana in a swimsuit enjoying the sunshine with Al Fayed aboard a yacht belonging to his father, Mohamed Al Fayed, on the French and Italian Rivieras. The couple had stopped in Paris en route for London and, at around 12:20am on 31 August, they left the Ritz Hotel to return to an apartment owned by Mohamed Al Fayed in rue Arsène Houssaye.

The hotel's acting Head of Security, Henri Paul, drove them in a black Mercedes-Benz S280 through Paris where they were pursued by paparazzi. Entering the tunnel under the Place de l'Alma in the centre of the city, he lost control of the car,

which smashed into a pillar at an estimated speed of 105kph (65mph). It then spun and hit a stone wall before coming to a halt.

DEAD AT SCENE

Al Fayed and Henri Paul died at the scene but Diana and her bodyguard, Trevor Rees-Jones, were cut from the wreckage and rushed to hospital. They were unable to save her and she died in the early hours of the morning. Of the four people in the car, only Rees-Jones survived. None of them had been wearing seat belts.

The news of the Princess's death – officially declared at 3.00am

(BST) – stunned the world. Newsreaders were visibly choked, stumbling over their words. And the story made the later editions of that day's Sunday newspapers.

Prince Charles broke the news of their mother's death to Princes William and Harry at Balmoral Castle in Scotland where the royal family had been spending the summer.

In a statement, Buckingham Palace said the Queen and the Prince of Wales were 'deeply shocked and distressed'.

STUNNED DISBELIEF

Her death caused overwhelming public grief in Britain, the like of which had never been seen before. The traditional British 'stiff upper lip' was replaced by tears and a general stunned sense of disbelief.

Diana's home at Kensington Palace became a focal point for mourners, many of whom were surprised by the overriding emotion that compelled them to pay their respects. They shared their grief with each other as one bouquet after another was laid on the ground. People also brought flowers to Diana's ancestral home, Althorp Park, in Northampton.

Around one million people lined the streets to see the Princess's funeral cortège as it made its way from Kensington Palace to Westminster Abbey for the service on 6 September.

Inside, Diana's brother, Earl Spencer, criticised the media and took a sideswipe at the royal family's behaviour towards Diana. He pledged to play a greater role in the upbringing of the two princes.

'It is a point to remember that of all the ironies about Diana, perhaps the greatest was this – a girl given the name of the ancient goddess of hunting was, in the end, the most hunted person of the modern age,' he said, in a voice trembling with emotion.

The Earl promised that he and what he called her 'blood family' would look after the welfare of her sons.

'GOODBYE ENGLAND'S ROSE'

Diana's friend, Elton John, memorably sang a re-written version of his hit song, 'Candle in the Wind', replacing lines such as 'Goodbye Norma Jean' with 'Goodbye England's rose.'

The service was watched by an estimated worldwide audience

of 2.5 billion people – one of the biggest televised events in history.

Outside the Abbey and in Hyde Park crowds watched and listened to proceedings on giant outdoor screens and huge speakers.

Afterwards, the hearse made its way to Althorp as people lined the roads, and so many flowers were thrown that the driver had to use the windscreen wipers to clear his view. And at one point the cortège stopped to remove some of the flowers that were piling up on the car.

Inside the estate, the Princess was buried in the idyllic and peaceful setting of an island in a lake where she had played as a child. ●

CLINTON ADMITS TO LEWINSKY RELATIONSHIP

(*Washington Post*, 18 August 18 1998)

BILL CLINTON BECAME the second U.S. President to be impeached since Andrew Johnson in 1868 after lying about an affair with 22-year-old White House intern Monica Lewinsky in 1998.

In an affair that gripped a worldwide audience, Clinton finally admitted that he had misled the public in an earlier statement in which he had denied any involvement with Lewinsky. His position as President hung in the balance as the Senate tried him for perjury and obstruction of justice.

Clinton had first got to know 22-year-old Lewinsky in 1995 when she was an unpaid intern at the White House. According to her, they became sexually involved that November. In December she landed a paid position in the Office of Legislative Affairs. But by the following spring, those close to the 49-year-old President were concerned about her hanging around the West Wing so much and what they perceived as her obvious infatuation with him.

LEWINSKY'S NEW FRIEND

Evelyn S. Lieberman, then deputy White House chief of staff, had her transferred to the Pentagon in April 1996, where she struck up a friendship with another employee named Linda Tripp.

That summer Lewinsky confided in Tripp about her intimate relationship with Clinton and, in the autumn of 1997, Tripp began secretly taping their conversations. On 17 December, Lewinsky was subpoenaed by lawyers for Paula Jones who was suing Clinton on sexual harassment charges dating back to when he was Governor of Arkansas. Kathleen Willey, another former White House staffer had recently testified about alleged unsolicited sexual advances made by Clinton in 1993.

LEWINSKY ON TAPE

On 12 January, Tripp made contact with independent counsel Kenneth Star who had been investigating Clinton and his wife Hillary over possible fraudulent land deals when Clinton was Governor of Arkansas. Tripp handed him her tape recordings, which allegedly had Lewinsky talking about her affair and indicating that Clinton asked her to lie about it.

Now working with Starr, Tripp again secretly recorded conversations with Lewinsky. On 17 January 1998, Clinton gave his deposition in the Jones lawsuit, in which he denied having a sexual relationship with Lewinsky and repeated his denial a week later in a live TV address, watched the world over, in which he stressed, 'I did not have sexual relations with that woman, Miss Lewinsky.'

In April, the Paula Jones case was dismissed by Judge Susan Webber Wright but Clinton continued to feel the heat.

On 6 August 1998, Lewinsky told a grand jury investigating Clinton's conduct that she had an 18-month sexual relationship with him and that the pair had discussed ways of concealing the relationship. She also presented one of her dresses as evidence, stating it had been stained with Mr Clinton's semen during one of their sexual encounters.

CLINTON ADMITS DECEPTION

On 17 August, Clinton himself testified before the jury. After the questioning at the White House was finished, he again went on national TV but this time to admit he had an inappropriate relationship with Lewinsky and deceived the American people about it. But he defiantly challenged Kenneth Starr to stop 'prying into private lives'.

He explained that he had not been candid because he wanted to protect himself and his family from embarrassment.

'I did have a relationship with Miss Lewinsky that was not appropriate,' he confessed. 'In fact, it was wrong. It constituted a critical lapse in judgement and a personal failure on my part for which I am solely and completely responsible.' He added, 'I misled people, including even my wife. I deeply regret that.'

Clinton's defence of his statements in the Jones sexual harassment lawsuit appeared to rely on the interpretation of 'sexual relations'. He maintained that it did not include oral sex.

After Starr submitted his report and supportive documents to the House of Representatives, the Judiciary Committee announced that it would begin an impeachment inquiry against President Clinton. It began on 7 January 1999 and ended on 12 February when senators voted to acquit him of the impeachment charges of perjury and obstruction of justice. •

U.S. ATTACKED

HIJACKED JETS DESTROY TWIN TOWERS AND HIT PENTAGON IN DAY OF TERROR

(*New York Times*, 12 September, 2001)

THIS DRAMATIC HEADLINE screamed across the *New York Times* above a big picture of the Twin Towers of the World Trade Center ablaze and billowing thick, black smoke.

When a plane hit the first tower it was initially thought by many to be a tragic accident. But a similar incident on the second tower just 17 minutes later left no one in any doubt that it was a terrorist attack.

On the morning of 11 September 2001, 19 Islamic terrorists, linked to al-Qaeda, hijacked four American passenger planes. At 8.38am local time (12.38pm GMT), the Federal Aviation Administration alerted NORAD (North American Aerospace Defense Command) that American Airlines Flight 11 had been hijacked. Eight minutes later, at the height of New York's morning rush hour, the plane crashed into the north tower of the World Trade Center, where thousands were already working at their desks.

News teams rushed to the site where the scenes of shock and despair were beamed around the world. The news media assumed it was an accident but as they kept cameras on the plane sticking out of the building, millions of viewers around the globe watched in horror as a second plane crashed into the south tower.

Some of those in the south tower had left the building after the first plane crash but many more were still inside. Meanwhile, hundreds of fire-fighters and police were doing their best to rescue those in both buildings.

PENTAGON HIT

More reports of hijackings began to filter through and at 9.37am a plane carrying 64 people crashed into the Pentagon in Washington, causing one section of the building to collapse. All airports across the U.S. were ordered to be shut down and commercial flights grounded. And the White House and the Capitol were evacuated, amid further threats.

Passengers aboard a fourth plane struggled with the hijackers above Pennsylvania, causing it to crash 80 miles (128km) southeast of Pittsburgh, killing everyone on board. The target was believed to have been either the Capitol or the White House.

As the public was struggling to take in all this incredible news, TV pictures relayed the sickening sight of the south tower of the Trade Center suddenly collapsing, sending a wall of smoke into the air and hundreds of people on the streets running for their lives. Twenty-nine minutes later, the north tower also fell.

The intense heat caused by the explosions had melted the steel structural cores in the towers, causing them to collapse. Hundreds of fire-fighters, police officers and people who were trying to escape the towers were crushed.

PRESIDENT VOWS REVENGE

President George W. Bush made an emergency statement on TV in which he pledged to 'hunt down and find those folks who committed this act'.

On the evening of that fatal day, which was to become known as 9/11, after the month and day, President Bush addressed the nation on TV again, in which he stated that 'our military is powerful and it's prepared', adding, 'The search is underway for those who are behind these evil acts. We will make no distinction between the terrorists who committed these acts and those who harbour them.'

The attacks killed 2,974 people. Suspicion quickly fell on al-Qaeda but the group's leader, Osama bin Laden, denied involvement until three years later when he claimed responsibility, citing U.S. support of Israel, the presence of U.S. troops in Saudi Arabia and sanctions against Iraq as motives for the attacks.

The U.S. responded to the attacks by launching the War on Terror.

On 7 October 2001, American and British forces initiated aerial bombing of Afghanistan, targeting the Taliban who had harboured al-Qaeda members. This was followed by an invasion of ground troops.

President Bush's popularity at home soared as Americans united in backing his fight against terrorism. •

BLOODBATH ON HOLIDAY ISLAND

(*New Zealand Herald*, 14 October 2002)

A **TERRORIST BOMB caused carnage on the idyllic holiday island of Bali in Indonesia after it exploded in a busy tourist area.**

It killed 202 people, mostly tourists, 88 of them holidaymakers from Australia. The death toll included 38 Indonesian citizens and 24 British visitors. A further 240 people were injured.

The bomb was placed in a van outside the Sari Club in downtown Kuta and was detonated just after 11.00pm local time on Saturday, 12 October 2002, when all the bars along the street were packed with customers enjoying themselves.

The blast destroyed the Sari Club and the resulting fire then engulfed a neighbouring bar, Paddy's Pub. Other buildings and several cars were also damaged in the blast and ensuing fire. Barely a shop front was left intact along a 500m stretch.

Rescuers worked through the night and into the following day, pulling the injured from the wreckage, along with dead bodies.

An Indonesian police chief said it was the worst act of terror in his country's history.

TOO FEW AMBULANCES

Bali's emergency services struggled to cope with the scale of the disaster. With so many injured, ambulances were in short supply to transport them to Sanglah Hospital, 10 miles away in the capital, Denpasar.

The hospital was ill-equipped to deal with the situation as more and more injured arrived needing treatment. Dozens of tourists volunteered to give blood or help in any way they could.

Many of the injured were burns victims who had to be flown to hospitals in Australia to receive specialist treatment.

Just prior to the main bomb a much smaller explosive had been set off in Paddy's Bar, which caused many to rush out into the street. Twenty seconds later, the huge van bomb was detonated across the road.

SLEEPING ON THE BEACH

Dozens of tourists, fearing more bombs, left their hotels to sleep on the beach that night, where they felt safer in the open space.

Another, smaller, explosion occurred in Denpasar, close to the United States Honorary Consulate, but there were no injuries.

The violent Islamic group Jemaah Islamiah, considered to be al-Qaeda's Southeast Asian arm, was suspected of being behind the bomb attack.

Although most of their victims in the Bali atrocity were unlikely even to have heard of Jemaah Islamiah, the group had been active for many years, with its roots stretching back to the 1940s. The group's modern incarnation dates back to 1993 and its stated aim is to establish an Islamic superstate incorporating Indonesia, Malaysia, the Philippines, Brunei and Singapore.

In 2001, the security services foiled a Jemaah Islamiah plot to bomb American, Australian, British, Israeli and Singapore diplomatic personnel at embassies, missions and schools in Singapore. At that time, 15 Jemaah Islamiah activists were arrested in Singapore, leading to a further 26 arrests elsewhere over next 36 months.

Bali – a predominantly Hindu island popular with Western tourists – was thought to represent a soft and tempting target for Islamist extremists linked to al-Qaeda

TERRORISTS JAILED

Three men were eventually sentenced to death for the bombings – Amrozi bin Nurhasyim, his brother Mukhlas and Imam Samudra. A fourth, Ali Imron, was sentenced to life imprisonment.

Muslim cleric Abu Bakar Bashir, widely thought to have been one of the masterminds behind the attack, was found guilty of conspiracy and sentenced to two and a half years imprisonment.

On 1 October 2005, Bali was targeted again when three suicide bombers blew themselves up in tourist areas, killing at least 19 people, mostly Indonesians. The incidents happened almost simultaneously just before 8.00pm local time. More than 50 others were injured as blasts ripped through three restaurants – two in the Jimbaran beach resort, the third in Kuta.

Police claimed to have discovered a further three bombs designed to be triggered by signals from cell phones. These failed to detonate as the island's mobile phone network was shut down as a precaution immediately after the initial blasts.

Once more Jemaah Islamiah was suspected of being behind the attack. •

THE TYRANT IS NOW A PRISONER

(*Independent*, 15 December 2003)

HE WAS THE president who brought education, electricity and welfare to his country but also death and destruction to anyone who opposed his regime.

Saddam Hussein had become involved in politics after joining the Arab socialist party, Ba'ath, while at college. After the overthrow of the monarchy in 1958, during a military coup, General Abdul Karim Kassem became the country's new leader but his moderate polices lost him the support of the Ba'ath Party. In 1959, Hussein had to flee to Egypt after being part of a discovered plot to assassinate Kassem. But he returned when Kassem was executed in another military coup in February 1963.

Colonel Abdul-Salam Arif became the new president but he was killed in an air crash in 1966 and was replaced by his brother General Abdul Rahman. Another military coup on 17 July 1968 brought to power Ahmad Hasan al-Bakr and the Ba'ath Party. Over the next ten years, Saddam rose quickly through the ranks of government and became the number two figure behind al-Bakr.

The Ba'ath government ruthlessly suppressed opposition but it did agree to enter negotiations with the Kurdish Democratic Party and, in March 1970, the government promised to grant the Kurds, in the north of the country, a degree of autonomy. But four years later, when nothing had changed, fighting broke out between the Kurds and Iraqi armed forces. Kurdish villages were destroyed and the inhabitants were resettled in specially constructed villages surrounded by barbed wire and fortified posts.

SADDAM BECOMES PRESIDENT

In 1979, Saddam became president after al-Bakr retired, and the ruthlessness continued as he put to death any opposition. He also created the Republican Guard, a presidential security force.

Increasing oil revenues provided him with the money to build schools, hospitals and clinics and start a literacy project, as well as creating an electricity network throughout the country.

Statues and posters of the president appeared all over the country. Some depicted him in military dress, others in traditional garb and others in casual wear with his family or with a young child on his knee, looking like a benevolent father figure.

Seeing himself as the leader and unifying force of Arabs, he poured his army across the border into Iran in September 1980 in an attempt to gain control of the Shatt al Arab Waterway that runs along the border of both countries.

Iraq's war with Iran received support from Britain, the U.S., Soviet Union and France. Iran fought back far more ferociously than anticipated and the war was to last eight years, costing the lives of hundreds of thousands before a ceasefire was agreed.

POISON GAS REVENGE

In an effort to gain their independence from Iraq, the Kurds supported Iran during the war. Saddam's retribution in the spring of 1988 was to send his air force over the Kurdish region releasing poisoned gas, resulting in 5,000 deaths.

But despite this long and bloody war, just two years later, Saddam ordered his army into neighbouring Kuwait – where he had long wanted to extend his territory – after lengthy disputes over oil.

The United Nations immediately imposed economic sanctions on Iraq and demanded a withdrawal from Kuwait. But Saddam refused and in January 1991 a United States-led coalition of 32 countries launched an attack on Iraq. Saddam called it 'the mother of all battles'. It eventually led to a ceasefire on 28 February.

In April he agreed to accept the U.N. resolution calling on him to destroy weapons of mass destruction and begrudgingly allowed U.N. inspectors into his country to monitor the disarmament.

OPERATION DESERT FOX

Convinced that he was hiding biological and chemical weapons, the U.S. and Britain launched Operation Desert Fox in December 1998 – a four-day intensive air strike aimed at destroying Iraqi military bases, weapons factories and airfields. The following month, U.S. and British aircraft began regular bombing attacks on Iraq.

With the arrival of George W. Bush as U.S. President in 2001, and the al-Qaeda attacks on the World Trade Center in September of that year, the War on Terror was stepped up. Bush described Iraq, Iran and North Korea as the 'axis of evil'.

In March 2003, Bush, with the support of British Prime Minister Tony Blair, ordered the invasion of Iraq on the pretext that Saddam was concealing 'weapons of mass destruction', despite having no U.N. resolution authorising the action. In the event, no such weapons were ever found. But it was the beginning of the end for Saddam. His reign was toppled with the fall of Baghdad on 9 April when he went into hiding. News footage of Iraqi civilians hacking away at a towering statue of Saddam in central Baghdad, which was eventually pulled down by U.S. troops, was shown around the world. It was a highly symbolic moment.

SADDAM CAPTURED ALIVE

In December 2003, following a tip-off from an intelligence source, U.S. forces found the wanted dictator hiding in a cramped bunker on a farm near Tikrit, where he was born. The U.S. administrator in Iraq at the time, Paul Bremer, told reporters, 'Ladies and gentlemen, we got him. The tyrant is a prisoner.'

Saddam's two sons, Uday and Qusay, were both killed during the invasion of Iraq when U.S.

special forces, acting on a tip-off, discovered their hiding place in a house in the town of Mosul.

Uday was Saddam's elder son and had been tipped to succeed his father as president, but he was also a notorious torturer, rapist and murderer. He suffered severe injuries in an assassination attempt in 1996 and was eventually deemed too unstable to take over from Saddam, but was in charge of a newspaper and TV station.

Qusay took over from his brother as heir to the presidency. He did not adopt the playboy lifestyle of his brother but tended to keep a low profile, although he was head of the elite Republican Guard and the Special Security Organisation. His 14-year-old son died alongside him in the gunfight that also killed Uday and a bodyguard.

Saddam survived to stand trial in Iraq for crimes against humanity but remained defiant throughout, refusing to accept the legality of the proceedings. He was found guilty, and executed on 30 December 2006. •

'WE SAW THE SEA COMING, WE ALL RAN. BUT GOD SAVES LITTLE'

(*Times of India*, 28 December 2004)

ONE OF THE WORLD'S deadliest natural disasters occurred on the morning of 26 December 2004 when an earthquake under the Indian Ocean caused a huge tsunami, killing more than 200,000 people in 14 countries.

The quake, which occurred off the west coast of Sumatra, Indonesia, at 7.58am local time, measured between 9.1 and 9.3 on the Richter scale, causing the sea floor to jolt vertically by about 10m (33ft). This sent surges of water roaring towards coastlines, travelling at speeds of up to 800kph (497mph). The huge tsunami took everyone by surprise as waves up to 30m (98ft) high smashed down onto beaches, villages and towns on the coasts of countries including Indonesia, Sri Lanka, India and Thailand.

MASSIVE DEATH TOLL

Over 200,000 people were killed – around 170,000 in Indonesia alone – including local people as well as many tourists who had been enjoying holidays in some of the most picturesque locations in the world.

There was little or no warning

that the tsunami was coming. Tragically, there were no tide gauges in the Indian Ocean as there are in the Pacific. If they had been in place, then tens of thousands of lives could have been saved.

The only visible sign was the waterline suddenly retreating on some beaches, causing bewilderment amongst those who saw it. Unfortunately, many were so intrigued by this unusual occurrence that they walked further out to sea to explore when they should have been running away. Other victims drowned after running to retrieve fish stranded on the beach.

SUMATRA HIT FIRST

The tsunami came in several waves with intervals of between 5 and 40 minutes. Sumatra was hit first with Sri Lanka and India roughly 90 minutes to 2 hours later.

In the Sumatran city of Banda Aceh people were going about their business as the sun was rising but within moments they were fighting for their lives when the first gigantic wall of water hit. It surged through the city, sweeping anyone and anything along, causing widespread devastation.

Many witnesses described how the sea appeared suddenly to 'seethe and boil' as it engulfed thousands of miles of coast. Others likened the first sighting of a spec on the horizon which grew and grew into a mountain of water as being 'like something out of a disaster movie'. By the time people realised what was coming it was largely too late. Some managed to flee to higher ground but all too many were washed away.

Many on the beaches, enjoying the sunshine, were engulfed. A woman on honeymoon in Sri Lanka said, 'It was terrifying. The water behind us was ripping through the trees as we ran up a hill to safety.'

BODIES ON THE BEACHES

In the aftermath, the beaches were lined with bodies, and cries and wails filled the air as emergency services did their best to tackle the appalling devastation.

There was a massive international response to the calls for help, with governments pledging aid in rescue operations, supplying food and water and sending in teams to help clear the devastated towns and villages. Ordinary members of the public, all over the world, appalled by the news stories and images, donated large sums of money.

The earthquake was the largest for 40 years and was a shocking reminder of how terrifying the power of nature can be.

The energy released by the initial earthquake has been estimated at the equivalent to 26 megatons of TNT – roughly 1500 times more powerful than the atom bomb that devastated Hiroshima in 1945.

The resulting tsunami was actually a rare occurrence in the Indian Ocean, despite the number of earthquakes in the area. In 2005 a quake of magnitude 8.7 happened in roughly the same area, but produced no major tsunami. In fact, the last tsunami in the region to cause a serious problem was when Krakatoa erupted in 1883.

Nevertheless, in 2005 the United Nations began work to provide the Indian Ocean Tsunami Warning System and by June 2006 the system was active, although the information it provides will only become an effective warning when a tsunami alert can be broadcast by the authorities to everyone in the coastal area danger zones. ●

KATRINA STORMS ASHORE

'BIG ONE' LASHES AT NEW ORLEANS

(*Atlanta Journal-Constitution*, 29 August 2005)

THE HURRICANE THAT New Orleans was dreading finally arrived and, as expected, the impact was devastating.

It caused widespread flooding when it ripped through the old city, tearing roofs off buildings, upturning trees and cars and killing over a thousand people. It was the worst natural disaster in the United States for decades.

There had been plenty of warning that it was going to strike. It began as a low pressure weather system which increased to a tropical storm and then a hurricane as it built up over the Bahamas. It then moved towards the Florida coast on the evening of 25 August 2005. By now it was classed as a Category 1 hurricane with 80mph (130 kph)

winds. Passing through Florida, it caused flooding, uprooted trees, caused structural damage and cut off electricity supplies. It resulted in 14 fatalities.

WORSE TO COME

President Bush declared a 'major disaster' in Florida. But there was far worse to come. After leaving Florida, Katrina blew over the warm waters of the Gulf of Mexico, strengthening rapidly overnight.

It had grown to Category 5 by the time it started its approach to the Louisiana coast but had weakened early on Monday, 29 August to Category 4 with sustained winds of 145mph.

New Orleans Mayor Ray Nagin ordered the city of 485,000 to evacuate and warned that the storm could topple its century-old levee system, leaving New Orleans under water.

Homes and buildings were shuttered and boarded up throughout the city and the motorway was jammed with people desperate to get out. But thousands took refuge in the city's Superdome arena. These were people too poor, sick or elderly to be able to leave and others doggedly determined to stay and sit the storm out.

NEW ORLEANS FLOODED

When Katrina finally hit New Orleans it had dropped to Category 3 but the force was still terrifying and immensely damaging, with winds of 125mph (205kph). Boats, bridges, houses and cars were washed inland along the Louisiana coast, New Orleans bearing the brunt of it. Up to 80 per cent of the city was flooded after defensive barriers were overwhelmed.

Howling winds and lashing rain ripped holes in the Superdome

but thankfully the roof held and those inside remained frightened but safe.

With the streets flooded, people were trapped in their attics or even on their roofs once the worst of the winds had passed. But rescue took time because emergency workers were hindered by the swift-moving floodwater. Supplies of fresh water and food began to run short in the aftermath of the disaster. Sanitary conditions quickly deteriorated, bringing the risk of diseases such as cholera and typhoid, and military units were despatched to bring emergency aid. The floodwaters lingered for weeks.

DEADLIEST SINCE 1928

At least 1,836 people died, making Katrina the deadliest U.S. hurricane since the 1928 Okeechobee storm that killed nearly 3,000.

The economic effects of the disaster were crippling, oil platforms and refineries having been destroyed as well as roads, homes, businesses and farm land. Thousands of residents were left homeless and unemployed.

The effect on the environment was catastrophic. There was substantial beach erosion, sixteen national wildlife refuges had to close and oil spillage estimated at 7 million gallons (26 million litres) had to be cleaned up.

Over seventy countries pledged money and physical aid as a mammoth undertaking got underway to re-build New Orleans. ●

MICROSOFT SAYS GOODBYE TO BILL GATES

(*Seattle Times*, 28 June 2008)

AN OBSESSION WITH computers led Bill Gates to world domination of the software market with his mighty Microsoft company changing the daily business operations and leisure lifestyles of millions around the world.

Along the way, he became the richest man in the world and one of the most influential. He departed from Microsoft after 33 years to devote his life to philanthropy, using his great wealth to help ease global suffering.

Born in Seattle, Washington, on 28 October 1955, he became fascinated by his school's computer as a 13-year-old. Together with three fellow students, including Paul Allen, they explored their interest and Gates wrote a program for a game of noughts and crosses

that could be played on it. By the age of 17 he had sold his first program – a timetabling system for the school, earning him $4,200.

THE PAYROLL PROGRAM

The four students were later hired by a company to write a payroll program for them. Gates then enrolled at Harvard College where he continued to spend much of his time understanding the workings of computers. He remained in contact with Paul Allen and took time out to write a program with Allen for computer company MITS, which was a version of the programming language BASIC (Beginner's All Purpose Symbolic Instruction Code). It was used for the Altair microcomputer.

Encouraged by their success, the two friends saw an opportunity to develop software for the next generation of computers and they formed their own company, Microsoft, in 1975. A year later, Gates dropped out of Harvard to concentrate on his work with his new company. Their big break came when computer giant IBM asked them to provide an operating system for a new personal computer they were developing. It was given the code name Project Chess and the team consisted of twelve people directed by Don Estridge with chief designer Lewis Eggebrecht.

GATES' FIRST FORTUNE

Gates adapted a system already in existence called 86-DOS, which became known as MS-DOS. Showing a flair for business he crucially accepted a one-time fee of $50,000 for the system but retained the licensing rights and this was to earn him a fortune.

The IBM PC was launched on 12 August 1981 and revolutionised the home-computer market. The original press release described it as IBM's 'smallest, lowest-priced computer system', which was 'designed for business, school and home'. This 'easy-to-use system sells for as little as $1,565'.

IBM vice president and group executive, C. B. Rogers, said, 'This is the computer for just about everyone who has ever wanted a personal system at the office, on the university campus or at home.'

IBM and Gates fell out after he was asked to develop a separate operating system for them called OS/2. Although he did a first version of it, creative differences led to him focusing on something he had already been working on – a system called Microsoft Windows. Windows arrived on 20 November 1985. This quickly became the standard software for most personal computers around the world and Microsoft became a household name.

SHARP BUSINESS SENSE

Several commentators have said that Gates's real genius is not so much in being original and creative but in his sharp business sense, which has been described as 'aggressive' .

In 1987, Gates was officially declared a billionaire in the pages of *Forbes* '400 Richest People in America' issue, just days before his 32nd birthday, with a fortune worth $1.25 billion. He was the World's Richest Man from 1995 to 2007 and again in 2009. And in 2011 *Forbes* ranked him as the fifth most powerful person in the world.

Gates stepped down as chief executive officer of Microsoft in January 2000 to concentrate on The Bill & Melinda Gates Foundation, which, amongst other things, seeks to reduce global poverty, expand healthcare and encourage education.

On 27 June 2008, he said farewell to Microsoft as he finished his last full-time working day there, although he remained as non-executive chairman. •

OBAMA MAKES HISTORY

U.S. DECISIVELY ELECTS FIRST BLACK PRESIDENT

(*The Washington Post*, 5 November 2008)

DEMOCRATIC SENATOR Barack Hussein Obama defeated Arizona Senator John McCain on 4 November 2008 to become the 44th President of the U.S.

It was a particularly historic occasion for he was the first black President in the country's history.

During an exciting campaign en route to the highest office, he captured the public's imagination with his vitality and freshness. His commitment and determination to change things was stressed by his catchphrase, 'Yes we can', which became a rallying cry amongst his supporters.

After his Republican rival, Senator John McCain, finally and graciously admitted defeat, Obama paid tribute to the former Vietnam prisoner-of-war, calling him a 'Brave and selfless leader' who 'has endured sacrifices for America that most of us cannot begin to imagine'.

Appearing with his family before a crowd of tens of thousands in Chicago's Grant Park on the day of his victory, Obama embodied the

'American Dream' in which anything is possible. 'If there is anyone out there who still doubts that America is a place where all things are possible, who still wonders if the dream of our founders is alive in our time, who still questions the power of our democracy, tonight is your answer,' he said to a cheering crowd.

COMMITMENT FOR CHANGE

He was under no illusions about the difficult times ahead but stressed his commitment for change, with the support of the country.

'The road ahead will be long, our climb will be steep. We may not get there in one year or even one term, but America, I have never been more hopeful than I am tonight that we will get there. I promise you, we as a people will get there.'

Then, turning towards his young daughters, he switched comfortably from the role of being the most powerful figure in the land to that of ordinary father.

'Sasha and Malia, I love you both more than you can imagine, and you have earned the new puppy that's coming with us to the White House.'

Barack Obama was born in 1961 in Hawaii, the only American president to have been born on the island, where his father, Barack Obama Snr., met his mother, Ann Dunham while they were both studying at the University of Hawaii. Barack Snr was Kenyan, and the university's first African student, while Ann came from Kansas.

The couple divorced when Barack Jnr. was only three and his father returned to Kenya. His mother then married Indonesian Lolo Soetoro and Barack moved to live in Jakarta when he was six years old, living there until he was ten.

In 1971, Barack was sent back to Hawaii to live with his grandparents and, having excelled at school, studied at university in California and New York where he studied political science and international relations. He worked in Chicago with a communities organisation before studying law at Harvard where he made national headlines by becoming the first black president of the influential *Harvard Law Review*.

Barack Obama was a civil rights lawyer before pursuing a political career, working his way up the ladder to become Illinois State Senator.

On 10 February 2007, he formally announced his candidacy

for the 2008 Democratic presidential nomination. There followed a gruelling primary campaign, battling against his rival, former First Lady and then Senator from New York, Hillary Clinton, but he clinched victory on 3 June 2008.

As the world headed towards a financial crisis, the economy took centre stage and Obama's campaign agenda was one of reform and change in finance, education and healthcare.

After capturing Republican strongholds Virginia and Indiana and key battleground states Florida and Ohio the result in the race for the White House was a Democratic victory and Obama was inaugurated as President on 20 January 2009.

He cut taxes for working families, small businesses and first-time home buyers and lobbied allies to support a global economic stimulus package. He also managed to persuade Congress – in the face of united Republican opposition – to pass a bill for a complete overhaul in healthcare insurance, making it more easily available for all. •

WORLD TRANSFIXED BY THE GREAT ESCAPE

(*Daily Telegraph*, 14 October 2010)

THE DRAMA UNFOLDED like a Hollywood movie as millions around the world were united in watching live pictures of the Chilean miners great escape from their 'hell hole' underground.

One by one, the 32 miners emerged from the depths and took their first gulp of fresh air in 69 days, their relief and exhilaration shared by a global audience who were fighting with them every inch of the way.

The men had become trapped when part of the San Jose mine in Chile's Atacama Desert collapsed on 5 August 2010. A second collapse two days later blocked rescue access to the lower parts of the mine.

Not knowing whether the men were dead or alive, rescue teams began drilling exploratory bore holes, lowering listening devices. But as the days wore on, and there was no sign of life, hope began to turn towards despair.

RESCUERS FIND NOTE

Then, seventeen days after the accident, rescuers found a note from the miners attached to one of the listening probes saying, 'Estamos bien en el refugio los 33' ['All 33 of us are well inside the shelter.']

It referred to a refuge shelter 700m (2,300ft) down, where the men had been having lunch when the first collapse occurred.

News that the men were alive quickly spread around the world and the miners' families and friends set up camp around the mine, providing emotional support for each other during the ordeal. It was dubbed Campo Esperanza, or Camp Hope.

Communications were set up and emergency supplies and fresh water were sent down the borehole to the miners who had been surviving on rations. The longest and most complex mining rescue in history was about to take place as three different drills were tried out, called Plans A, B and C, to see which would work best. To save time, they bored down into the rock simultaneously.

FREE BY CHRISTMAS?

It was thought that the men would be freed by Christmas but the excellent progress by Plan B drill indicated that breakthrough would happen much quicker than expected. The man at the controls of this rig was an American named Jeff Hart, who had been in Afghanistan drilling water wells for the U.S. military's forward operating bases when he got the call to fly to Chile.

Meanwhile, food, drink, medicine and letters from loved ones were passed on to the miners via two narrow boreholes that became their lifelines.

Plan B drill finally broke through to the miners on 9 October and there was jubilation under and above ground in Campo Esperanza, as well as around the world.

Further good news came after a video inspection of the shaft showed the rock to be quite stable and only the first 96m (315ft) needed to be encased with steel pipes.

A rescue capsule was put in place attached to a winch and pulley and at 11.15pm local time on Tuesday, 12 October (2.15am GMT on Wednesday, 13 October), technical expert Manuel Gonzalez entered the capsule and was lowered down the shaft. He was warmly embraced by the miners as he stepped out the other end, and Florencio Avalos took his place for the return journey.

FITTEST FIRST

The men had been supplied with green boiler suits and sunglasses to wear and an order of rescue had been planned with the fittest and most experienced winched up first in case anything went wrong and a cool head was required. Next would come the weakest, either psychologically or physically, and finally those who were considered to be in good health but not expert mining equipment operators.

Avalos reached the surface at ten minutes past midnight local time on Wednesday, 13 October and was warmly hugged by his sobbing son and wife, along with Mining Minister Laurence Golborne and Chilean President Sebastián Piñera. He was then strapped onto a stretcher and taken away for health checks – a procedure followed for each of the miners.

Next up was the exuberant Mario Sepulveda, who hugged his wife, ran to the rescue workers to exchange 'high fives' and punched the air as he led the crowd in chants of 'Viva Chile!' He also handed Piñera and other dignitaries pieces of rock from his shoulder bag as mementos.

The rescue team was soon able to reduce the time between each ascent from an hour to between 16 to 25 minutes. TV cameras below ground showed remarkable pictures of the trapped men – looking surprisingly fit and healthy – stepping into the capsule and being brought to the surface, one-by-one, with clockwork precision.

The last of the 33 miners to be rescued was shift supervisor Luis Urzua. The very last man left below on his own was rescuer Manuel Gonzalez, who strapped himself into the capsule for its final ride to the surface. •

THE DAY THAT SHOOK JAPAN

(*Independent*, 12 March 2011)

JAPAN'S BIGGEST ever earthquake occurred on 11 March 2011 and triggered a huge tsunami that caused widespread devastation. Around 16,000 people died and a further 6,000 were injured.

The quake struck at 2.46pm local time beneath the seabed in the Pacific, 80 miles off Japan's east coast, sending terrifying waves 30ft high rushing towards coastlines at 500mph.

The tremor – the world's fifth biggest since records began in the 1800s – sparked a tsunami alert around the entire Pacific rim. Japan's early-warning system kicked in but things were happening at such a pace that there was little time to evacuate coastal populations.

The city of Sendai on Honshu island, close to the epicentre of the quake, took the worst hit as the tsunami crashed into 1,300 miles of coastline, smashing ships, demolishing houses and washing everything away as the water quickly surged ashore. Three thousand homes were destroyed and a petrochemical complex was set alight, sending huge orange fireballs into the air. Sendai Airport was flooded, causing severe damage.

The capital city of Toyko, some 170 miles away, escaped the worst horrors of the disaster but it was badly rocked. Office workers scrambled to hide under desks, people stumbled in the streets and falling debris caused havoc. At least 20 people were injured when the roof of a hall collapsed onto a graduation ceremony.

THOUSANDS STRANDED

With roads badly damaged, many found themselves unable to flee. All railway services were suspended in Tokyo, with an estimated 20,000 people stranded at major stations across the city.

To the east of the capital in Ichihara, Chiba, a huge fire broke out at an oil refinery. It raged for ten days before being extinguished.

The earthquake was followed by over a hundred 'aftershocks', which caused further damage. A dam burst in north-eastern Fukushima prefecture, sweeping away 1,800 homes.

There were further problems when three nuclear plants were affected by the quake and some were swamped. At the Fukushima Daiichi plant, the tsunami severed its main power supply and also flooded the emergency generator rooms. With no electricity to power electronics systems and the pumps that circulate cooling water around the reactors, they began to overheat.

Over the course of the next few days, three of the reactors went into meltdown and there were several explosions. Military helicopters were used to 'bomb' the reactors with sea water to try to cool them down. Workers battling to restore electrical power were exposed to radiation leaks and were evacuated until radiation levels became more tolerable.

It wasn't until 20 May, more than three months after the earthquake, that the situation was brought fully under control and personnel were able to re-enter the main Reactor Building.

EXTENSIVE DAMAGE

The earthquake and tsunami caused extensive structural damage in Japan, splitting roads, buckling railways and rupturing concrete. Tens of thousands of people were left homeless.

With gas and water pipes and electrical cables destroyed, people were left without power and there was a shortage of water and food.

The force of the quake and tsunami was felt in other countries, too. Russia evacuated 11,000 residents from coastal areas of the Kuril Islands and a tsunami warning was given along some coastal areas of America. In California and Oregon, 8ft-high waves damaged docks and harbours. Thousands of people fled beaches in Hawaii as it was swamped by 7ft waves.

In the aftermath of the disaster, many countries helped with supplies and in sending search-and rescue-teams.

Japanese Prime Minister Naoto Kan said, 'In the 65 years after the end of World War II, this is the toughest and the most difficult crisis for Japan.' •

GOT HIM!

(*New York Post*, 2 May 2011)

ALMOST A DECADE after the 9/11 terror attack on the World Trade Center and the Pentagon, al-Qaeda leader Osama Bin Laden was killed by U.S. forces in Pakistan. It had taken months of planning but the raid was all over within 40 minutes.

The death of America's 'most wanted' man was announced by President Barack Obama who called it 'the most significant achievement to date in our nation's effort to defeat al-Qaeda'.

It transpired that U.S. intelligence had intercepted a phone call the previous August from a trusted courier of Bin Laden who was identified as Abu Ahmed al-Kuwaiti. The mobile-phone number was traced to a compound in Abbottabad, Pakistan, which was put under surveillance by CIA operatives on the ground and by high-altitude spy planes, which were able to take pictures and video footage of the building undetected.

A man thought to be Bin Laden was often spotted walking up and down within the compound but the CIA were unable to positively identify him even after Obama gave the go-ahead for a raid, which took place in the early hours of 2 May 2011. The operation was top secret. No other country had been informed.

LIVE VIDEO FEED

Two Black Hawk helicopters flew to Abbottabad, carrying 23 Navy Seals who blasted their way through several walls to get into the buildings. Back in Washington, the live events were being watched as they unfolded by Obama and his security team via a video camera with which one of the Seals was equipped.

According to U.S. officials, al-Kuwaiti fired at the troops as they searched the inner confines. They shot him dead along with his wife who made a lunge for them.

They also shot dead al-Kuwaiti's brother and Bin Laden's adult son, Khalid Bin Laden.

COMMANDOS GIVE CHASE

Osama Bin Laden was found on the top floor of the three-storey building, around 20 minutes into the raid, standing at the end of the corridor. He ducked back inside a room and the commandos chased after him. Initial U.S. reports said that Bin Laden shot at them, using his wife as a human shield, but this was later retracted and U.S. officials described how the Seals found two women in front of Bin Laden, screaming and trying to protect him. One of the women was pushed aside and another Seal shot Bin Laden in the head and chest.

His body was taken aboard a helicopter and flown back with the Seals to the U.S. air base in Bagram, Afghanistan.

From there Bin Laden's body was transferred to a U.S. aircraft carrier in the north Arabian Sea where it was prepared for burial. After a Muslim funeral, his body was placed in a weighted bag and dropped into the water.

LOCALS SURPRISED

The large compound in which Bin Laden had been living had towering walls and a high metal security gate which led to inner walls and other security gates. The building was far bigger than any others in the neighbourhood and lay only about a kilometre from the Pakistan Military Academy. Yet the Pakistan security forces said they had no idea that Bin Laden had been living there and residents of the area also expressed their surprise. Some told how the occupants of the compound rarely went out and when they did so – in either a red Suzuki jeep or a van – they passed through security doors that closed immediately afterwards.

After the death of Bin Laden was announced, crowds gathered outside the White House in Washington, D.C., chanting 'USA, USA' and singing 'The Star Spangled Banner'.

Former U.S. President, George W. Bush, who had been in power during 9/11, commented, 'The fight against terror goes on, but tonight America has sent an unmistakable message: No matter how long it takes, justice will be done.' •

STEVE JOBS DEAD

APPLE ICON CHANGED THE WORLD

(*New York Post*, 6 October 2011)

VISIONARY, INVENTOR, maverick, designer, genius, salesman… Steve Jobs had been described as all of these things during a remarkable life in which he stood at the pinnacle of the electronics industry.

Born in San Francisco in February 1955 to unmarried students, he was given up for adoption to a Californian couple and grew up in Cupertino – later to become the headquarters of Apple, the world's most valuable technology company.

After leaving school he helped to design video games for Atari, earning enough money to fund a six-month travelling experience in India. On his return, he went back to work for Atari and joined a local computer club with his schoolfriend, Steve Wozniak, who was designing and building his own computer.

In 1976, he and Wozniak formed the Apple company in his parents' garage and that year they released Apple I – a computer lacking a keyboard and monitor. The following year they made a truly ground-breaking version with the Apple II – the first computer for personal use.

MOUSE AND GRAPHICS

The Macintosh computer in 1984 was a worldwide success with its use of a mouse to bypass the keyboard and its graphical user interface – allowing users to interact with images rather than text commands.

But within the company there were some concerns about Jobs's management style, said by some to be 'autocratic', and he was ousted from the company. However, this just spurred him on to do other things and he founded the NeXT computer development company in 1985, which aimed its products at the business and higher-education markets. A year later, he bought Graphics Group from the *Star Wars* director George Lucas, which had been producing expensive computer-animation hardware used by a number of film makers, including Disney. Jobs shifted away from manufacturing and began producing computer-animated feature films under the new name of Pixar.

HUGE PROFITS FOR PIXAR

The results were stunning. *Toy Story* was a massive hit, generating huge profits. It was followed by the likes of *Finding Nemo*, *Monsters Inc.* and *WALL-E*.

Apple paid more than $400 million for NeXT computers and, in 1996, Jobs was back with the company he founded, becoming CEO in 1997. And he was about to unleash a string of eye-opening technological marvels...

In 1998 he brought design to the forefront of desktop computers, ditching the traditional beige with the colourful iMac. Turning his attention to music, he revolutionised the market with iTunes and iPod, allowing the public to buy their favourite songs easily on the Internet and store and play them on a small portable device.

In 2005, Disney paid $7 billion worth of stock to buy Pixar from Jobs. Apple then entered the mobile-phone business with the sleek iPhone, its touch-screen control icons combining phone, media player, Internet and camera.

This was followed three years later by the iPad – a touch-screen 'tablet' computer providing the services of a laptop with the ease of use of an iPod.

FACE OF APPLE

Each new and exciting product was unveiled by Steve Jobs in theatrical style, wearing his trademark black turtle-neck jumper, faded blue jeans and trainers. He made his inventions look appealing to own and explained their functions in a simple way. He was the face of Apple with a flair for knowing what people wanted before they knew themselves.

His untimely death from pancreatic cancer at the age of 56 on 5 October 2011 robbed the world of one of the most influential men of his generation. He had been fighting cancer for eight years and had a liver transplant in 2009. He took medical leave in January 2011, before resigning as CEO in August, although he remained as Apple's chairman.

On the day of his death, Microsoft founder Bill Gates commented, 'The world rarely sees someone who has had the profound impact Steve has had, the effects of which will be felt for many generations to come.'

And U.S. President Obama said, 'By making computers personal and putting the Internet in our pockets, he made the information revolution not only accessible, but intuitive and fun.

'He transformed our lives, redefined entire industries and achieved one of the rarest feats in human history: he changed the way each of us sees the world.' •